THE GRAPHIC STORIES OF R.O. BLECHMAN

TALKING LINES

DRAWN AND QUARTERLY

MONTREAL

Jacket design by Tom Devlin.

Drawn & Quarterly
Post Office Box 48056
Montreal, Quebec
Canada H2V 4S8
www.drawnandquarterly.com

First edition: September 2009.
Printed in Singapore.
10 9 8 7 6 5 4 3 2 1

Library and Archives Canada Cataloguing in Publication
Blechman, R. O. (Robert O.), 1930–
Talking Lines / R.O. Blechman.
ISBN 978–1–897299–85–2
1. Blechman, R. O. (Robert O.), 1930–. 2. Artists—United States
—Biography. I. Title.
N6537.B563A4 2009   741.5'973   C2009–901651–6

Distributed in the USA and abroad by:
Farrar, Straus and Giroux
18 West 18th Street
New York, NY 10011
Orders: 888.330.8477

Distributed in Canada by:
Raincoast Books
9050 Shaughnessy Street
Vancouver, BC V6P 6E5
Orders: 800.663.5714

INTRODUCTION BY SETH

I have been waiting for this book for years. I always felt that it existed somewhere in the realm of potential, that it could someday materialize if the stars were properly aligned or the correct runes cast. I knew that a good number of strips by R.O. Blechman remained, until now, scattered in disparate magazines, newspapers, and books. The question was whether anyone would ever get around to collecting them.

I'm not entirely sure when I first encountered Blechman's work—probably back in the 1980s when I was discovering so many cartoonists for the first time. That was an exciting period for me—I was just coming of age as a cartoonist and was reaching out, greedily, with both hands into the great pool of 20th century cartoon art and grabbing up anything I saw. I wanted to know the works of every cartoonist and during that decade, wave after wave of them passed before my eyes: Arno, Hokinson, Addams, Gorey, Crumb, Spiegelman, Feiffer, Steinberg, Thurber, Herriman, Gray, Gould, Bemelmans, McKay, Briggs, Kurtzman, Bateman, and, of course, Blechman. I forgot about some artists in as much time as it took to read their strips, but I also developed a group of favorites that has remained fairly constant, whose works appeared in newspapers, magazine gags, adventure comics, and children's books. There was something unique and attractive in Blechman's work, and I wanted more. But in those pre–internet days, more wasn't easy to get and it took me about a decade to collect the small handful of books he had published.

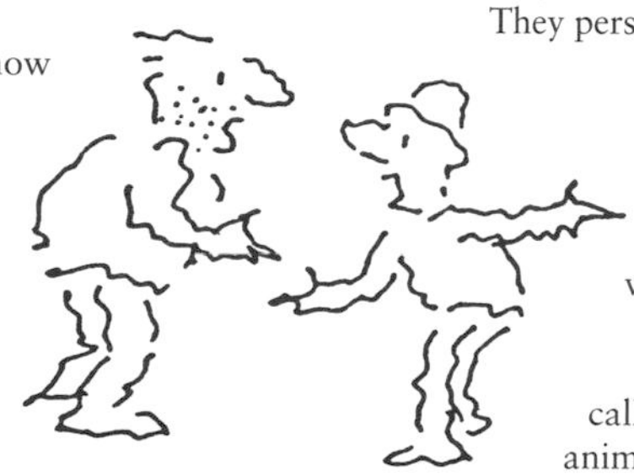

When I started looking, I wasn't even sure any Blechman books existed. I had to track them down, one by one, in the dusty humor sections of second–hand bookstores. I remember the day I found THE JUGGLER OF OUR LADY in an old bookstore. I knew very little about Blechman's work at the time, and the book was something of a revelation. I was surprised and delighted to have found a marvel of cartoon storytelling, ages ahead of its time. Later, I realized that THE JUGGLER OF OUR LADY (published in 1953) was a signpost on the way to the "graphic novel," like Freeman's IT SHOULDN'T HAPPEN, Dunn's EAST OF FIFTH, and Gropper's ALLEY OOP. All of these books were "graphic novel" anomalies done long before any one ever dreamed up that awful modern term.

Reading through TALKING LINES, I'm struck by how perfect Blechman's work is. It's an embodiment of the less–is–more maxim. There's really almost nothing on the page. A few wiggly lines make up a man or a dog or a building, a clutch of words written by an equally shaky hand. There is rarely a background, and there aren't even any panel borders. This is cartooning boiled down to its elemental form. At this level there's the danger of barrenness, the danger that there simply isn't enough on the page to convey ideas and emotions. Miraculously, Blechman breathes life into his microscopic world. His little figures, because of their very shakiness, call out to us for sympathy. They personify human frailty, human foolishness. This is cartooning at its best. Blechman's lines do not represent real people—they are real people. His pen opens a window to the dimension where these little wiggly folk live.

A few years ago, Blechman called me up to do some work for his animation studio. We never met face to face, so whenever we spoke on the phone, I imagined him looking just like one of his drawings. I felt shy talking to him and wanted to let him know how well I regarded his work but I did a pretty poor job of it. He on the other hand was very kind and encouraging toward me. It was a nice thing on his part. I was sorely tempted to take advantage of his generous spirit, but asking a busy artist to photocopy and mail his uncollected work to you is simply not done. I kept my mouth shut and kept hoping that a collection would someday appear.

And here we are; that day has arrived. The book is wonderful. After reading it, one can't help but conclude that Blechman is a clever and sophisticated man. But more importantly, one comes away with the feeling that he must be a kind man. There is a great sympathy extended toward his little people. Blechman infuses them with real human gentleness. Even the most hard–hearted of them seems merely misguided. When one gazes down on their tiny features; dotted eyes and potato noses, shapeless bodies and little hands and feet, one can't help but wish them the very best as they make their way out into the world. I certainly do.

R.O. BLECHMAN

THE FOLLOWING IS A TRANSCRIPT OF AN INTERVIEW CONDUCTED BY ZINA SAUNDERS IN 2006.

As a kid, I had no interest in being an artist whatsoever. I wasn't even a cartoonist except in high school and that was just to show off. It only occurred to me very recently that the only reason I went to the High School of Music and Art was that I was in love with my next door neighbor, a beautiful blonde French girl who was an artist. I loved her. She painted her walls and had murals everywhere. She'd painted a donkey's behind on the wall and the switch was where his ass was and she would ask me to, "Turn on the lights please." This, to me, was what art was all about!

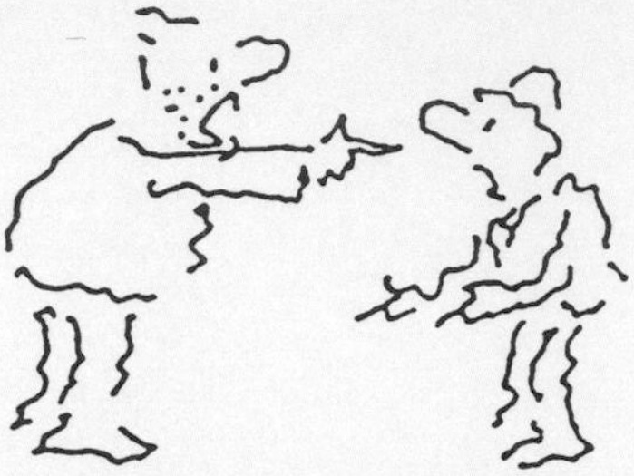

When I was in college at Oberlin, I was doing political cartoons, but it wasn't art, it was really junky stuff. But I liked the idea of making political comments with my artwork. And there was a class ball, I guess you'd call it, and I remember that I decorated the entire hall with my own murals on paper, drawings of everything I loved; like I was crazy about the film ALEXANDER NEVSKY, so one mural was of that. But again, I never thought of myself as an artist.

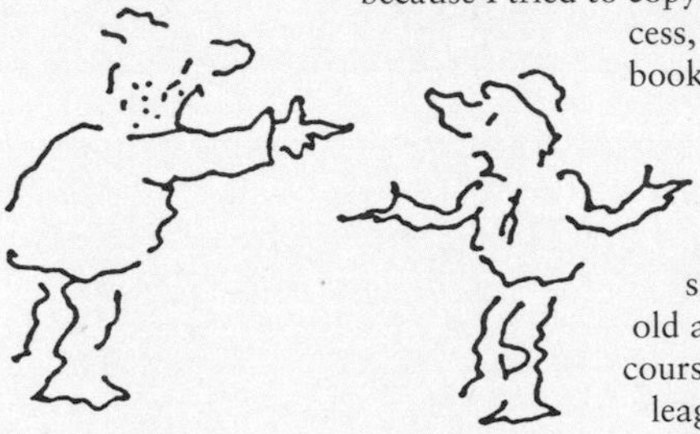

The Korean war was on, and after I got out of college I knew I'd be drafted. I didn't know if I'd be called up in a few months or a year, so I figured what the hell, I'll just goof off and do what I enjoy doing, never thinking that it might be a career.

I wasn't so much an artist as a cartoonist. My ideas were brighter and funnier than they were beautiful, because I just didn't know how to draw well. And I wasn't, nor am I now, a natural artist. I am very visual, but I don't have the hand. I work very, very hard to get things, which is probably true of many, many artists.

I was shopping around my stuff and surprisingly selling it. I'm still amazed it sold, but the stuff was, again, very bright, because I'm clever, and very funny, because I had to compensate for the fact that it looked like hell. I've made a career based on the whole notion of breaking free of the text and interpreting it; I was on the cusp of that and that helped me a hell of a lot.

Now this was a really crazy thing—in 1953 I did what's now called a graphic novel, that was immensely successful. I mean, I couldn't believe it. It was called THE JUGGLER OF OUR LADY and it was about a person who couldn't do anything in life but juggle. I suppose I thought I couldn't do anything in life but draw funny cartoons. THE HERALD TRIBUNE, which was then comparable to THE NEW YORK TIMES, gave it a full front page write–up. I was interviewed and blah, blah, blah and of course, it put my career in a tailspin, because I was too young to have that kind of success. For the next ten years I didn't come out with anything because I tried to copy what brought me the success, thinking that it was the book, not the person who made the book.

Filmmaking has always been my real passion. When I was 19 years old and in college, I took a course in humor taught by a colleague of Buñuel, Augusto Centeno. And at that point, in a flash, it occurred to me that the future of our business is animation. I thought, "This is what I have to do."

So, after college and my big book success, I freelanced a little and I went into the army for two years. And then, when I came out, my very first job was with an animation studio, Storyboard Studios. I was doing storyboards, but the storyboards were then given to artists to re–render because my stuff was considered unanimatable, because of the broken, jagged line I use.

After that I was a freelance animator and illustrator, and in 1960, because I loved graphic design, and because I was bright and restless, I was part of a design team and we had our own studio for a short time, called Blechman and Palladino, which I loved.

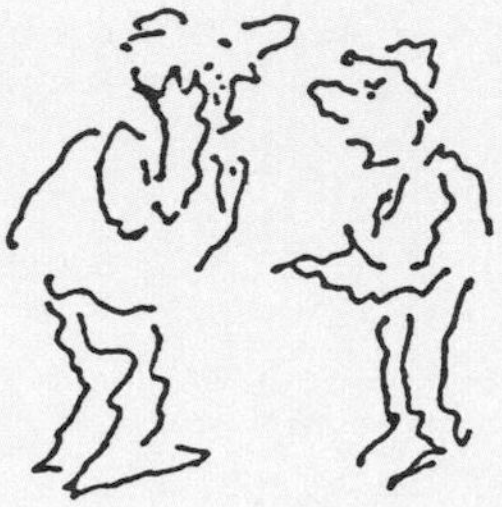

That broke up after a year. So I was doing commercials and a few books thrown in, and nothing much was happening in my career, but then I was lucky enough to produce an hour–long Christmas show for PBS called SIMPLE GIFTS. It was tremendously gratifying because I was able to use the artwork of many people I admire like James McMullan and Seymour Chwast and Maurice Sendak. Being the producer and director, I did one of the segments, myself.

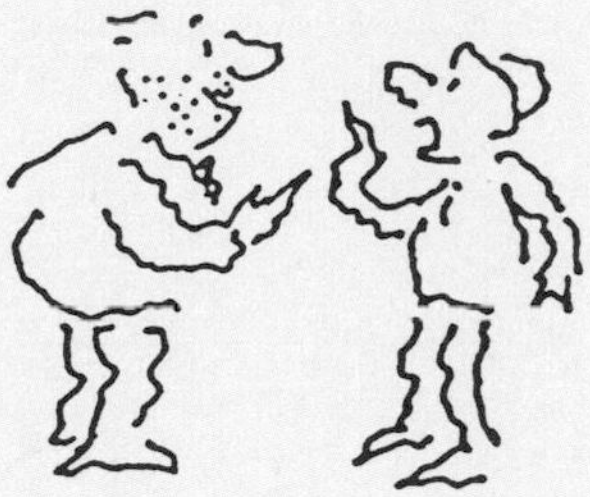

After that I founded an animation studio called The Ink Tank. And that lasted up until a few years ago. I loved working with other artists, and I still do as a matter of fact. And it's fun to commission good stuff. I was able to do a few things of significance there, and the Stravinsky film, THE SOLDIER'S TALE, was the most gratifying of all the things I was able to do.

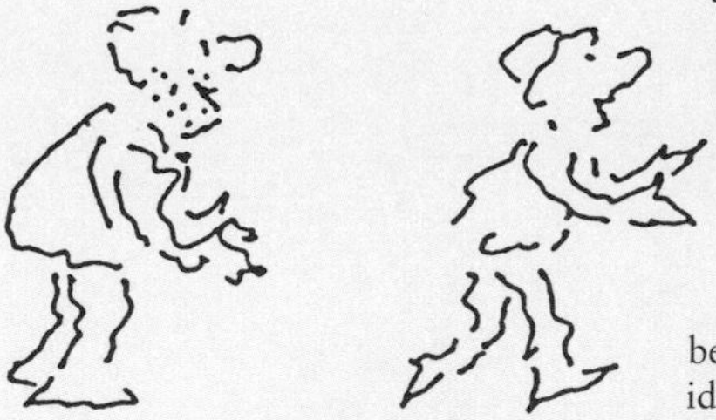

I always felt that my skills, such as they are, are as much literary as visual—maybe even more literary than visual, because I always enjoyed language a lot. As for my drawing skills, if I work hard I can do very well. But I am very lazy, and I am not interested in art that much. I'm really not. I mean, I love it, but unless somebody says, "Go do," I don't.

I love both drawing and writing, but again, I tend not to draw unless I'm asked, but I write just because it's immensely satisfying. I love it. I wrote a biography of Steinberg, that almost got published. I got a contract and an advance, but I ran into trouble with the Steinberg Foundation. It was tough when it fell through, but I'm used to a lot of failures like that. I mean, I was blessed with a difficult childhood that prepared me for the freelance life. I had a psychotic mother: occasionally she'd lie on the floor and go into a spasm. I would run upstairs to the doctor who lived in our building, and he'd be eating and I'd say, "Would you please go down, my mother is just lying on the floor screaming!" and he would finish his appetizer and main course and he would then finish his dessert. He knew my mother. She was a nut.

My father was very cut off. Listen, if you were married to a crazy like that, you would be cut off, too. And he wasn't a nice guy. He was a mean son of a bitch, particularly to my older brother. We were not the happiest family, but it prepared me for the freelance life and all the rebuffs that would happen. I've had my share of them and that's the way it goes.

I've had some proud achievements in illustration, of course: some of my NEW YORKER covers were really very good and then the ten years I did every single cover for a magazine called STORY. I loved doing that stuff. It was fantastic. But I have not begun to fulfill my ideas about animation, which is my real passion. Even still, every few years, hey, I've got another idea for a feature, and it's got to be done and I'm still hacking away at it. I'll never stop.

TALKING LINES

HUMBUG

. . . .

HUMBUG, 1957-58

These were done for *Humbug*, a short-lived magazine of the late Fifties edited by the incomparable Harvey Kurtzman. It pains me to look at the drawings now -- those Sunnyside--up eyes (a simple dot does the trick now)! --that brittle linework! But for archival reasons I've agreed to include this early work in the book.

WATCHING THE WORLD SERIES

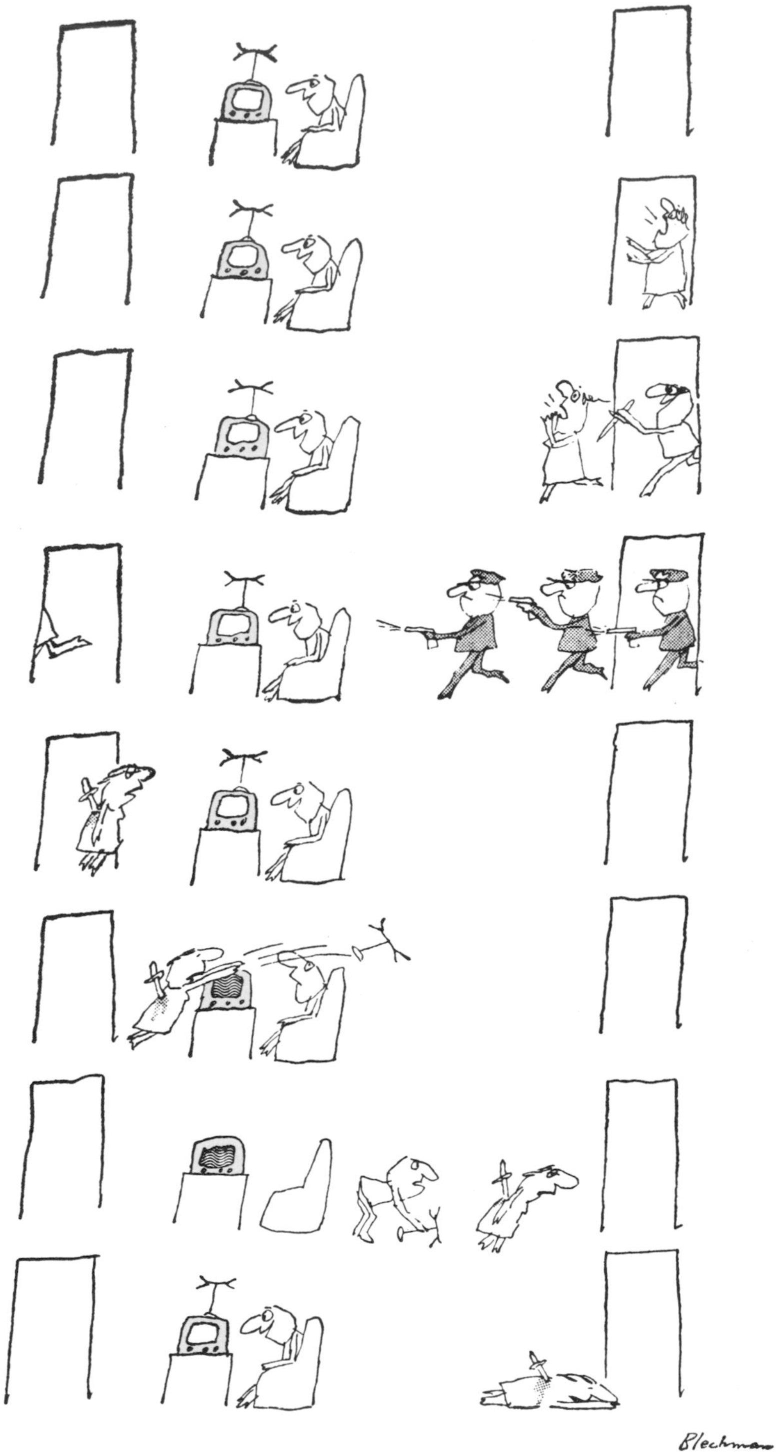
Blechman

THE TEMPORARY RECESSION

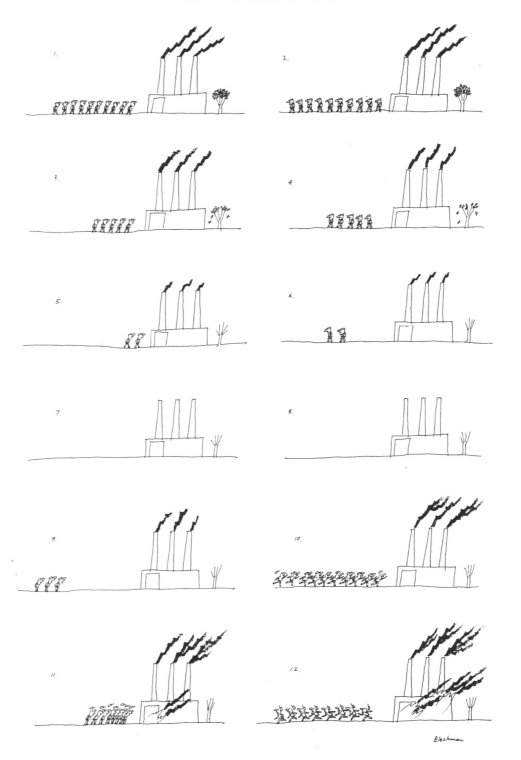

Blechman

A WHITE CHRISTMAS

1.
FOR RENT
2
FOR RENT
3.
4.

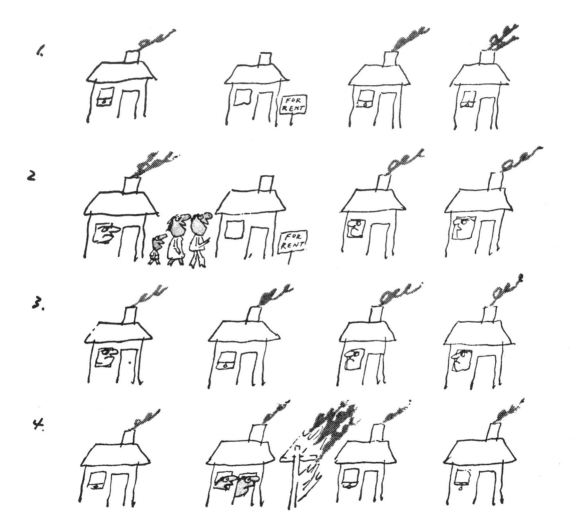

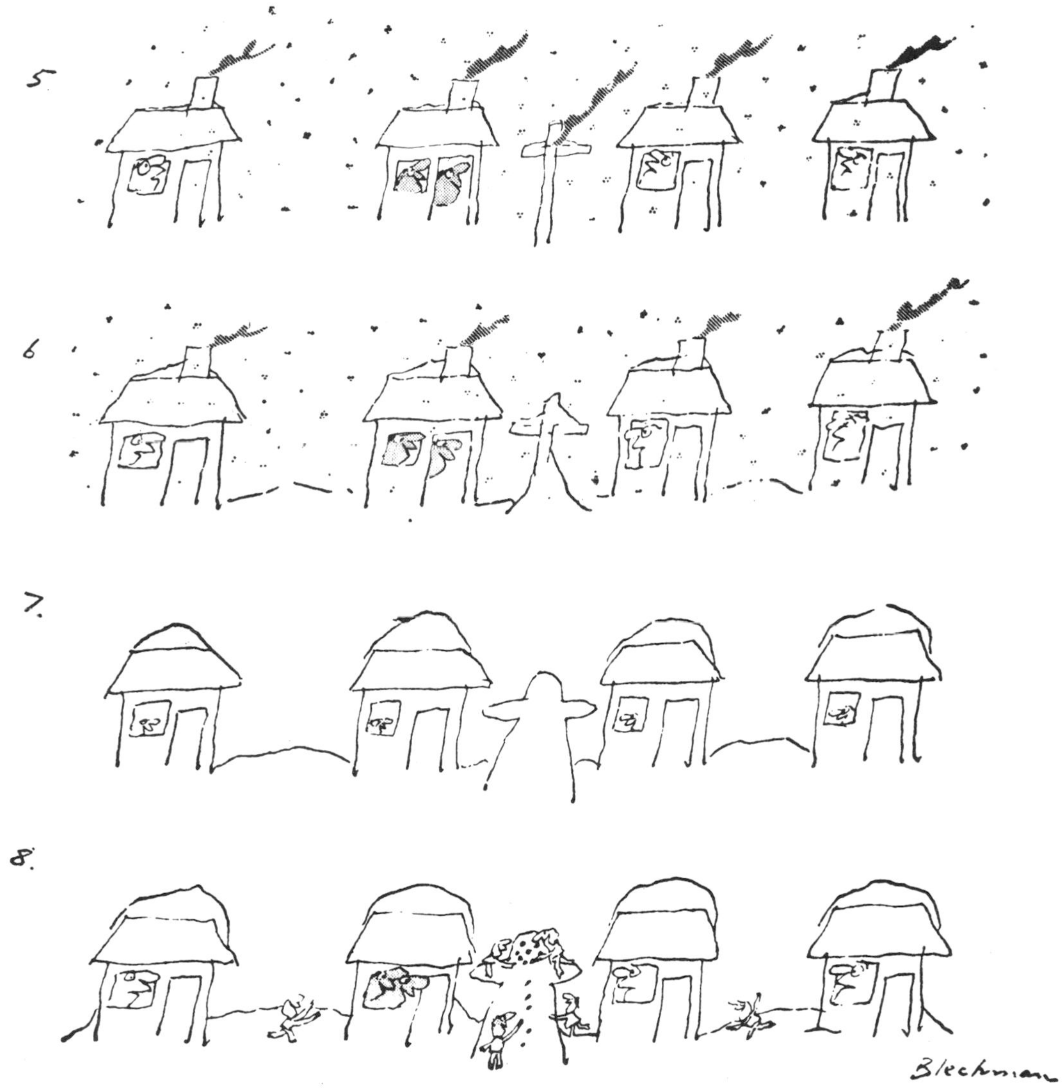
5.
6
7.
8.
Blechman

THANKSGIVING DINNER

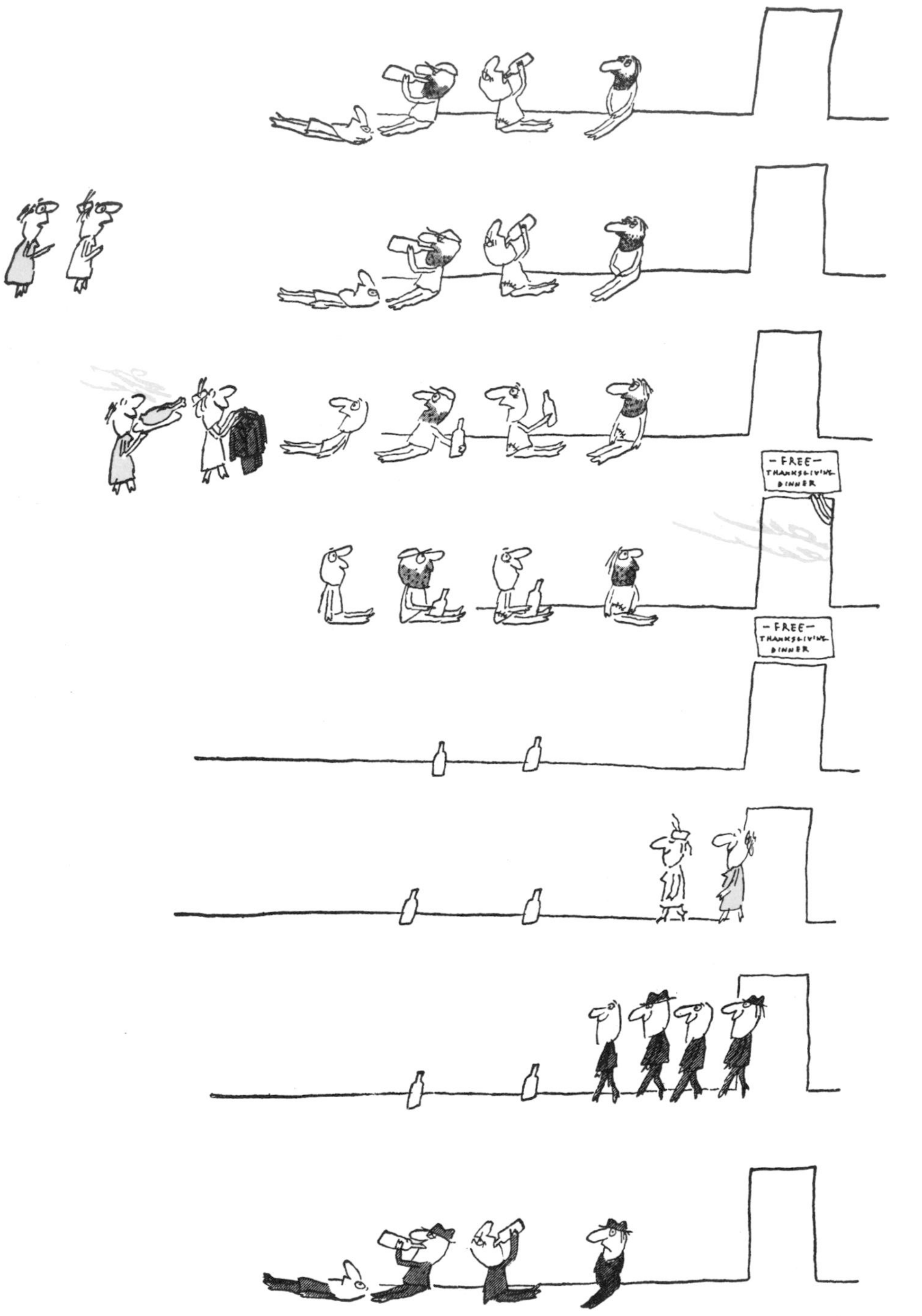

-FREE-
THANKSGIVING DINNER
-FREE-
THANKSGIVING DINNER
Blechman

A HUMAN INTEREST STORY

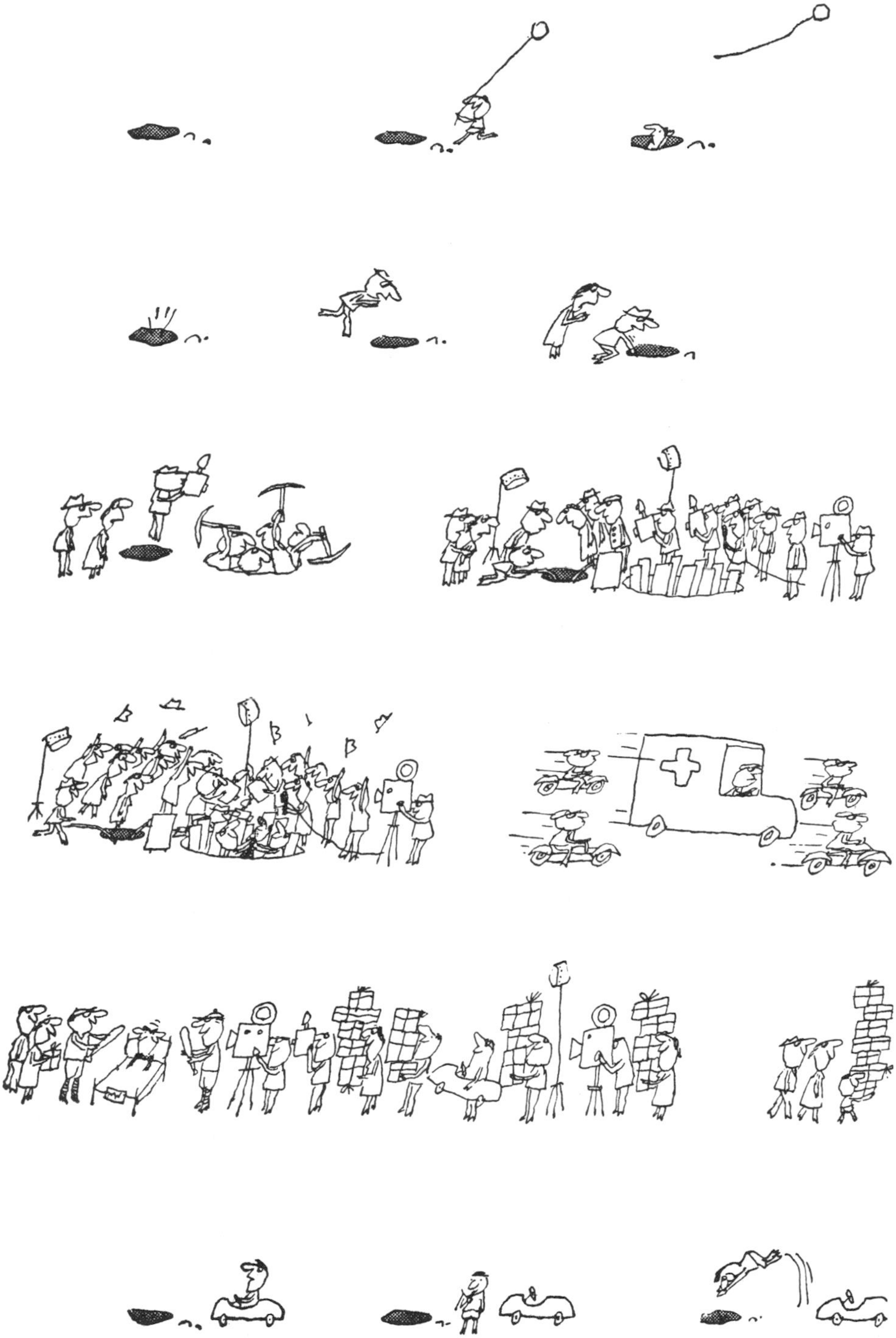

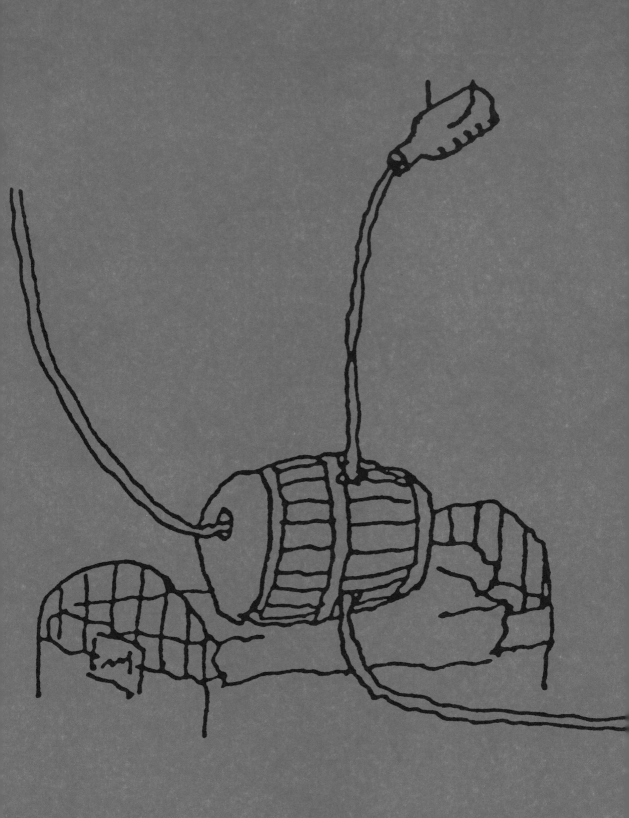

CONTAMINATION

ONION SOUP, 1964

Contamination was drawn in 1964, and appeared in a collection of short stories called *Onion Soup.* The flyleaf of the book described *Onion Soup* as "a pungent book, nicely garnished with the drawings of its author." To my present taste, the garnish has lost some of its allure, but I think its pungency remains.

The subject matter, nuclear weaponry, still retains its pertinence, in fact, now more than ever. In those days we held protest marches. Today we have replaced marching shoes with Nikes.

CONTAMINATION

When Simpson Eks finished the equation he could hardly believe it.

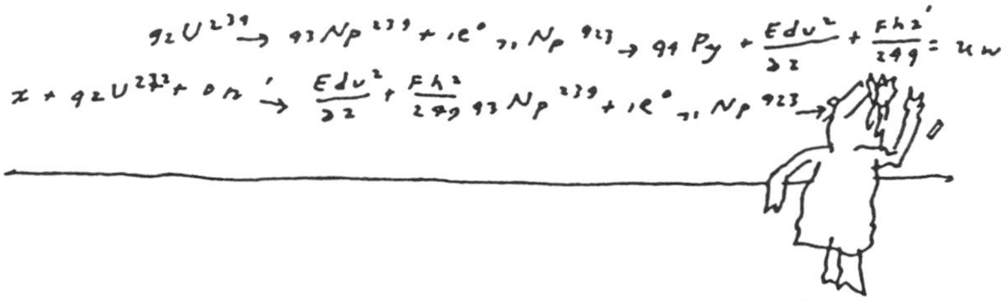

92U239 → 93Np239 + -1e0 71Np923 → 94Py + Edv2/∂z + Fh2/249 = uw
x + 92U232 + on' → Edv2/∂z + Fh2/249 93Np239 + -1e0 71Np923 → 9

He went over it carefully...

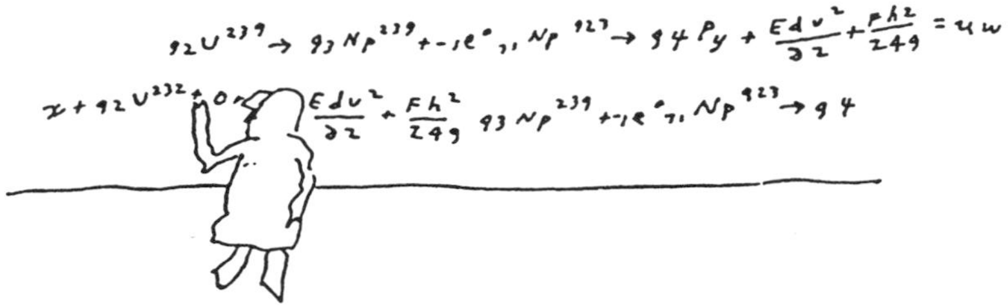

92U239 → 93Np239 + -1e0 71Np923 → 94Py + Edv2/∂z + Fh2/249 = uw
x + 92U232 + on Edv2/∂z + Fh2/249 93Np239 + -1e0 71Np923 → 94

... and it all checked out.

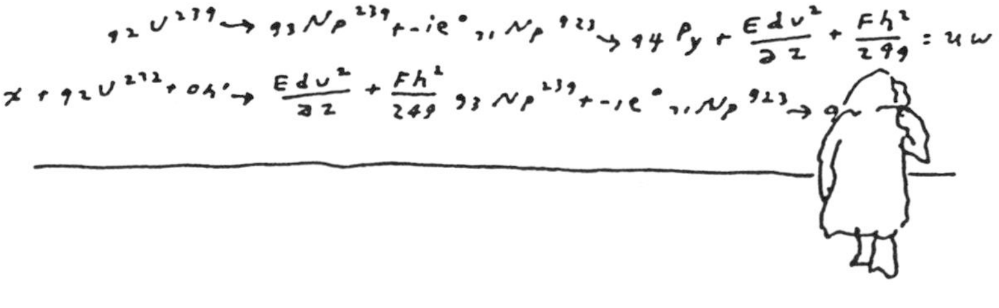

92U239 → 93Np239 + -1e0 71Np923 → 94Py + Edv2/∂z + Fh2/249 = uw
x + 92U232 + on' → Edv2/∂z + Fh2/249 93Np239 + -1e0 71Np923 → 9

He had discovered the ultimate weapon.

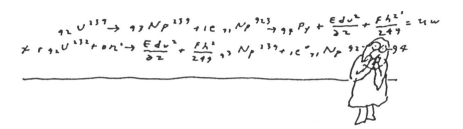

He copied the equation in his notebook,...

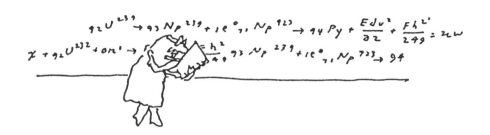

... and erased the blackboard...

... and washed it down with a
special no-trace liquid...

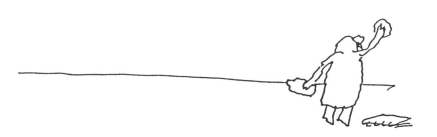

... and fainted.

That night he could not sleep.

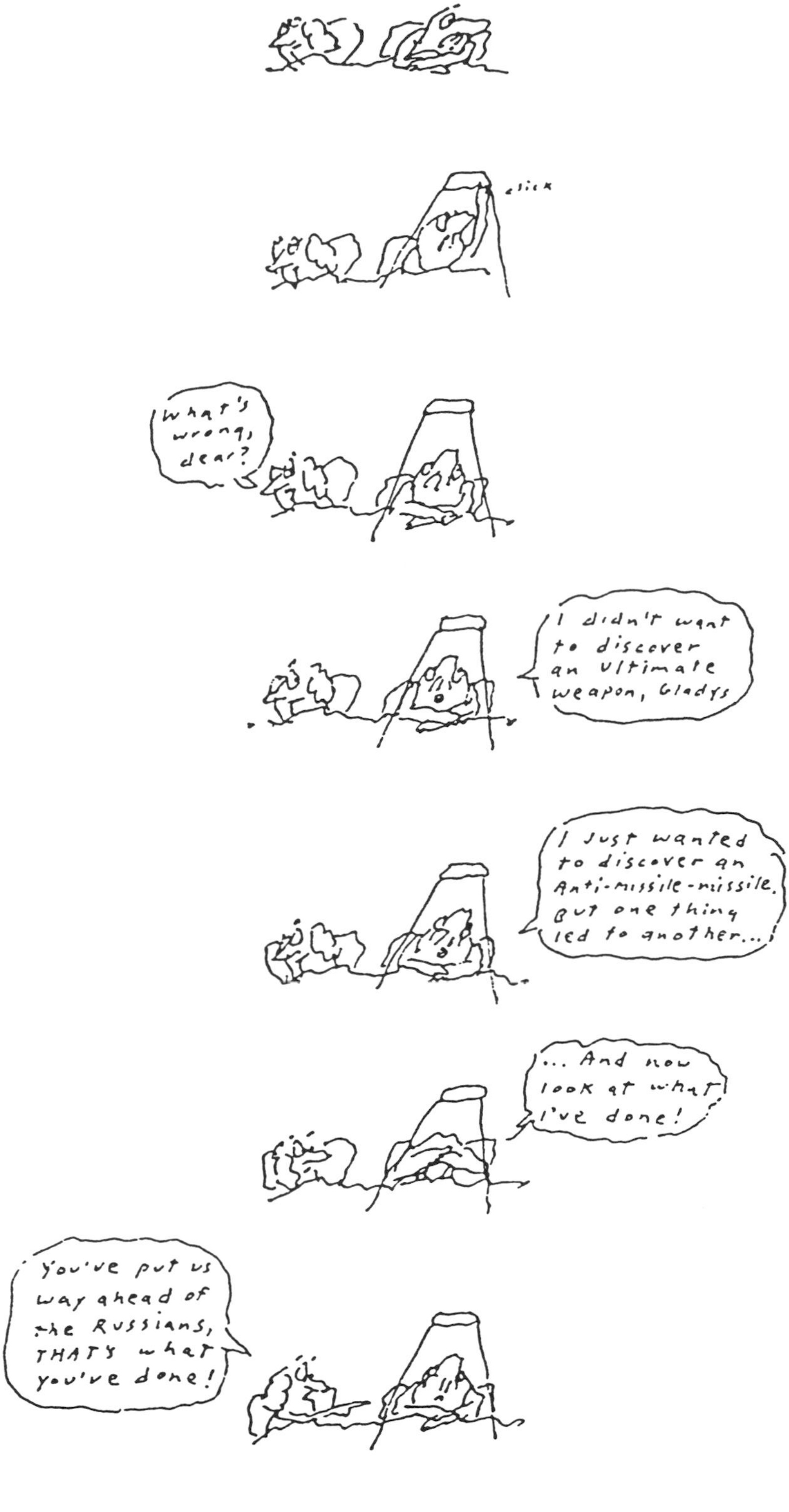
click
what's wrong, dear?
I didn't want to discover an ultimate weapon, Gladys
I just wanted to discover an Anti-missile-missile. But one thing led to another...
... And now look at what I've done!
You've put us way ahead of the Russians, THAT'S what you've done!

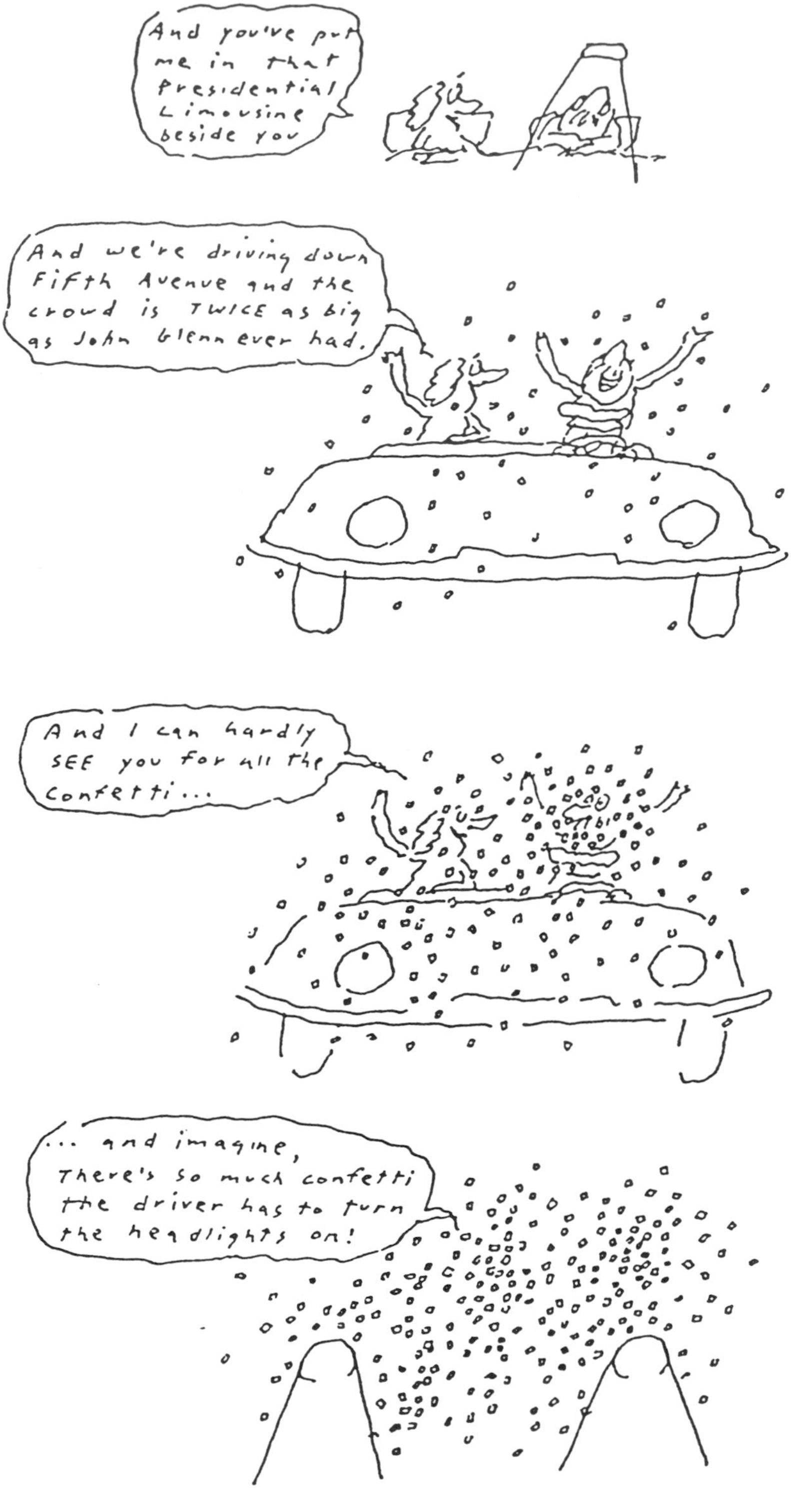
And you've put me in that Presidential Limousine beside you
And we're driving down Fifth Avenue and the crowd is TWICE as big as John Glenn ever had.
And I can hardly SEE you for all the confetti...
... and imagine, There's so much confetti the driver has to turn the headlights on!

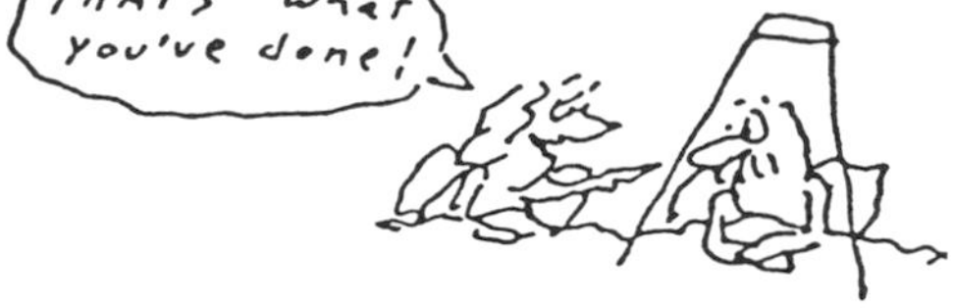
THAT's what you've done!

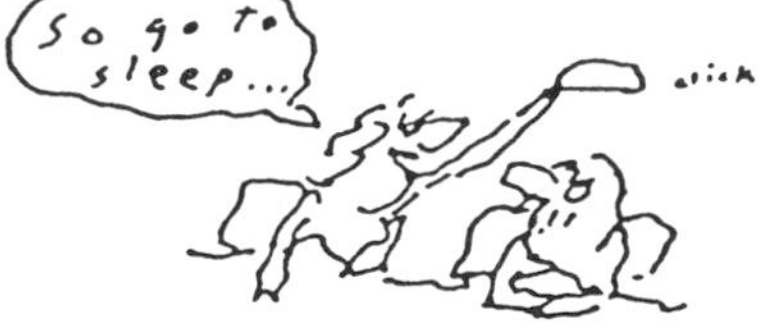
So go to sleep...
click

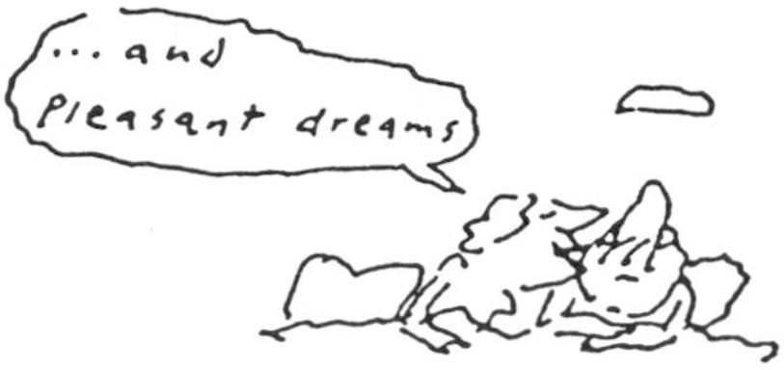
...and Pleasant dreams

In the morning his wife brought him breakfast.

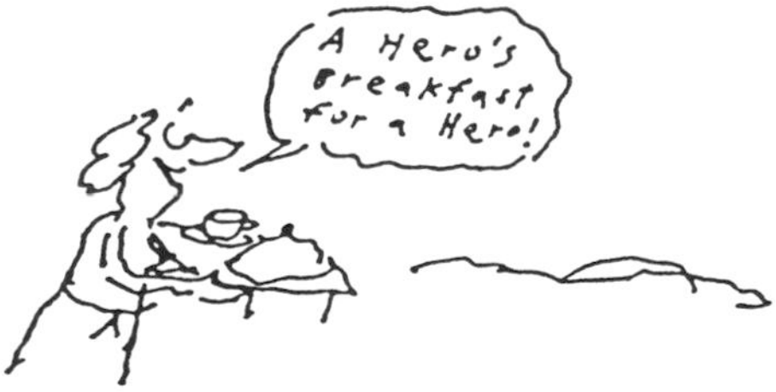
A Hero's Breakfast for a Hero!

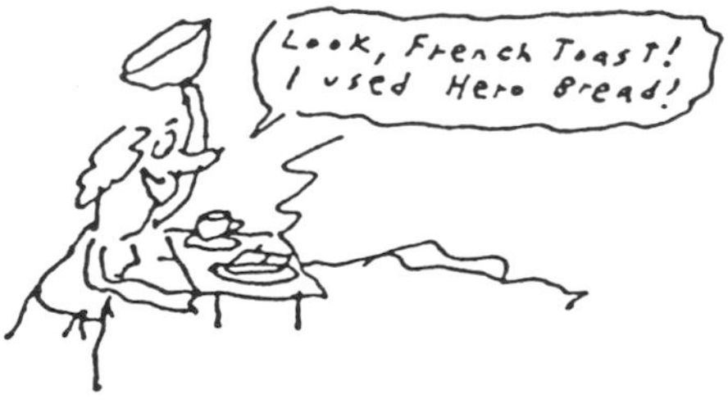
Look, French Toast! I used Hero Bread!

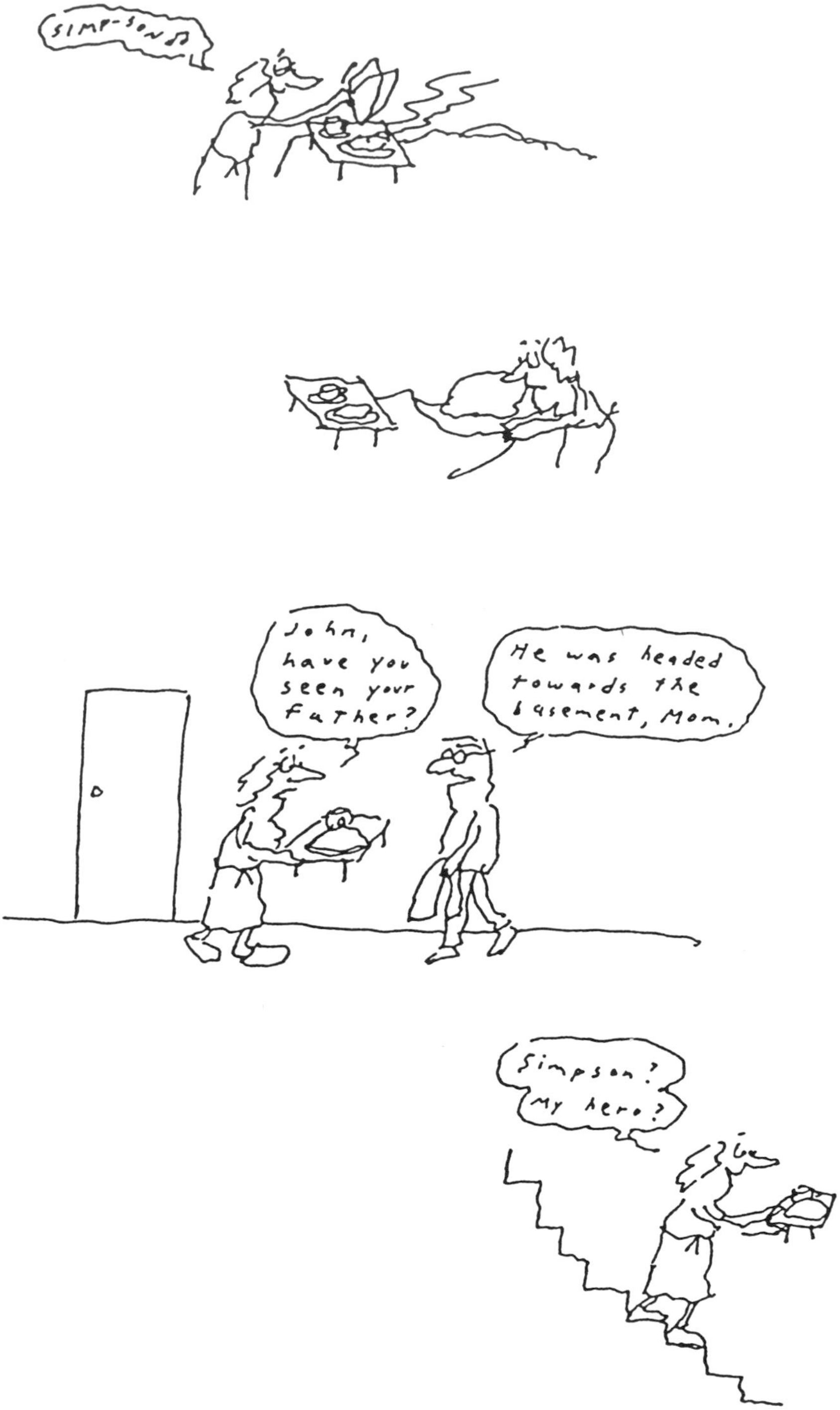
SIMP-SON
John, have you seen your father?
He was headed towards the basement, Mom.
Simpson? My hero?

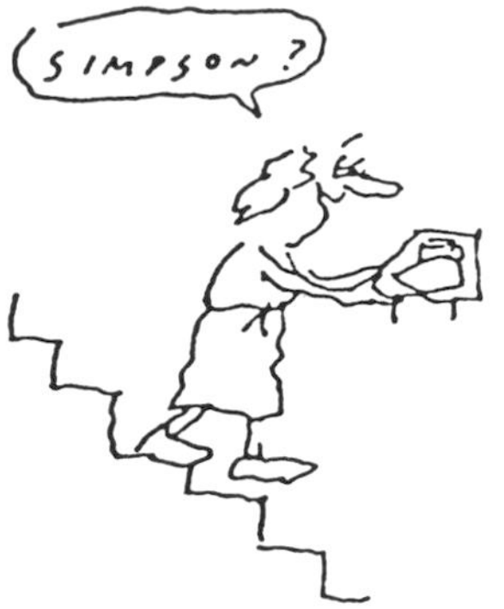
SIMPSON?

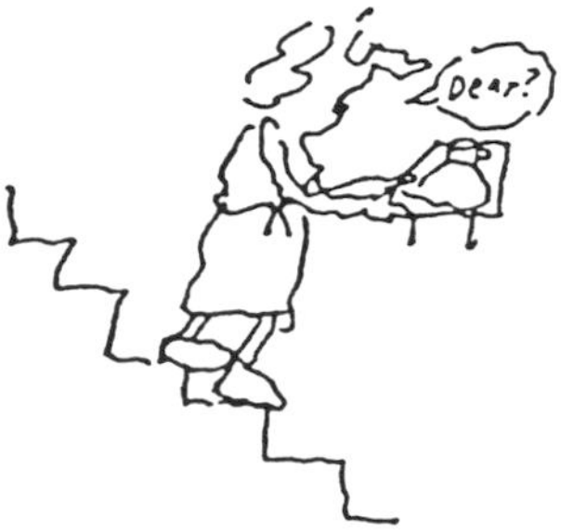
DEAR?

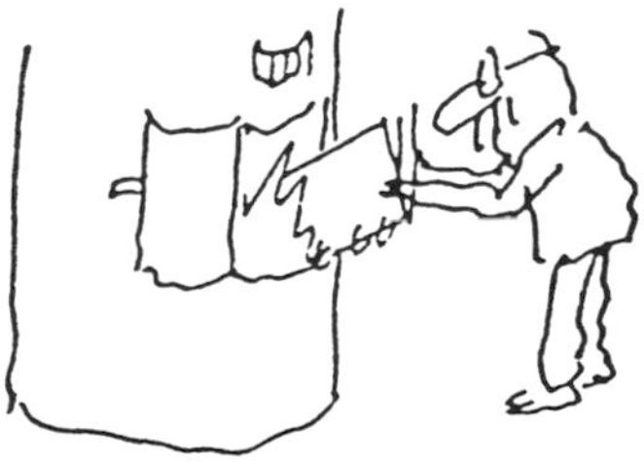

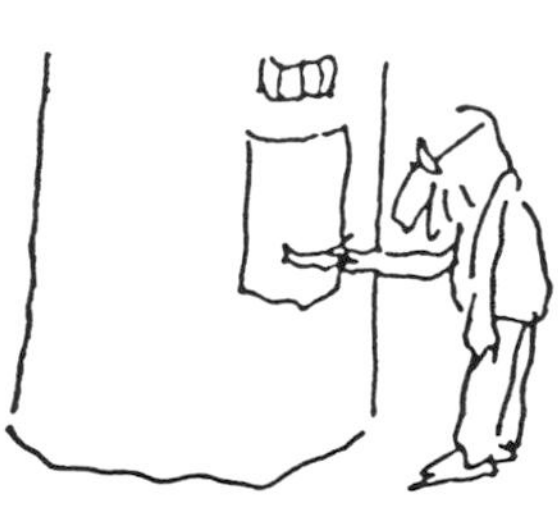

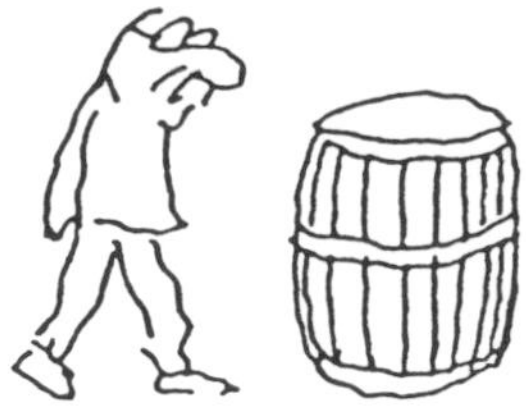

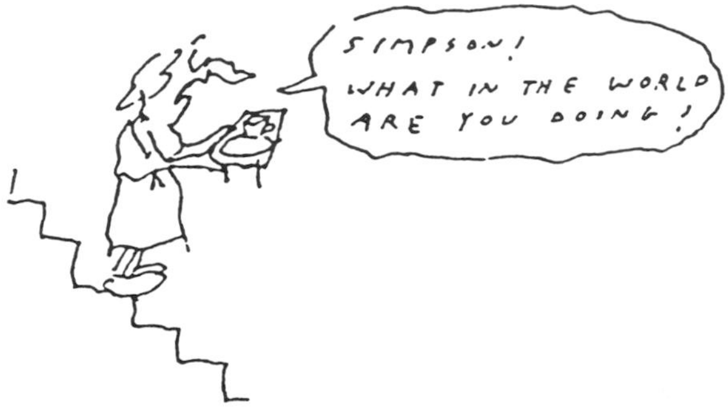
SIMPSON!
WHAT IN THE WORLD
ARE YOU DOING!

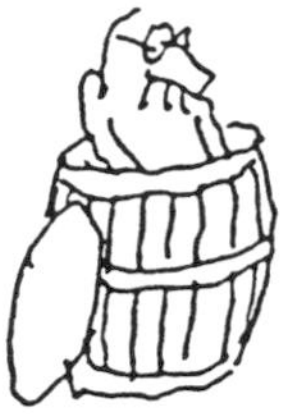

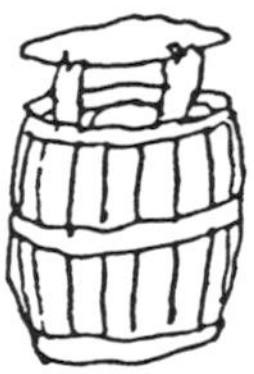

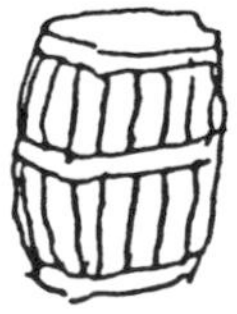

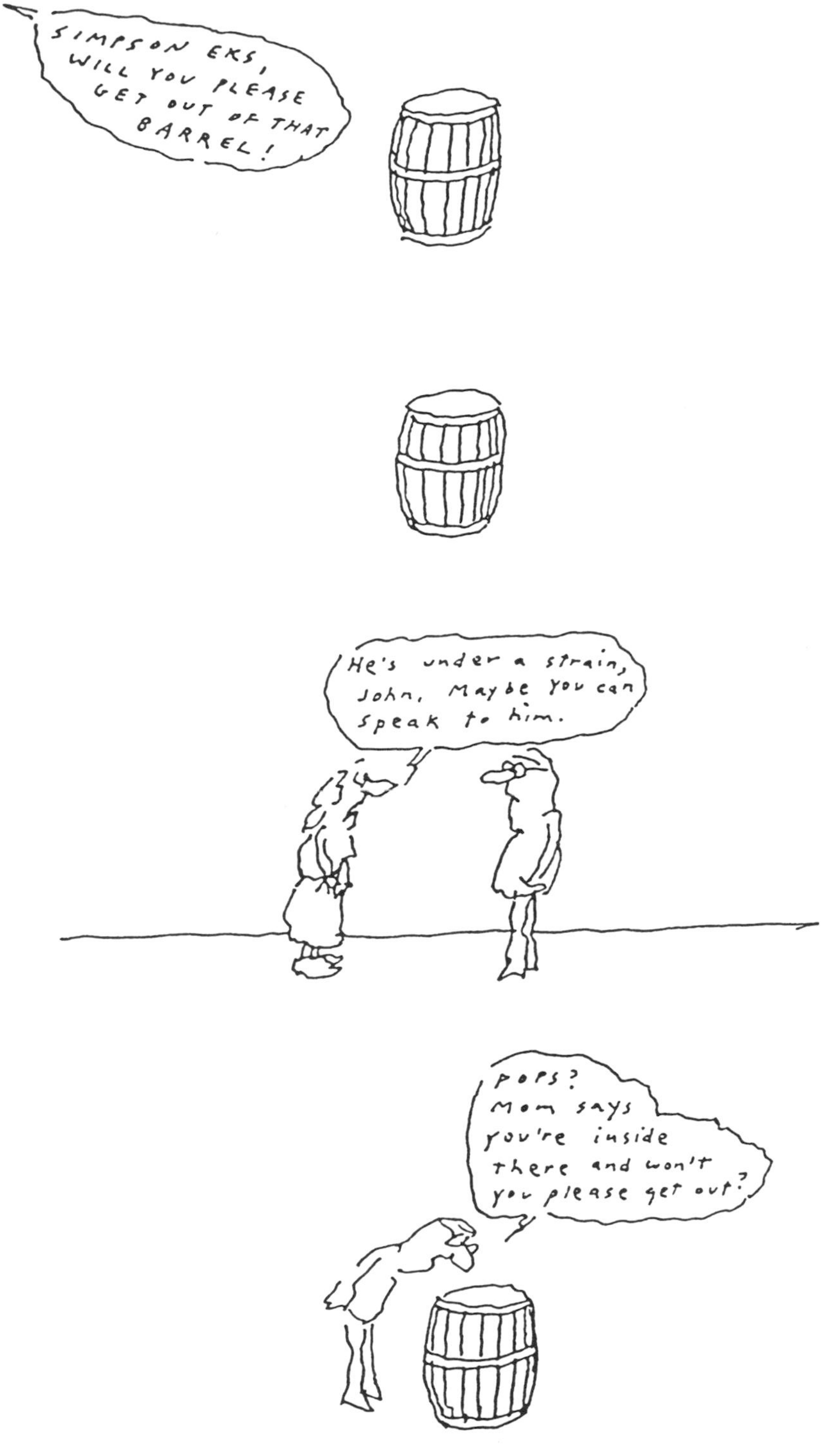
SIMPSON EKS, WILL YOU PLEASE GET OUT OF THAT BARREL!
He's under a strain, John. Maybe you can speak to him.
Pops? Mom says you're inside there and won't you please get out?

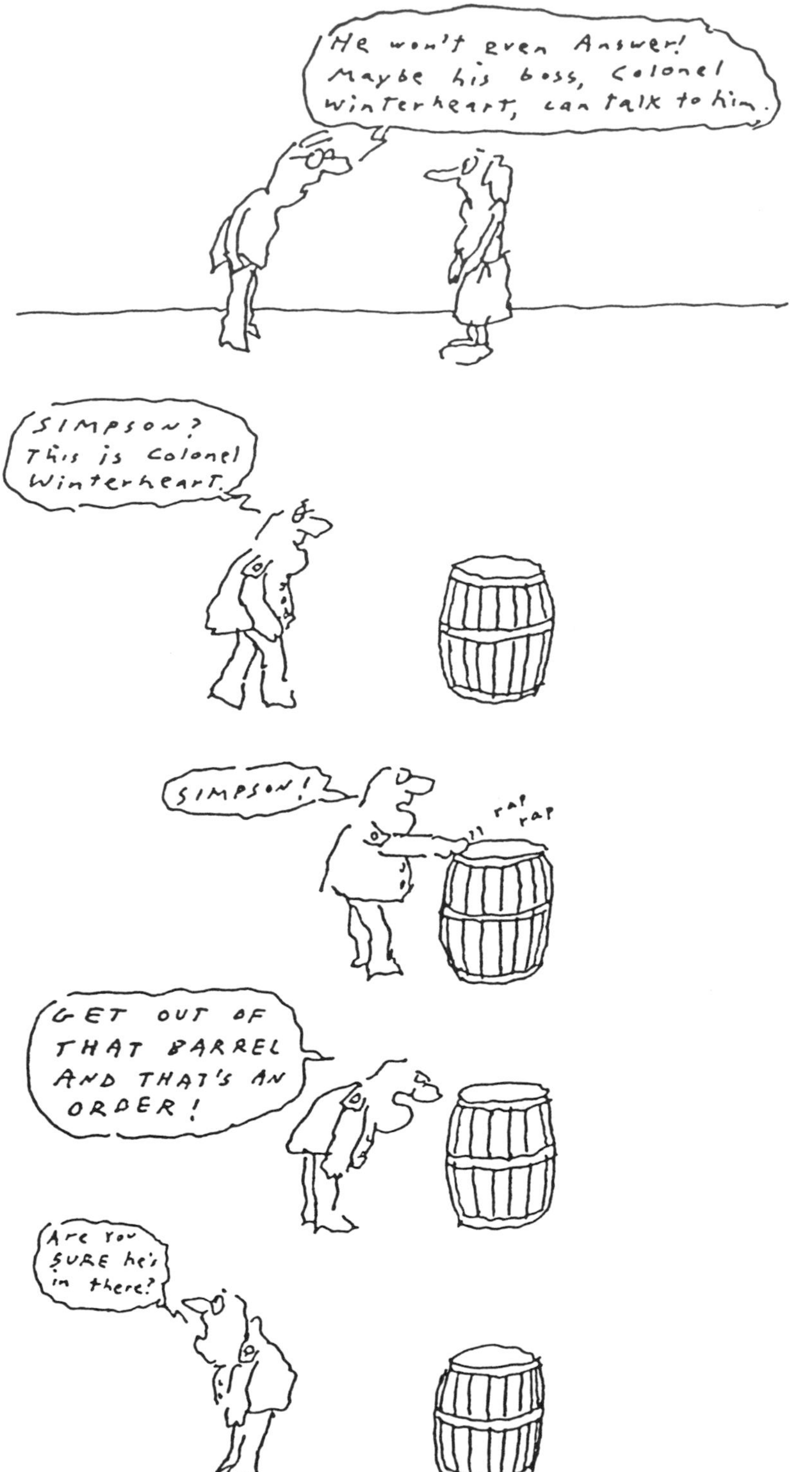
He won't even Answer! Maybe his boss, Colonel Winterheart, can talk to him.
SIMPSON? This is Colonel Winterheart.
SIMPSON!
rap rap
GET OUT OF THAT BARREL AND THAT'S AN ORDER!
Are You SURE he's in there?

That afternoon Simpson Eks was taken to the Bethlehem Naval Hospital for an examination.

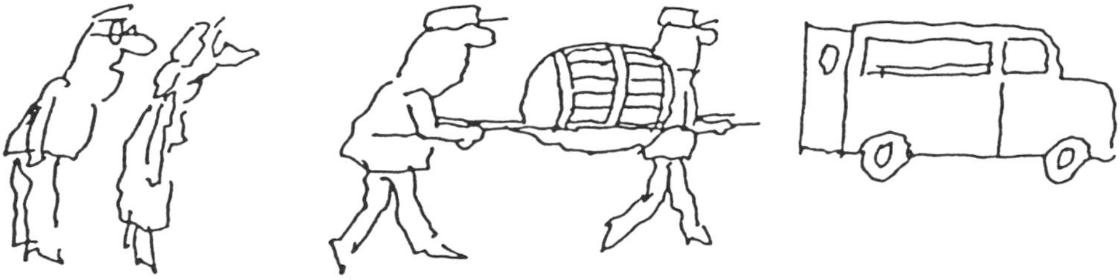

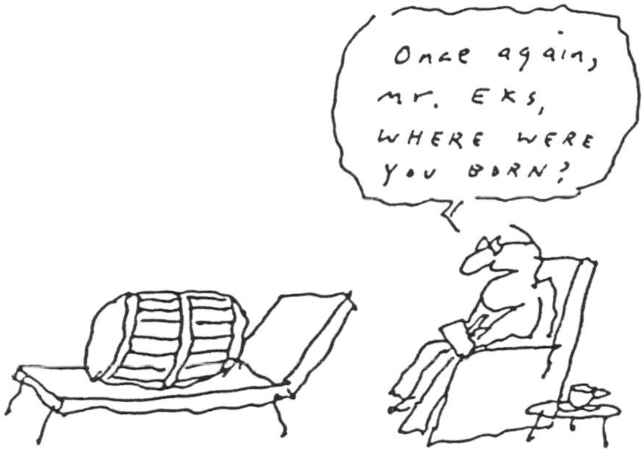
Once again, mr. Eks, WHERE WERE YOU BORN?

His wife and son visited the hospital.

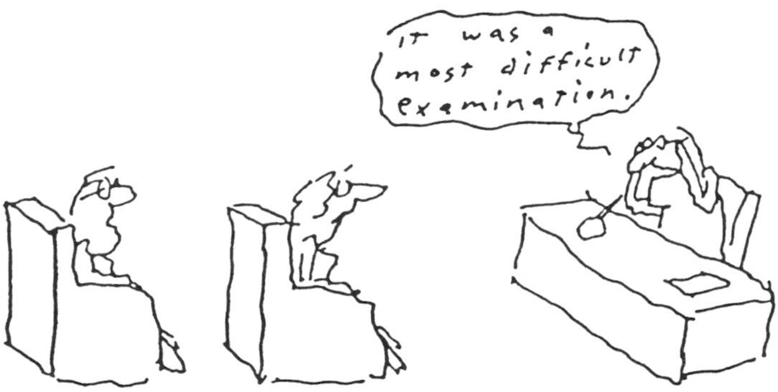
It was a most difficult examination.

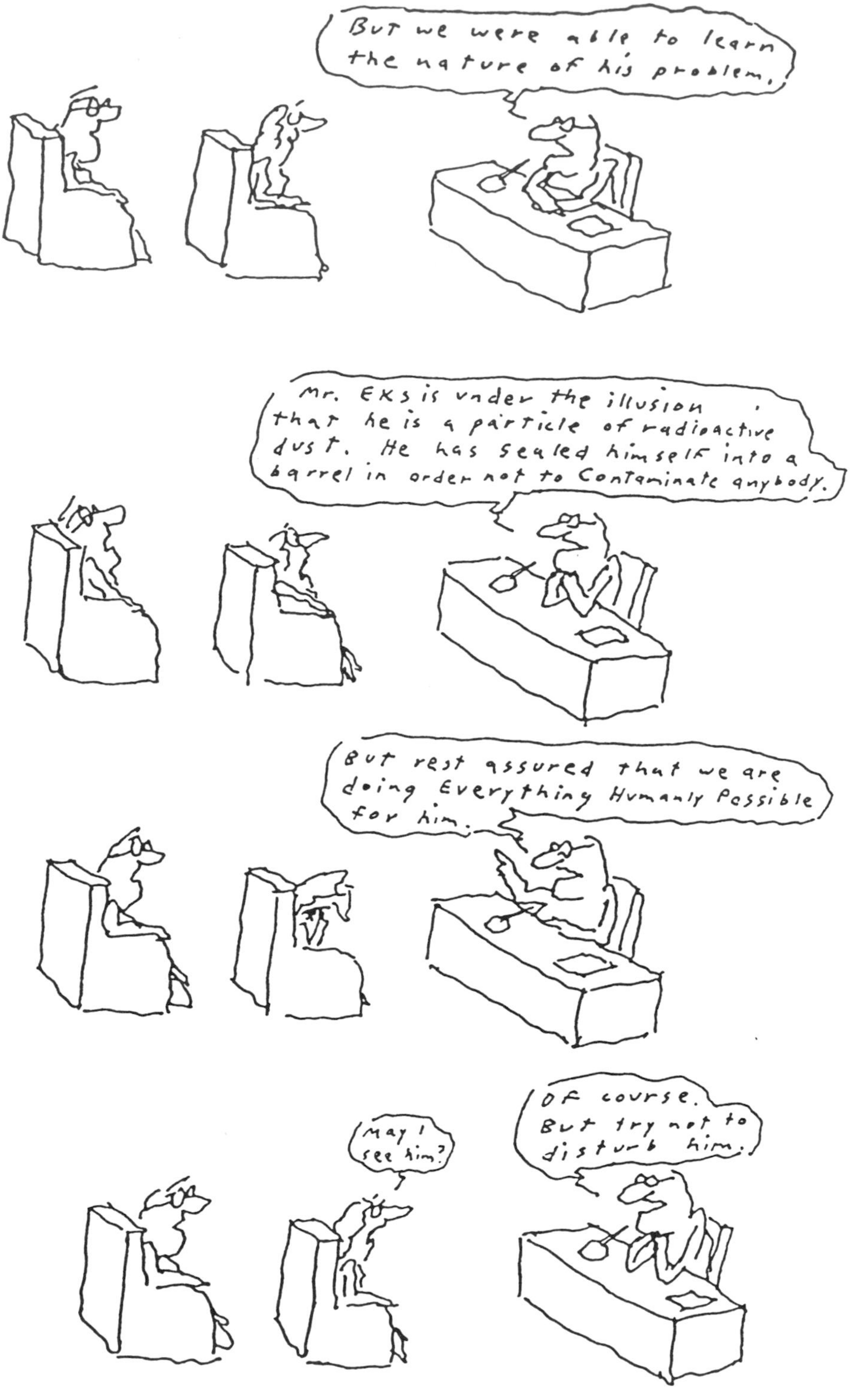
But we were able to learn the nature of his problem.
Mr. Eks is under the illusion that he is a particle of radioactive dust. He has sealed himself into a barrel in order not to Contaminate anybody.
But rest assured that we are doing Everything Humanly Possible for him.
May I see him?
Of course. But try not to disturb him.

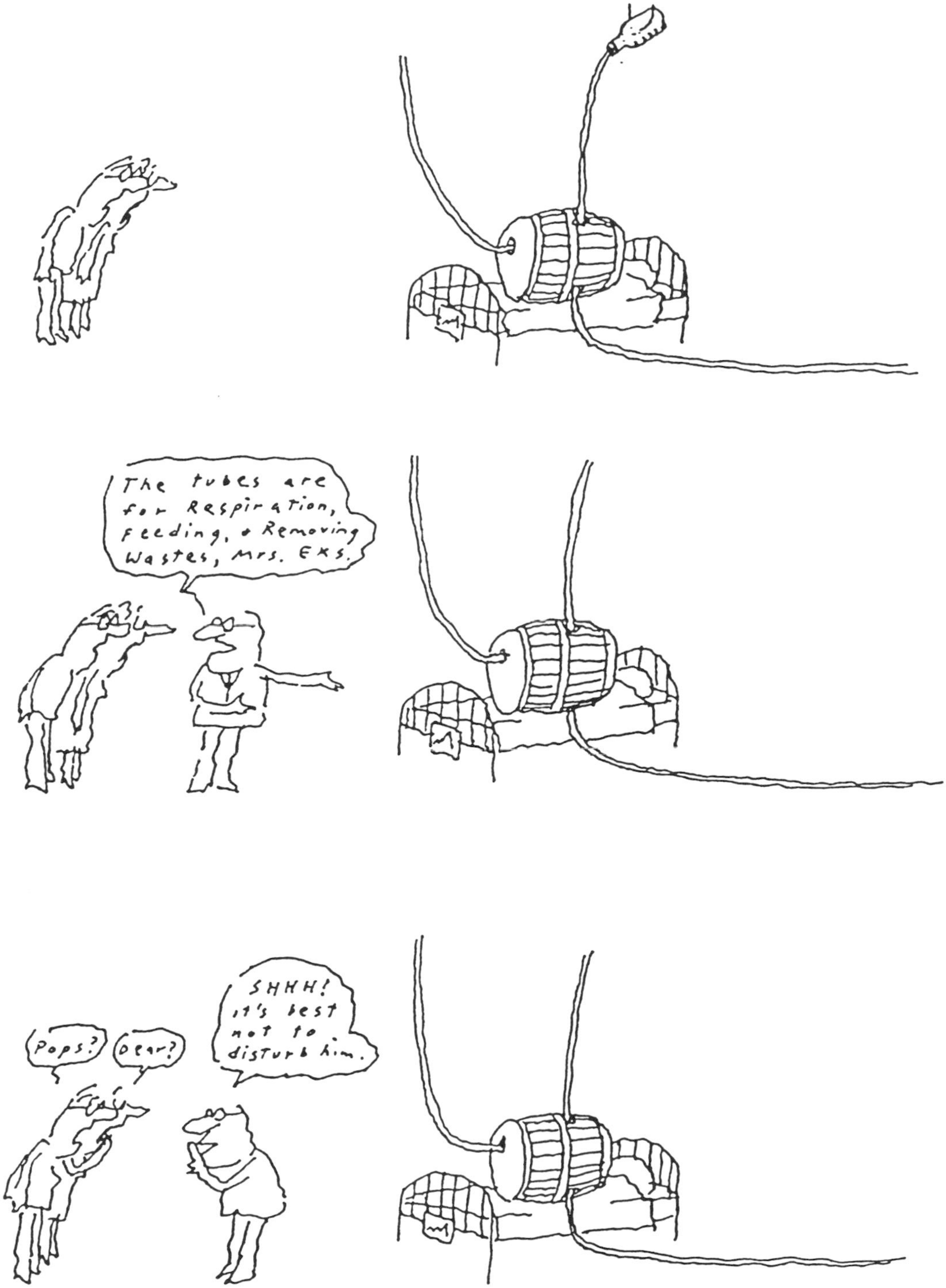
The tubes are for Respiration, Feeding, & Removing Wastes, Mrs. Eks.
Pops?
Dear?
SHHH! it's best not to disturb him.

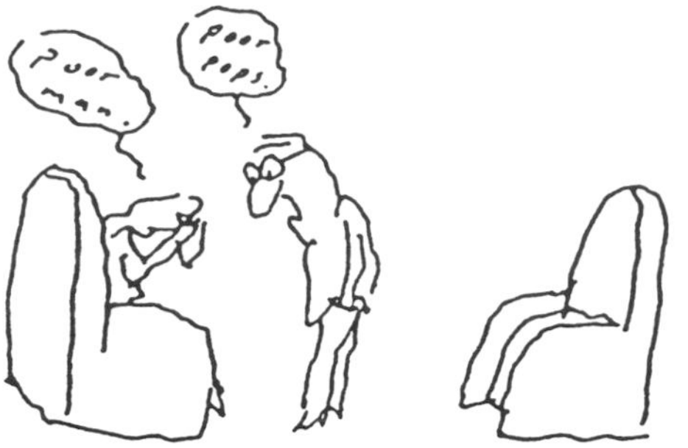
Poor man.
Poor pops.

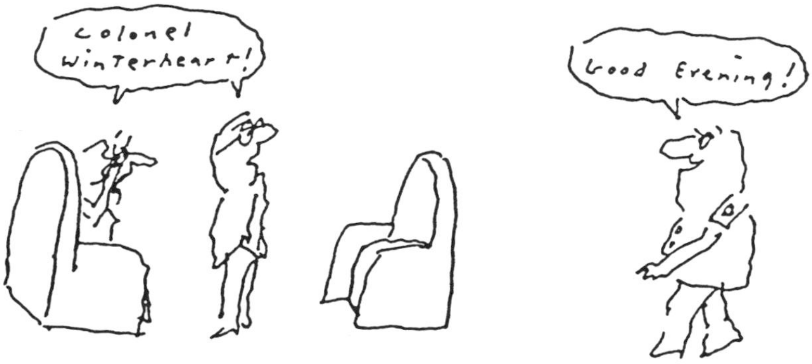
Colonel Winterheart!
Good Evening!

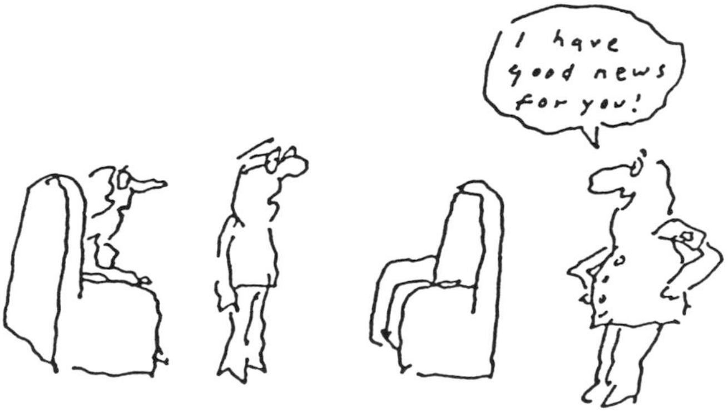
I have good news for you!

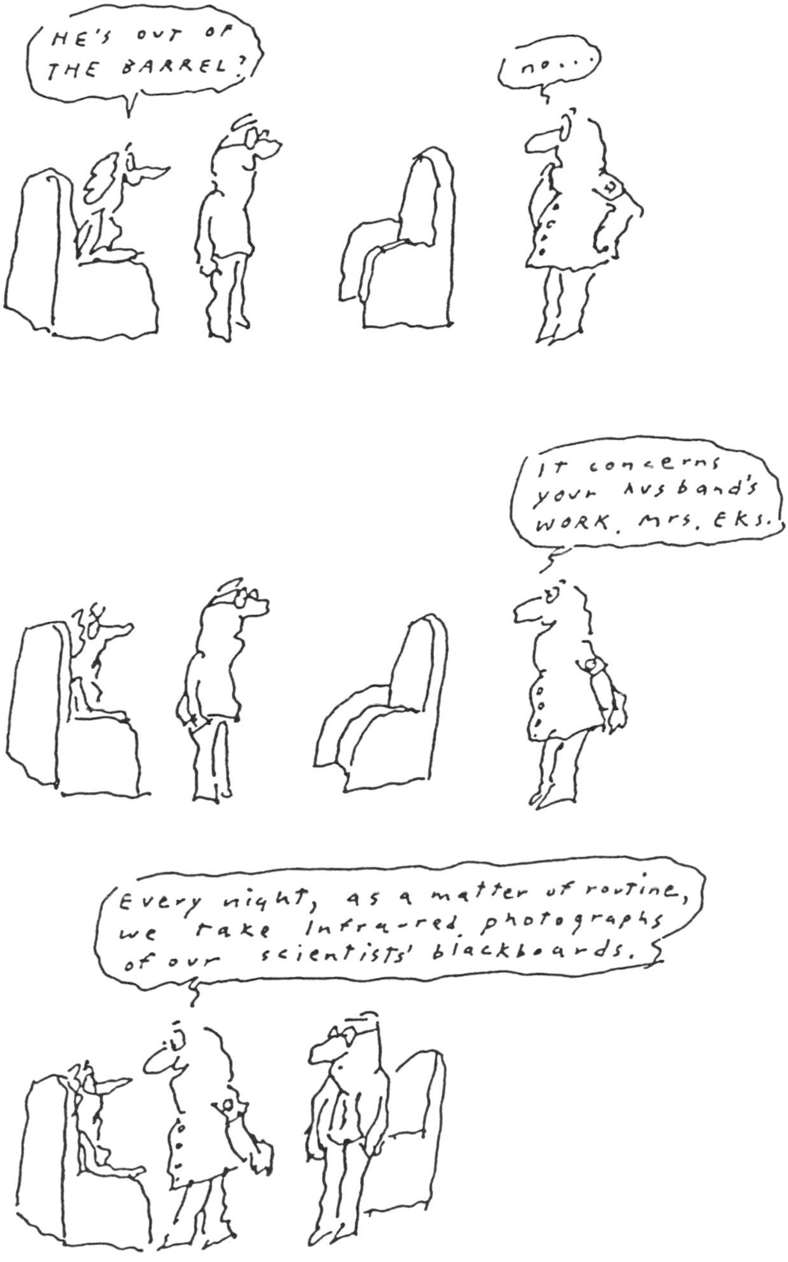
HE'S OUT OF THE BARREL?
no...
IT concerns your husband's WORK, Mrs. Eks.
Every night, as a matter of routine, we take infra-red photographs of our scientists' blackboards.

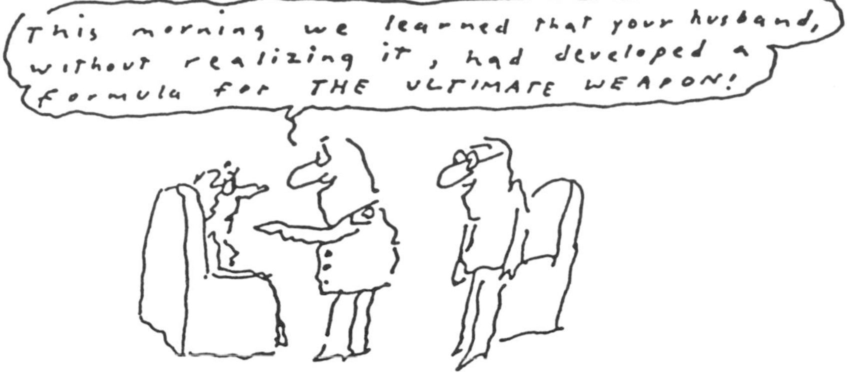
This morning we learned that your husband, without realizing it, had developed a formula for THE ULTIMATE WEAPON!

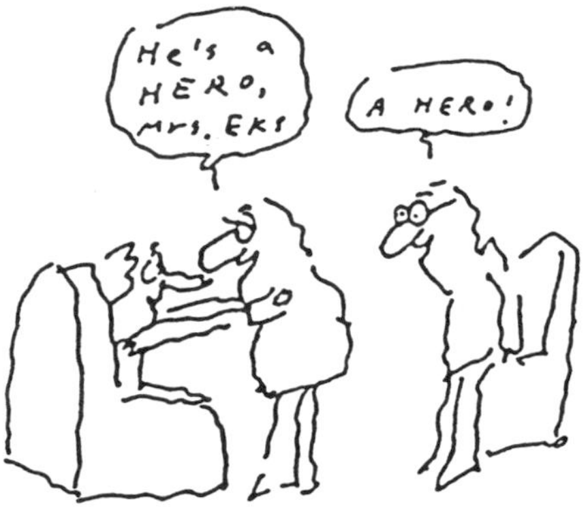
He's a HERO, Mrs. Eks
A HERO!

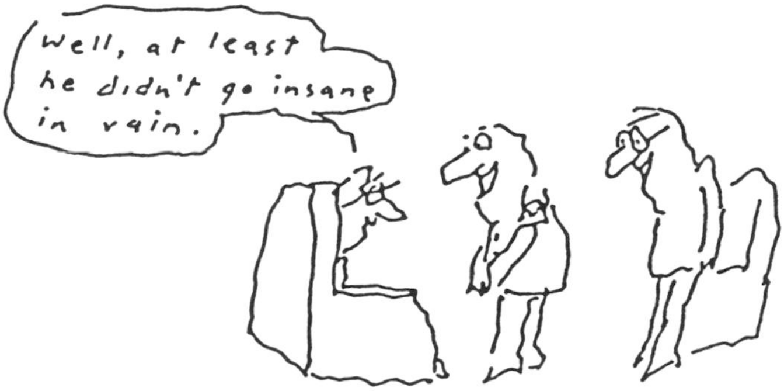
Well, at least he didn't go insane in vain.

MORAL: Even radioactive clouds have their silver linings.

VIETNAM

. . . .

THE VILLAGE VOICE, 1966

There's a saying to the effect that
one should walk the talk.
In this case my drawings did
the walking.

Vietnam

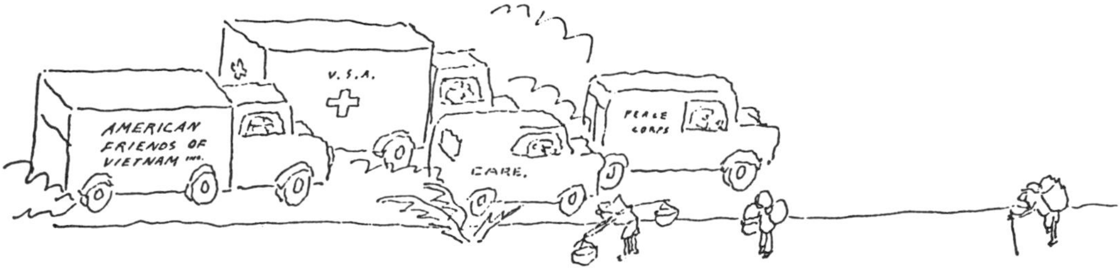

AMERICAN
FRIENDS OF
VIETNAM
U.S.A.
CARE.
PEACE
CORPS

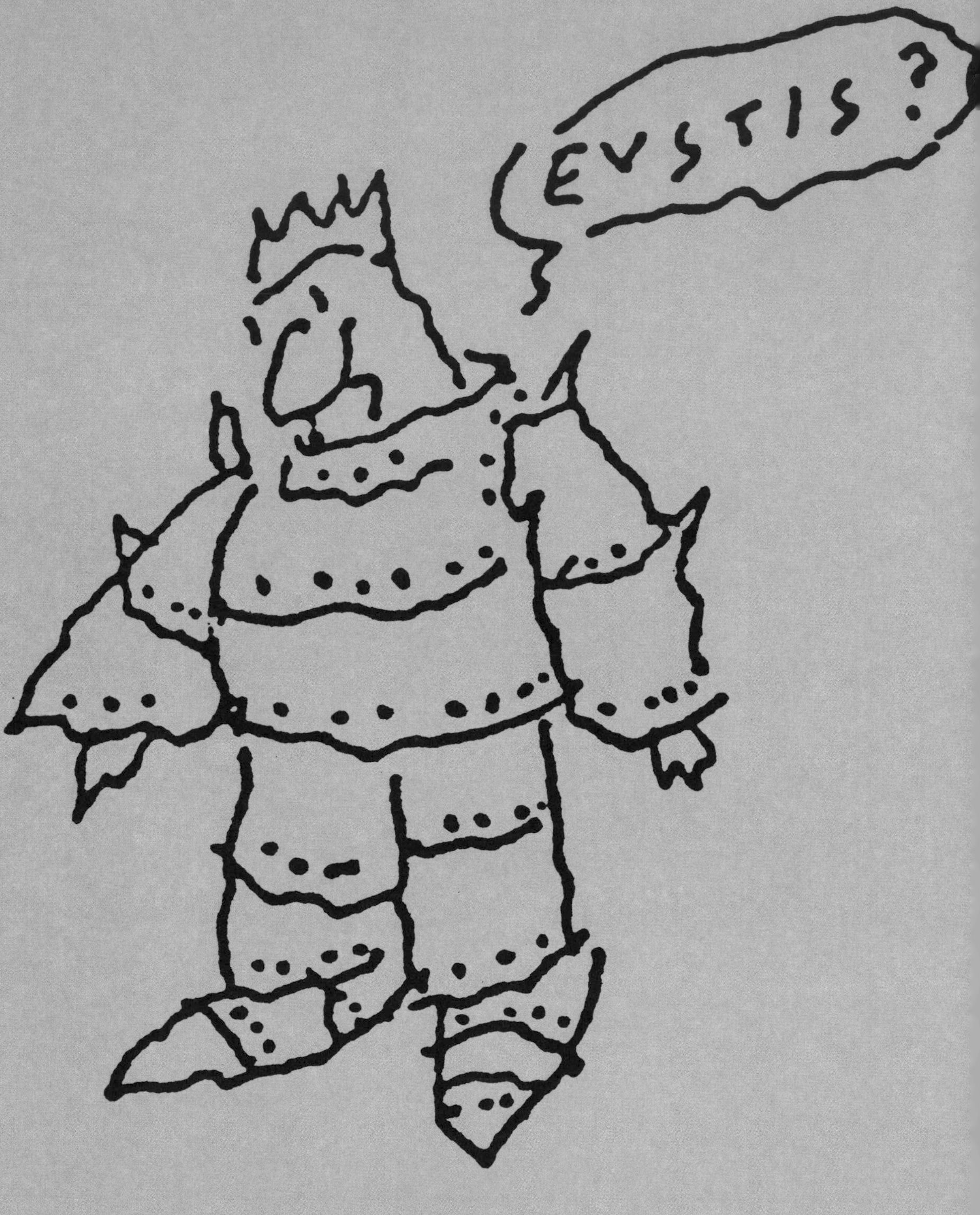
EVSTIS?

The Emperor's New Armor

VISTA MAGAZINE, 1968

My elder son, Nicholas, was born a year before this was published (It was printed in black and white with silver for the armor). I think his birth, and the Vietnam War, were the inspirations for this piece. It was later made into an animated film.

There once were Three Tailors who visited a King.

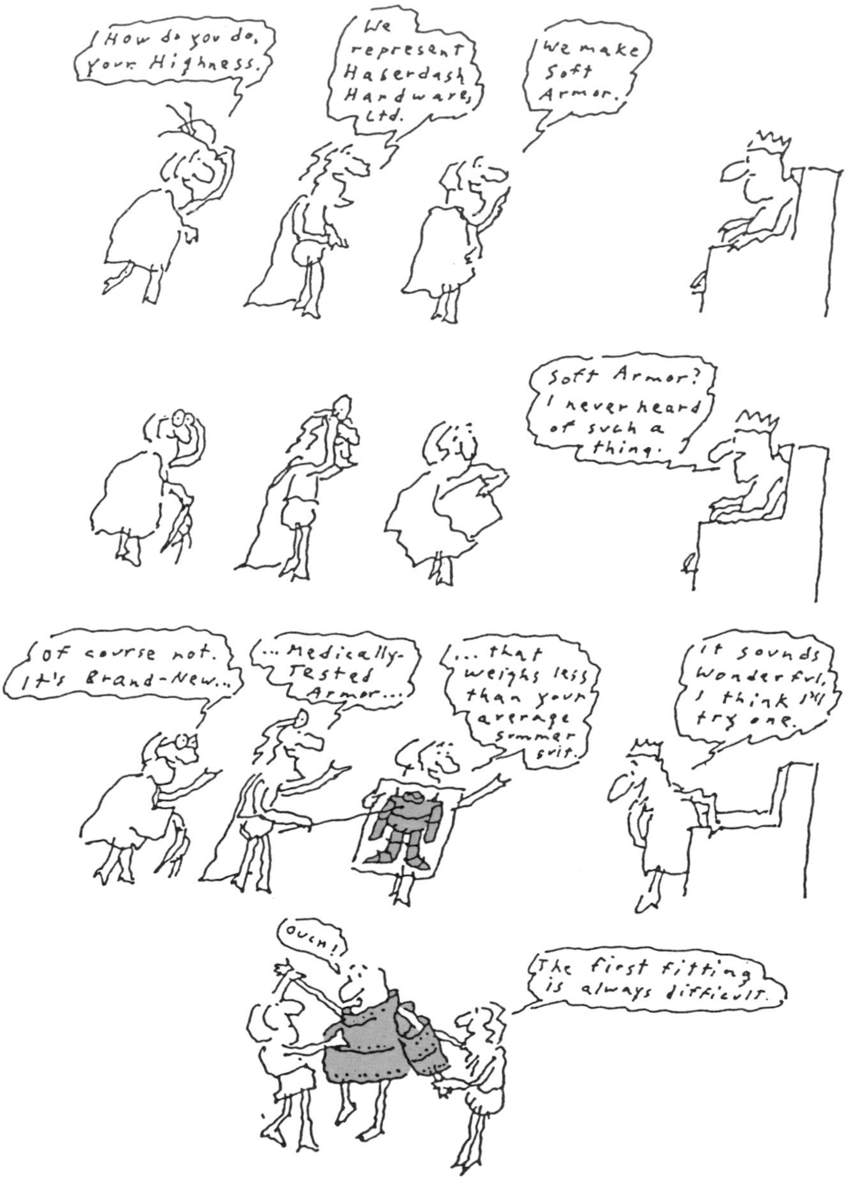
How do you do, Your Highness.
We represent Haberdash Hardware, Ltd.
We make Soft Armor.
Soft Armor? I never heard of such a thing.
Of course not. It's Brand-New...
...Medically-Tested Armor...
...that weighs less than your average summer suit.
It sounds wonderful. I think I'll try one.
Ouch!
The first fitting is always difficult.

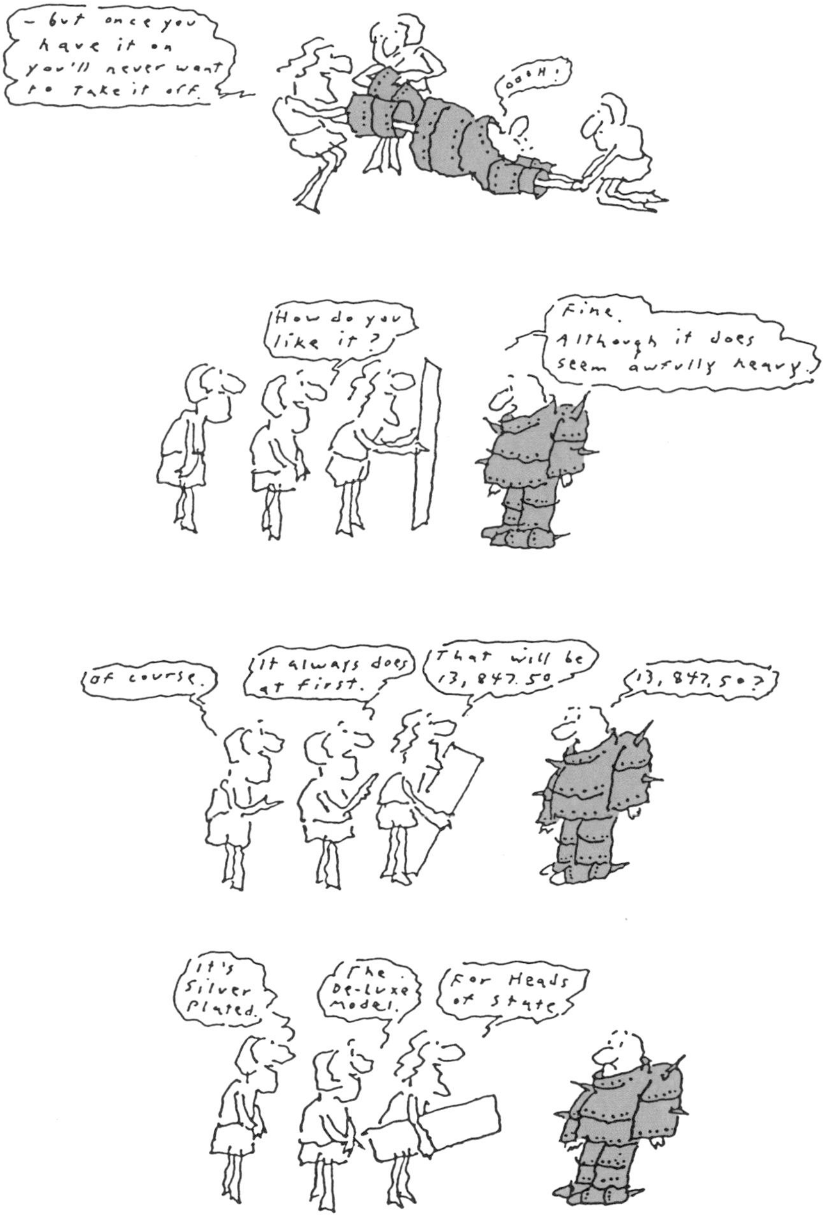
- but once you have it on you'll never want to take it off.
OOOH!
How do you like it?
Fine. Although it does seem awfully heavy.
Of course.
It always does at first.
That will be 13,847.50
13,847.50?
It's Silver Plated.
The De-Luxe model.
For Heads of State.

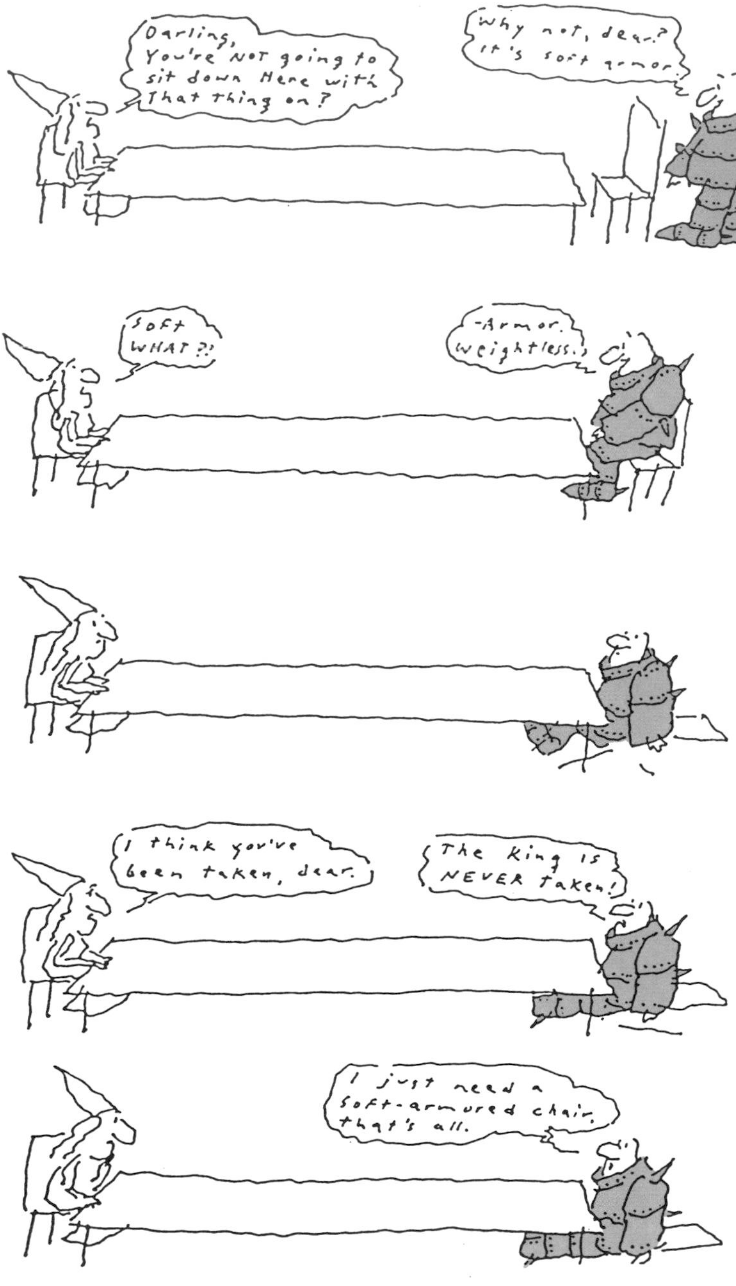
Darling, You're NOT going to sit down Here with That thing on?
Why not, dear? It's soft armor.
Soft WHAT?!
-Armor. Weightless.
I think you've been taken, dear.
The King is NEVER taken!
I just need a soft-armored chair, that's all.

Here's the chair, and how is the armor today, sir?
Lighter. Really much lighter.

Naturally. In a while it will weigh almost nothing...
That will be 1,798.00
Silver-plated, eh?

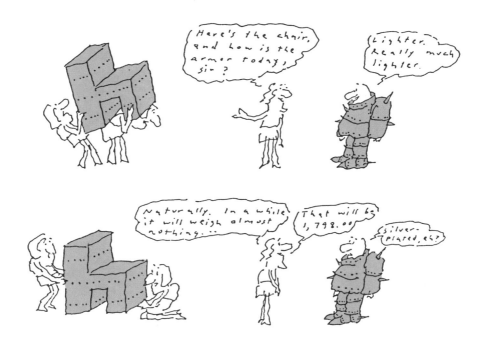

Soon the entire court learned about the King's soft armor, ...

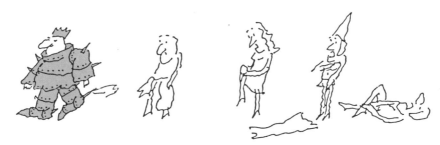

... and soon the entire court began wearing it.

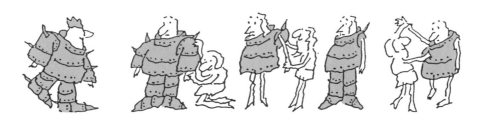

One evening, as the King sat down at his soft-armored table with his soft-armored wife . . .

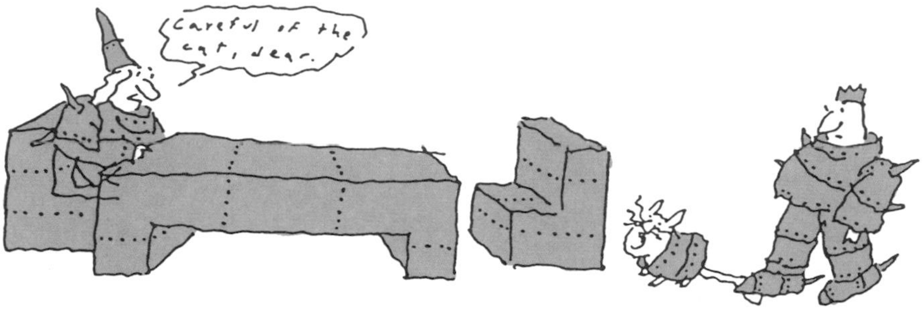
Careful of the cat, dear.

. . . their son unexpectedly returned from Harvard.

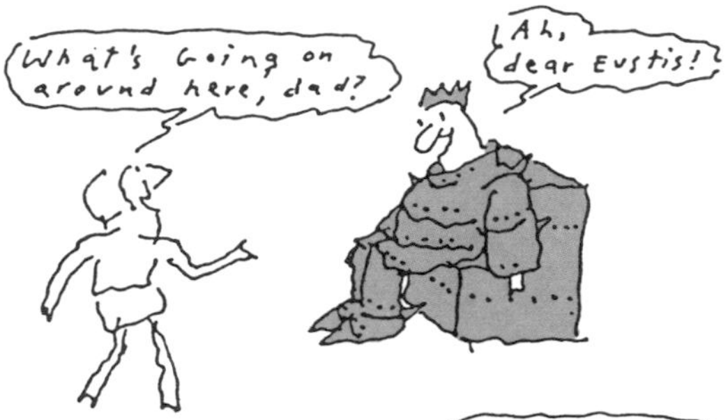
What's Going on around here, dad?
Ah, dear Eustis!

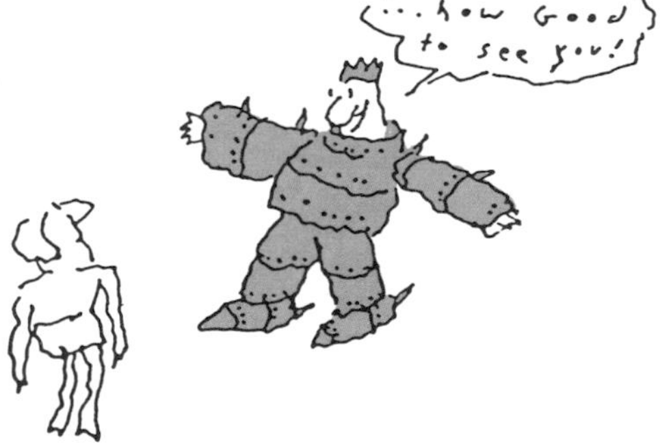
. . . how Good to see you!

snap!
crackle!
pop!
EUSTIS?
Could it be?
I'm dying.
THAT SOFT-ARMORED SUIT OF YOURS!
O, no...

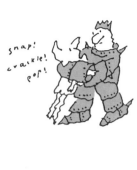

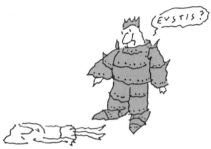

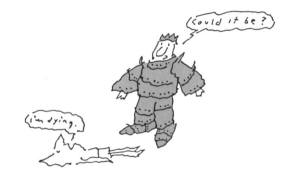

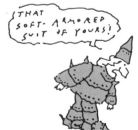

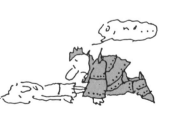

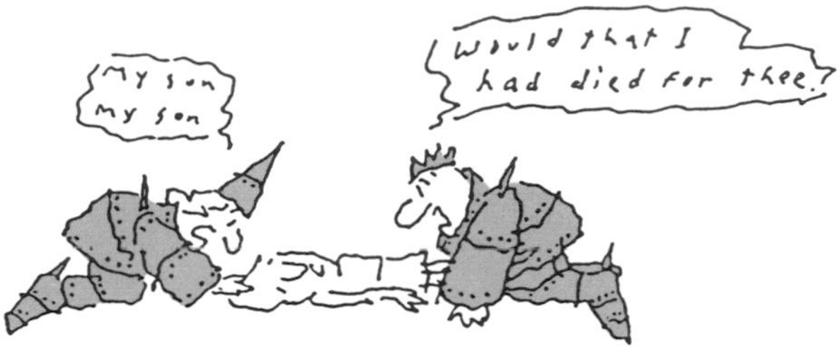
My son my son
Would that I had died for thee.

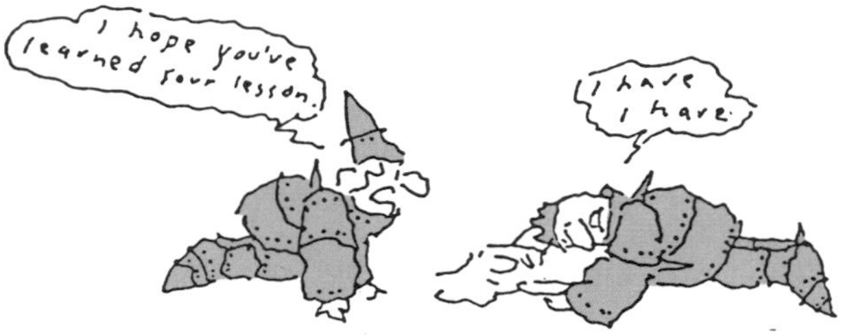
I hope you've learned your lesson.
I have I have.

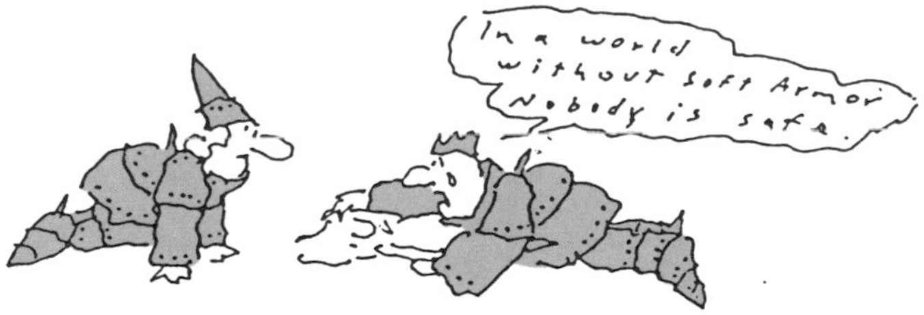
In a world without soft Armor Nobody is safe.

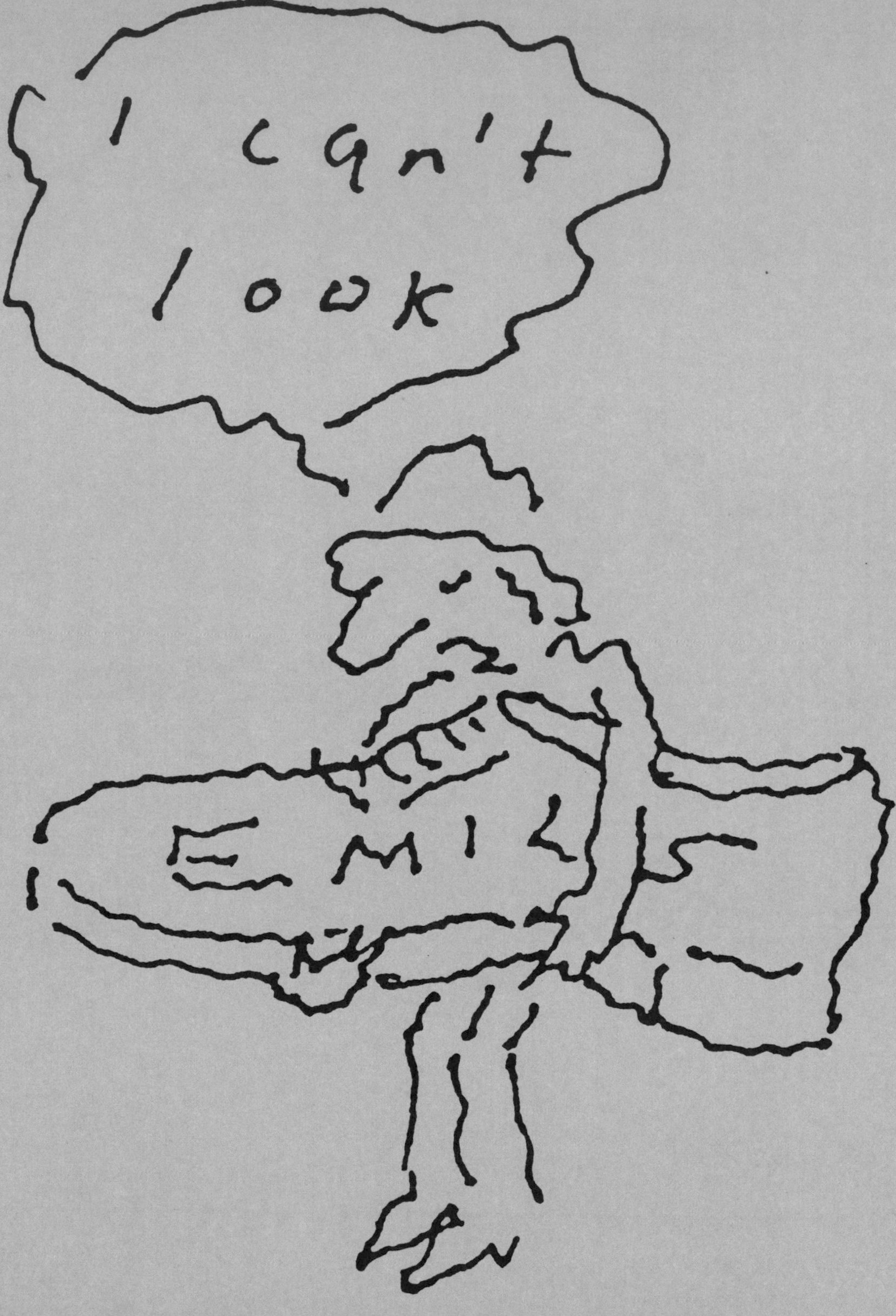
I can't look
EMILY

The Last Stand

UNPUBLISHED, 1998

During the Sixties and Seventies, thousands of Manhattan's single room occupancy buildings were destroyed. Not many occupants had the "happy" ending of Mrs. Ochs.

The Last Stand

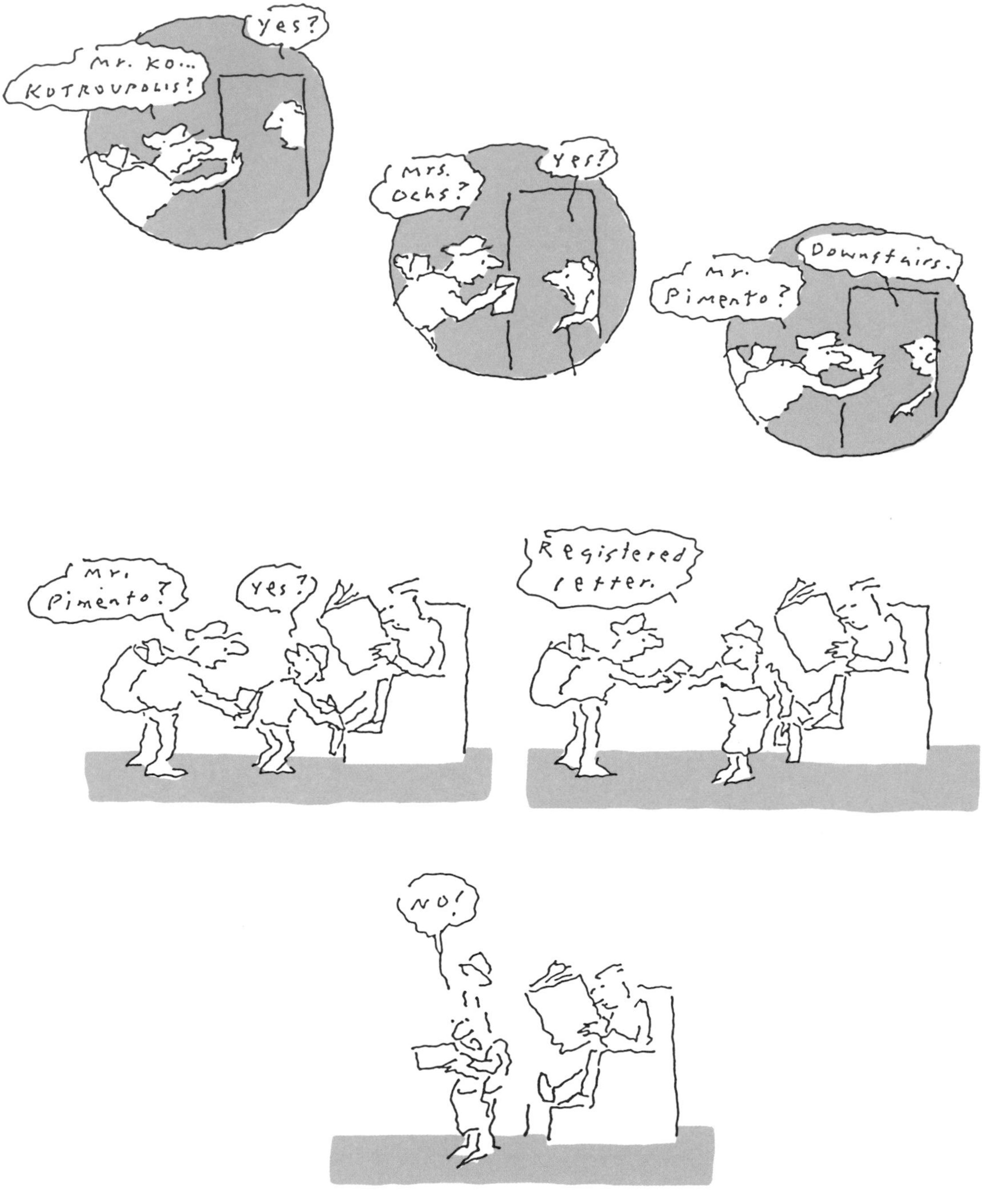

Mr. Ko...
KUTROUPOLIS?
Yes?
Mrs.
Ochs?
Yes?
Mr.
Pimento?
Downstairs.
Mr.
Pimento?
Yes?
Registered
letter.
NO!

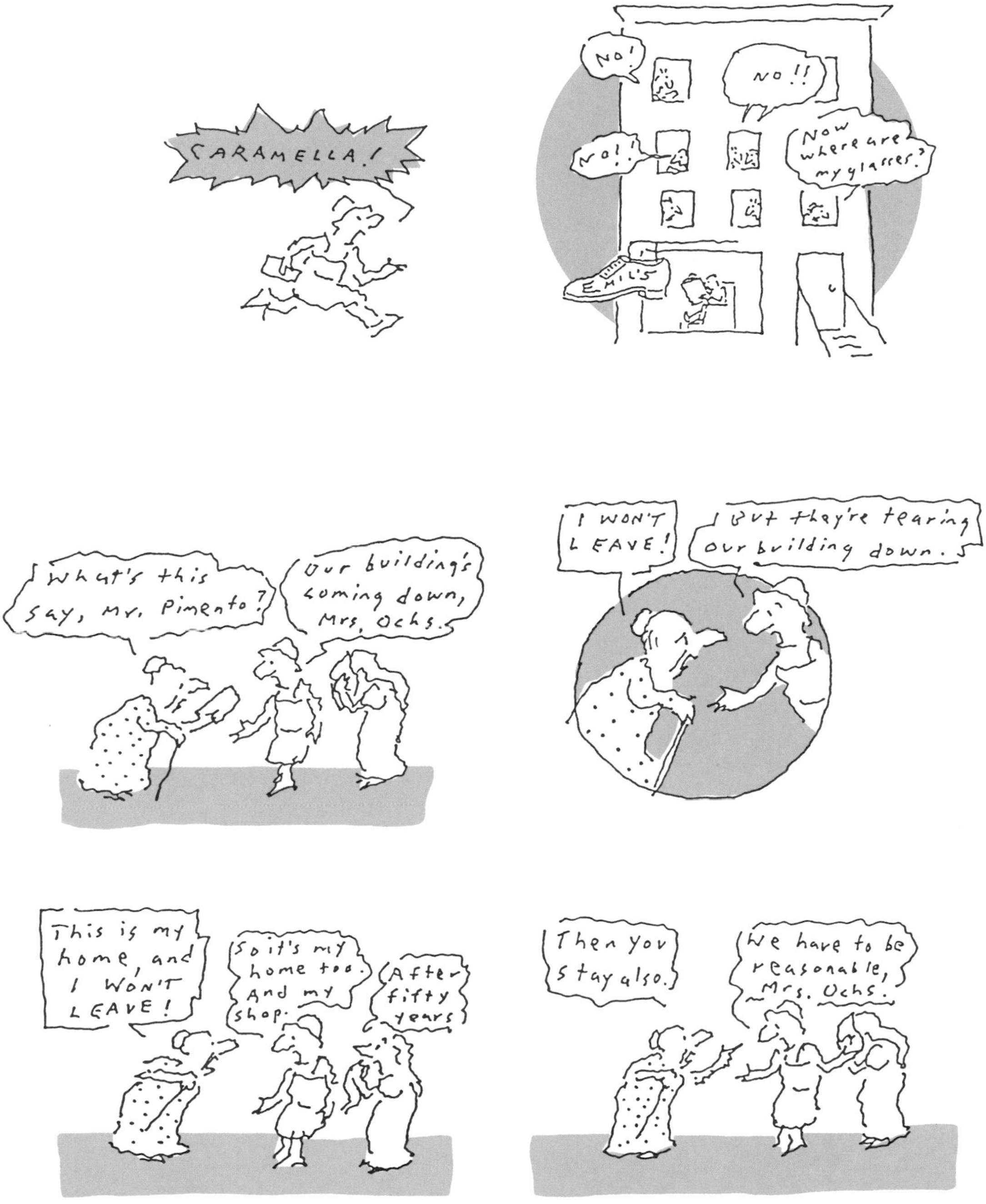

CARAMELLA!
No!
NO!!
No!!
Now where are my glasses?
EMIL'S
What's this say, Mr. Pimento?
Our building's coming down, Mrs. Ochs.
I WON'T LEAVE!
But they're tearing our building down.
This is my home, and I WON'T LEAVE!
So it's my home too. And my shop.
After fifty years
Then you stay also.
We have to be reasonable, Mrs. Ochs.

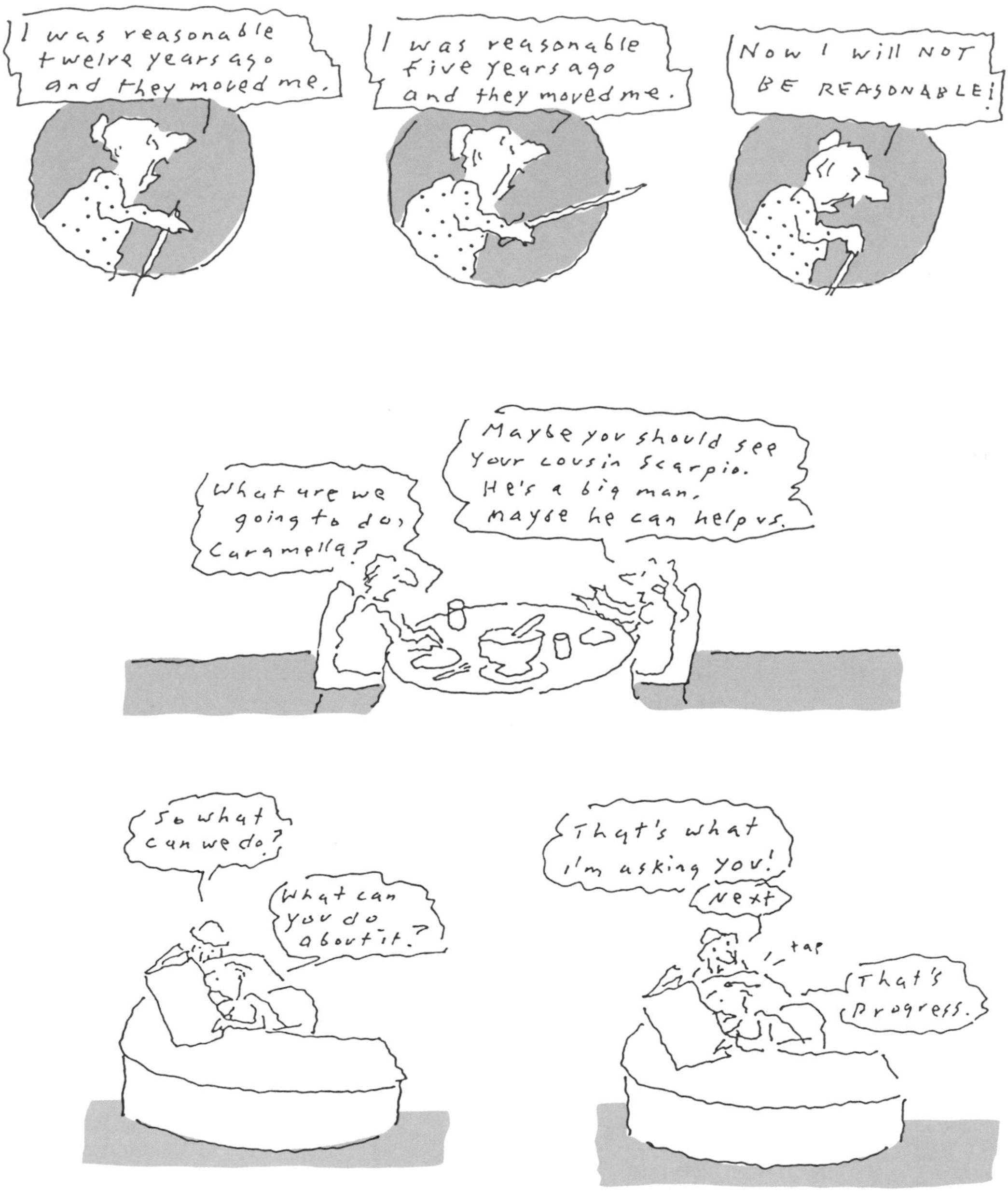
I was reasonable twelve years ago and they moved me.
I was reasonable five years ago and they moved me.
Now I will NOT BE REASONABLE!
What are we going to do, Caramella?
Maybe you should see your cousin Scarpio. He's a big man. maybe he can help us.
So what can we do?
What can you do about it?
That's what I'm asking you!
Next
tap
That's progress.

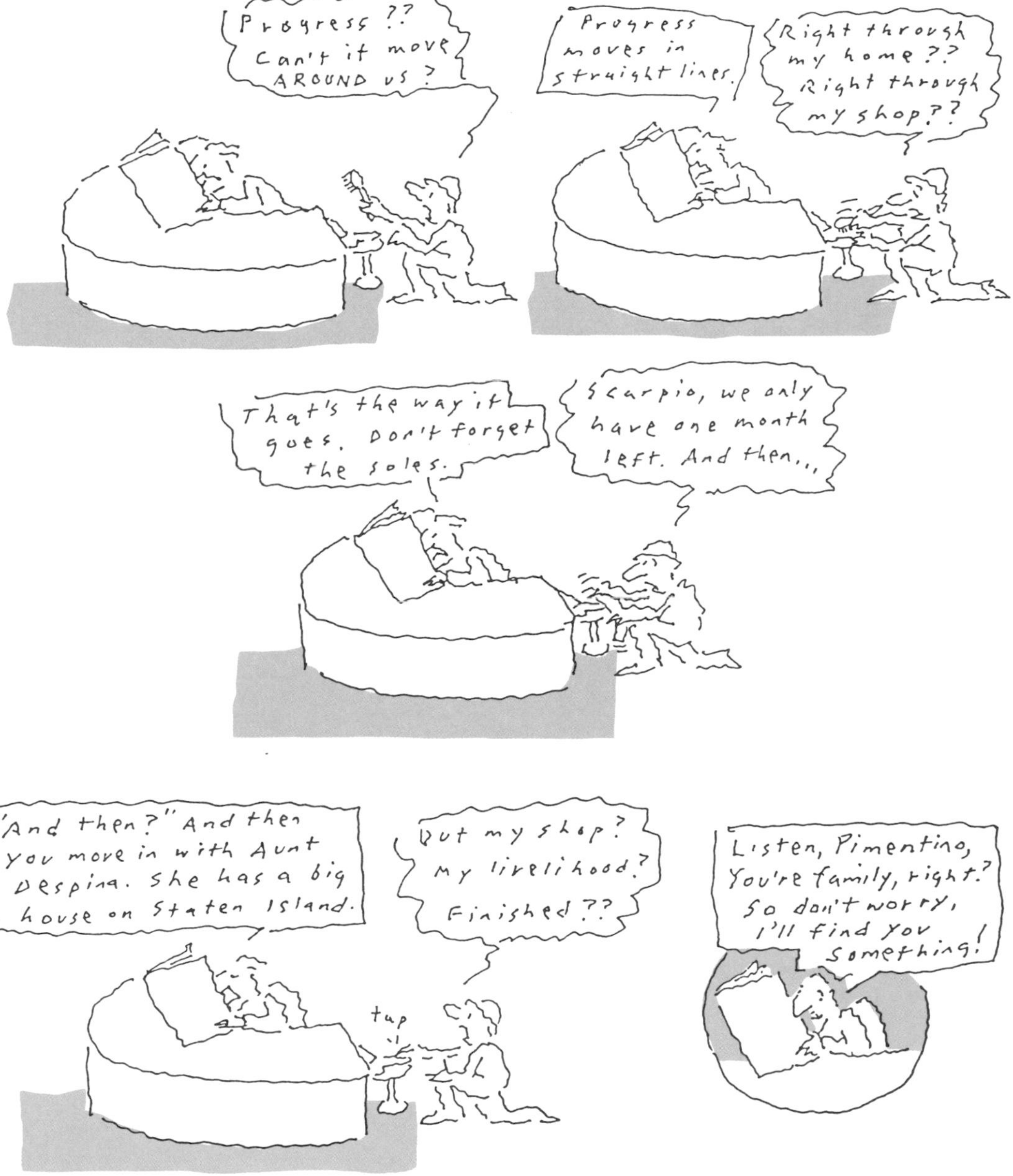
Progress?? Can't it move AROUND us?
Progress moves in straight lines.
Right through my home?? Right through my shop??
That's the way it goes. Don't forget the soles.
Scarpio, we only have one month left. And then...
"And then?" And then you move in with Aunt Despina. She has a big house on Staten Island.
Out my shop? My livelihood? Finished??
tap
Listen, Pimentino, You're family, right? So don't worry, I'll find you something!

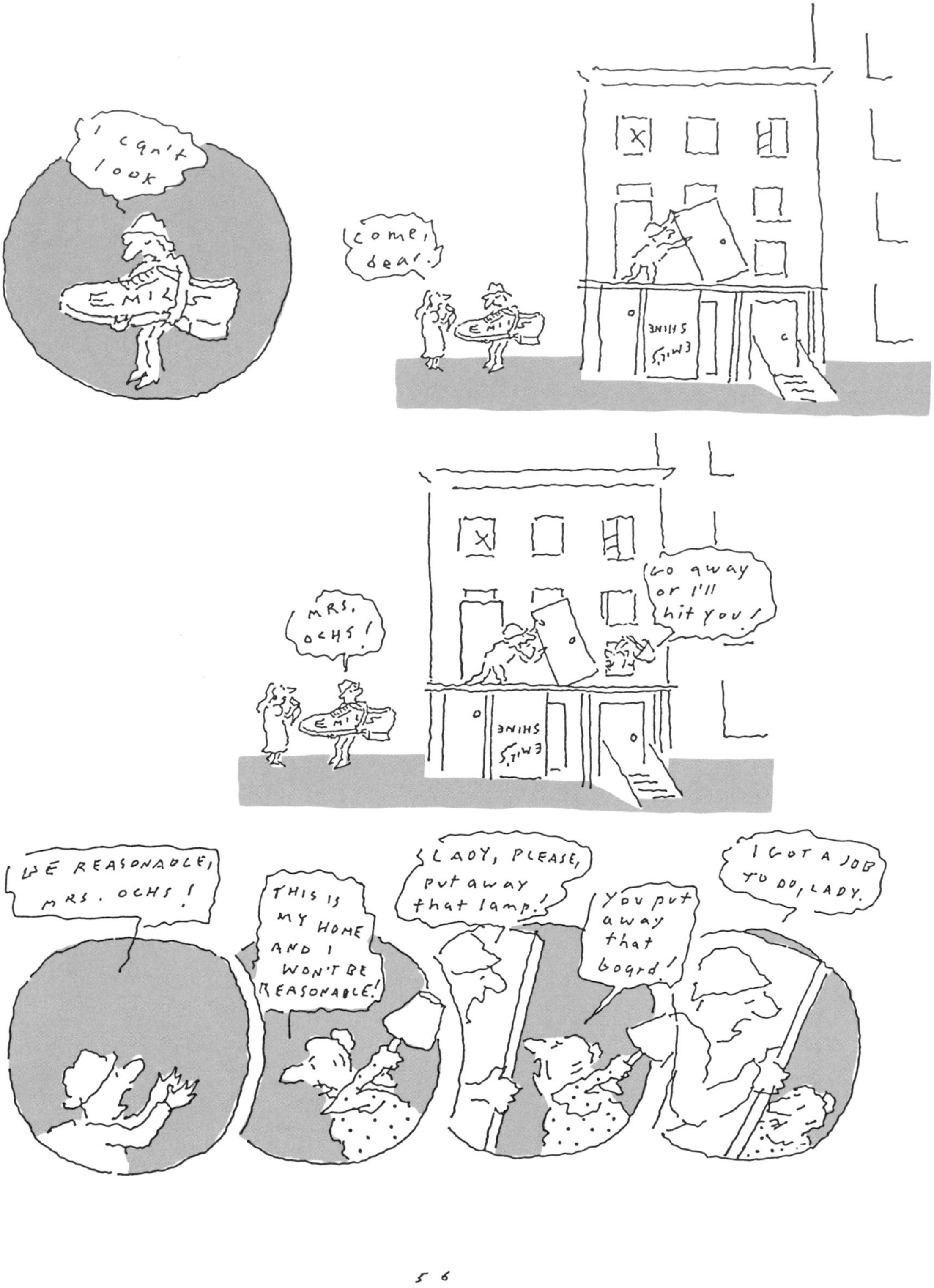
I can't look
Come, dear.
Mrs. Ochs!
Go away or I'll hit you!
BE REASONABLE, MRS. OCHS!
THIS IS MY HOME AND I WON'T BE REASONABLE!
LADY, PLEASE, put away that lamp!
You put away that board!
I GOT A JOB TO DO, LADY.

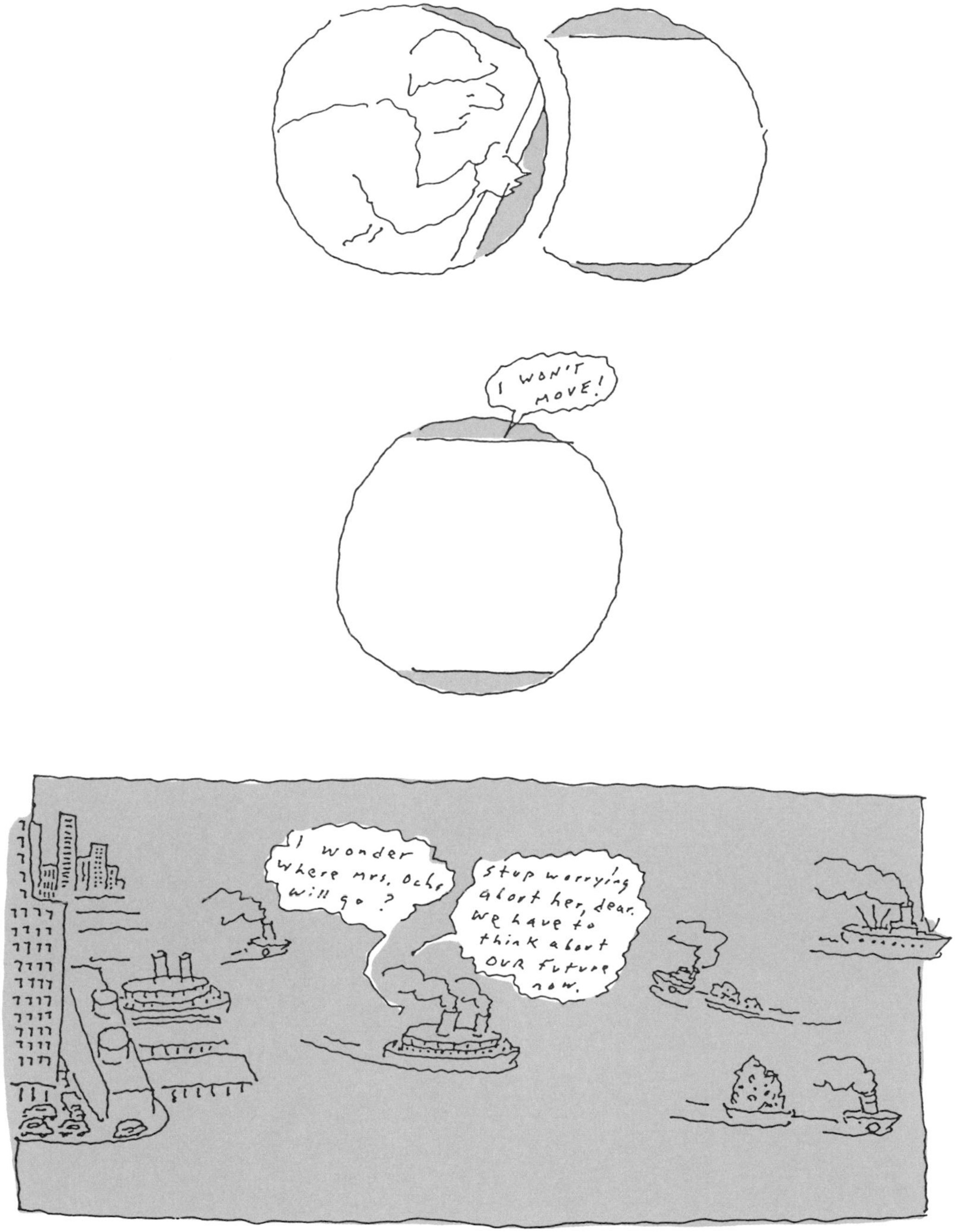
I WON'T MOVE!
I wonder where Mrs. Ochs will go?
Stop worrying about her, dear. We have to think about OUR future now.

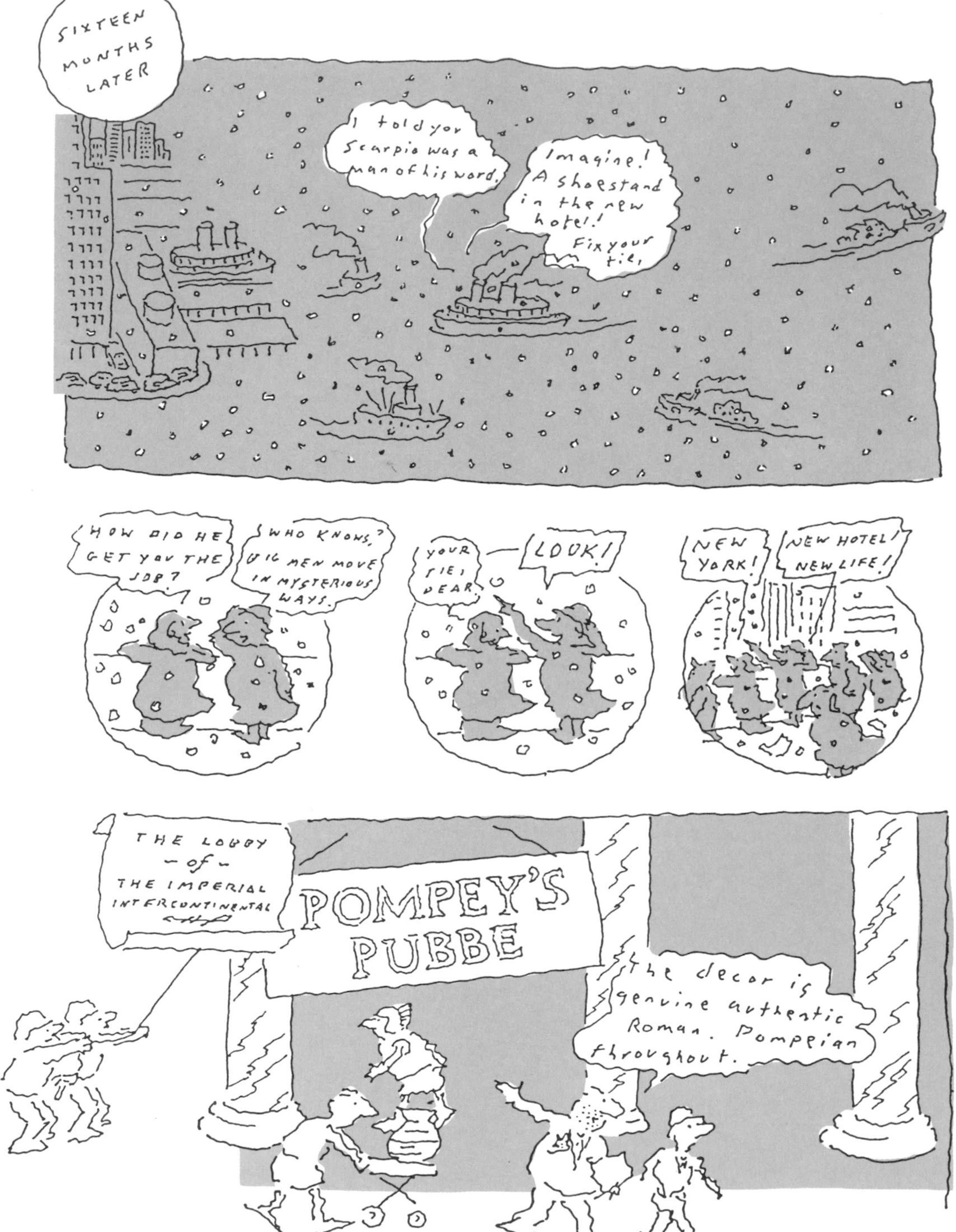
SIXTEEN MONTHS LATER
I told you Scarpio was a man of his word.
Imagine! A shoestand in the new hotel! Fix your tie,
HOW DID HE GET YOU THE JOB?
WHO KNOWS? BIG MEN MOVE IN MYSTERIOUS WAYS.
YOUR TIE, DEAR.
LOOK!
NEW YORK!
NEW HOTEL! NEW LIFE!
THE LOBBY - of - THE IMPERIAL INTERCONTINENTAL
POMPEY'S PUBBE
The decor is genuine authentic Roman. Pompeian throughout.

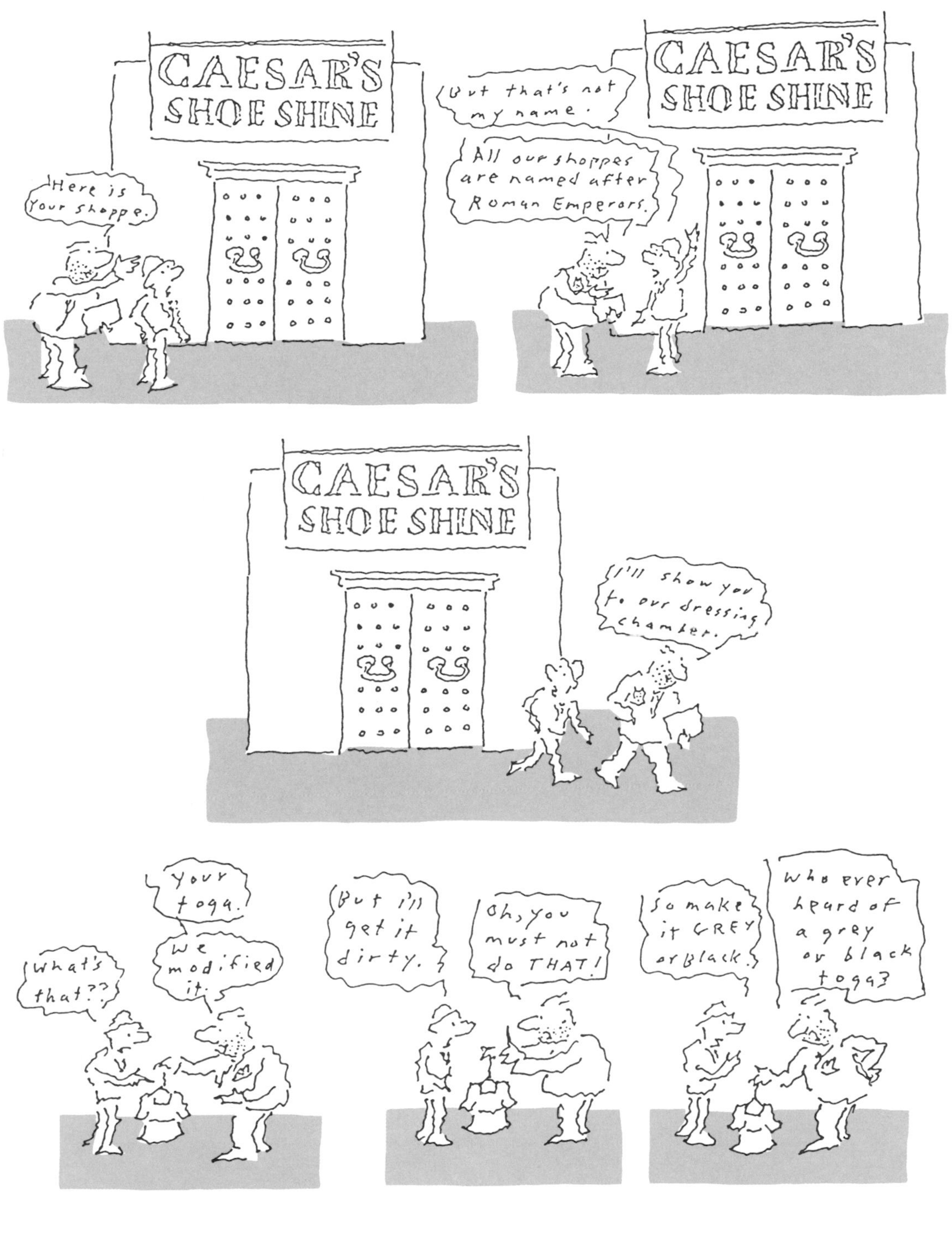
CAESAR'S SHOE SHINE
Here is your shoppe.
But that's not my name.
All our shoppes are named after Roman Emperors.
I'll show you to our dressing chamber.
What's that??
Your toga.
We modified it.
But I'll get it dirty.
Oh, you must not do THAT!
So make it GREY or Black.
Who ever heard of a grey or black toga?

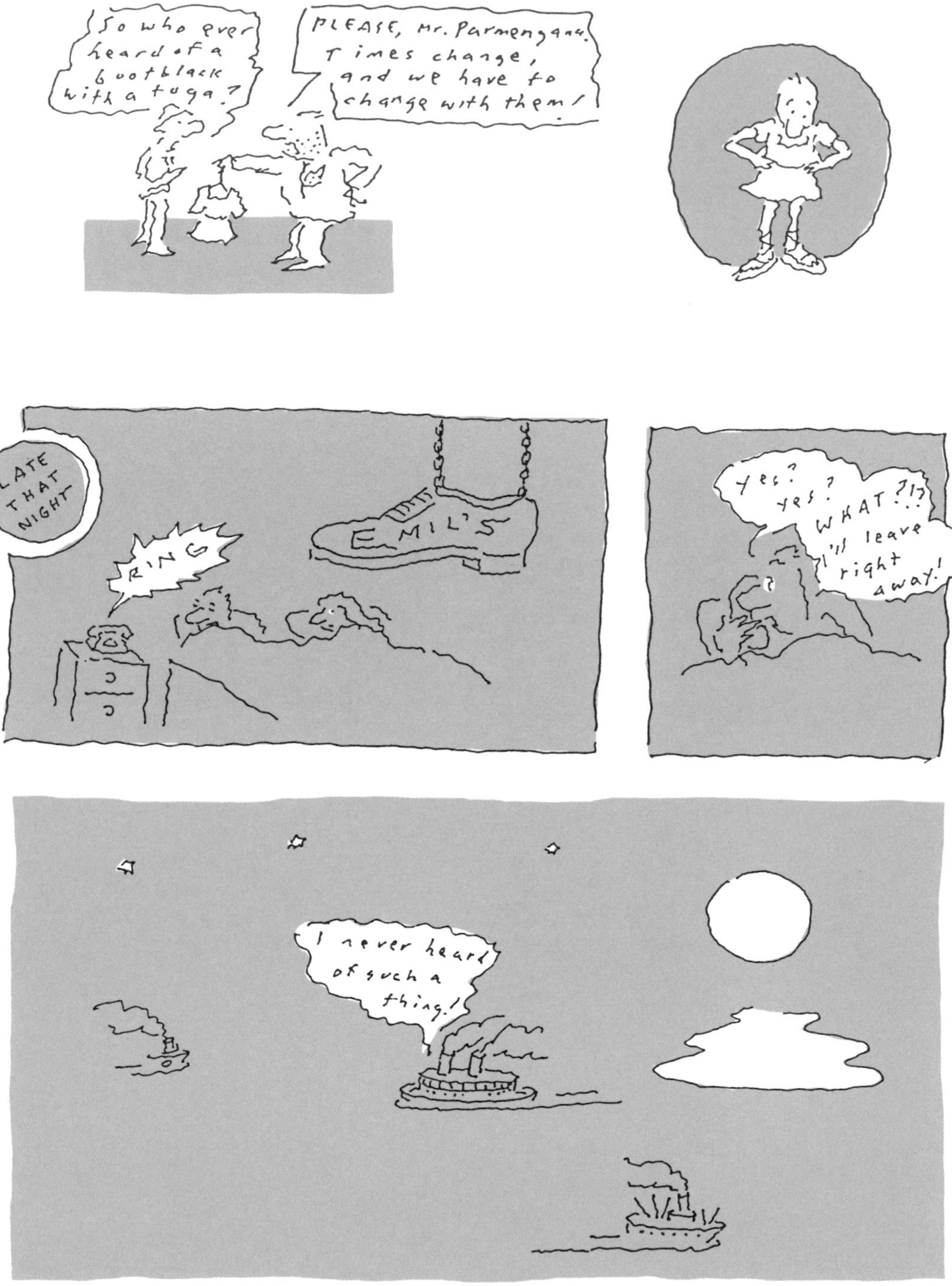

So who ever heard of a bootblack with a tuga?
PLEASE, Mr. Parmenganu. Times change, and we have to change with them!
LATE THAT NIGHT
EMIL'S
RING
Yes? Yes? WHAT?!?
I'll leave right away!
I never heard of such a thing!

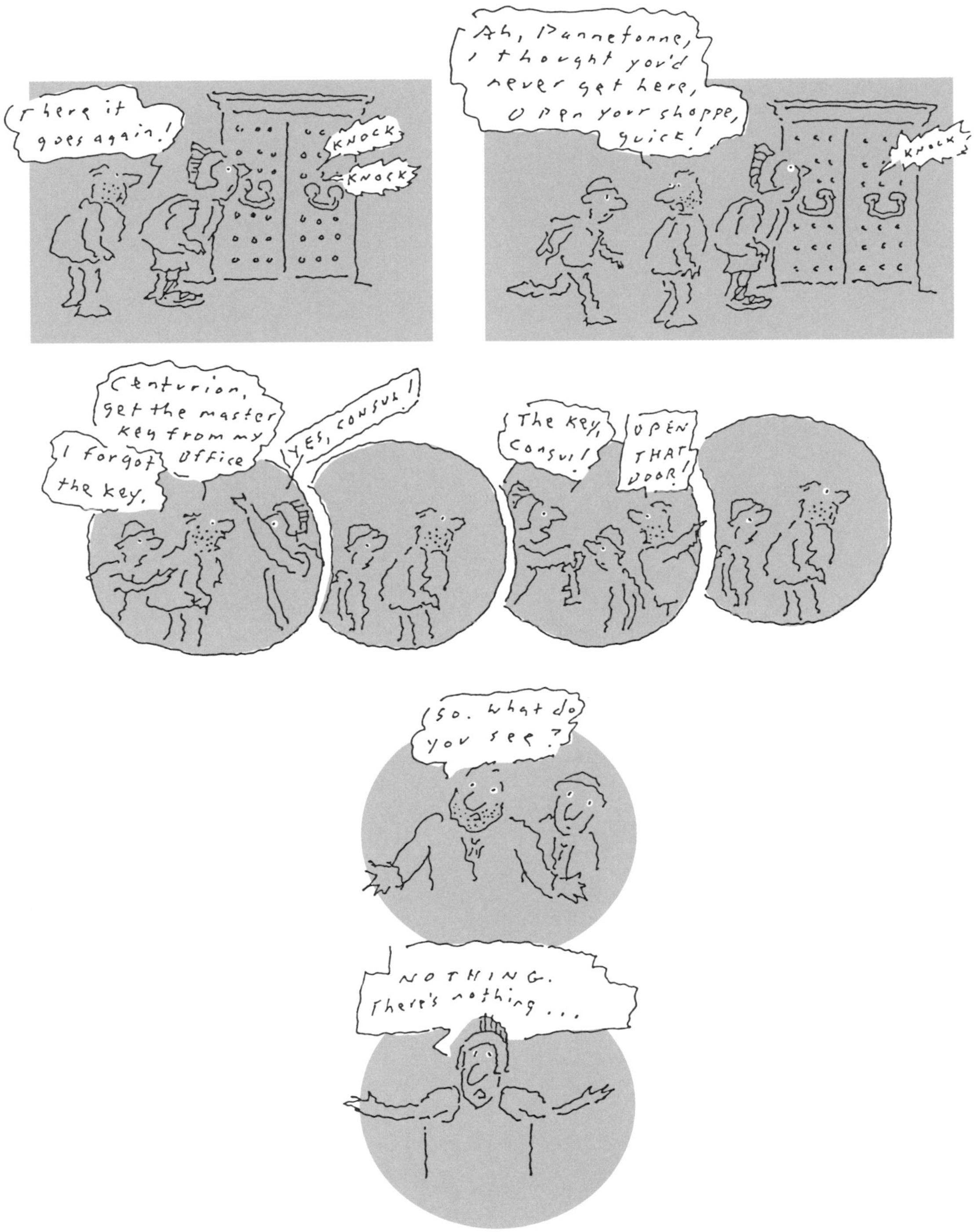
There it goes again!
KNOCK
KNOCK
Ah, Dannefonne, I thought you'd never get here, Open your shoppe, quick!
KNOCK!
Centurion, get the master key from my Office
I forgot the key.
YES, CONSUL!
The key, Consul!
OPEN THAT DOOR!
So. What do you see?
NOTHING. There's nothing . . .

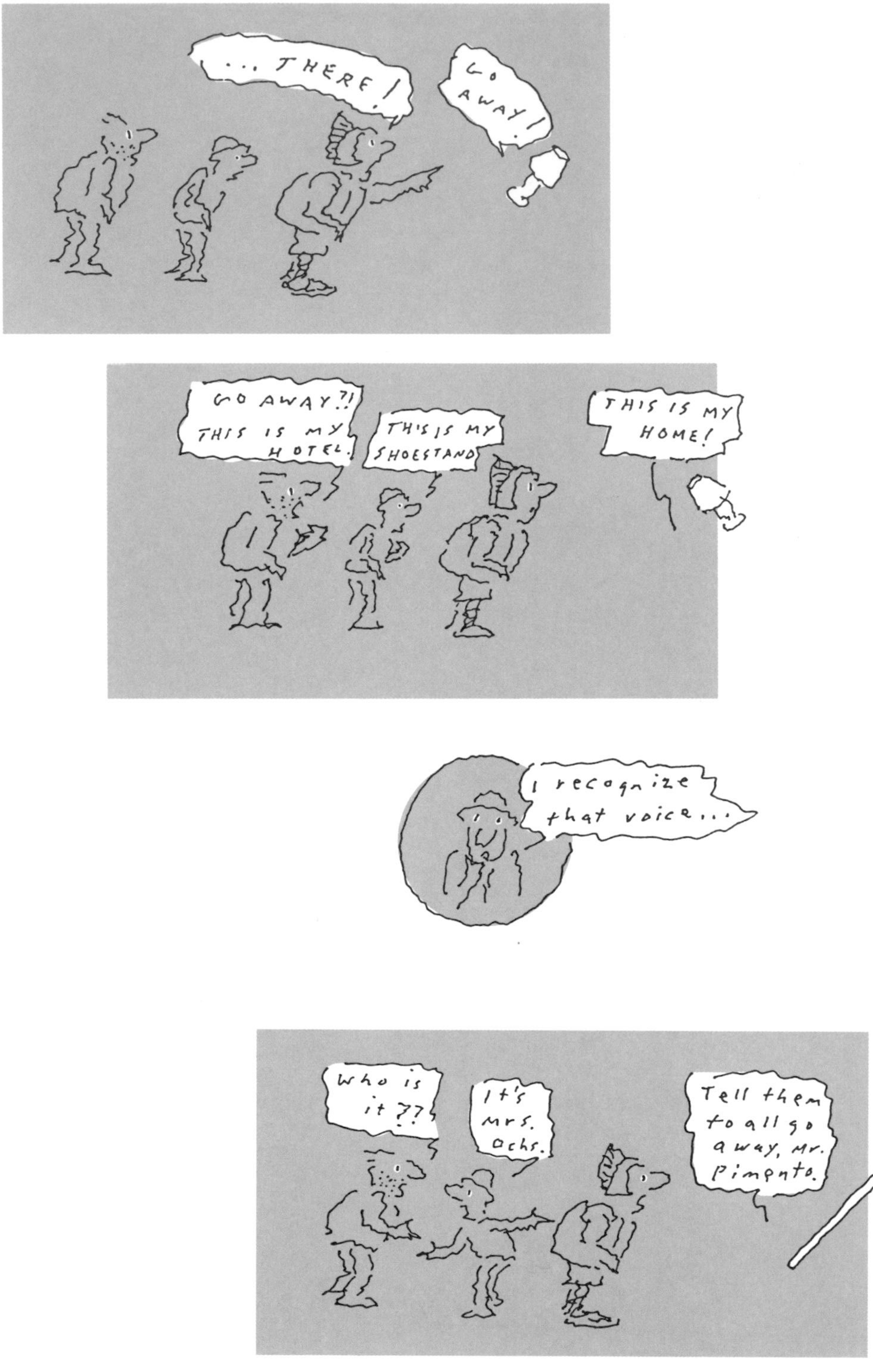
... THERE!
GO AWAY!
GO AWAY?! THIS IS MY HOTEL.
THIS IS MY SHOESTAND
THIS IS MY HOME!
I recognize that voice...
Who is it??
It's Mrs. Ochs.
Tell them to all go away, Mr. Pimento.

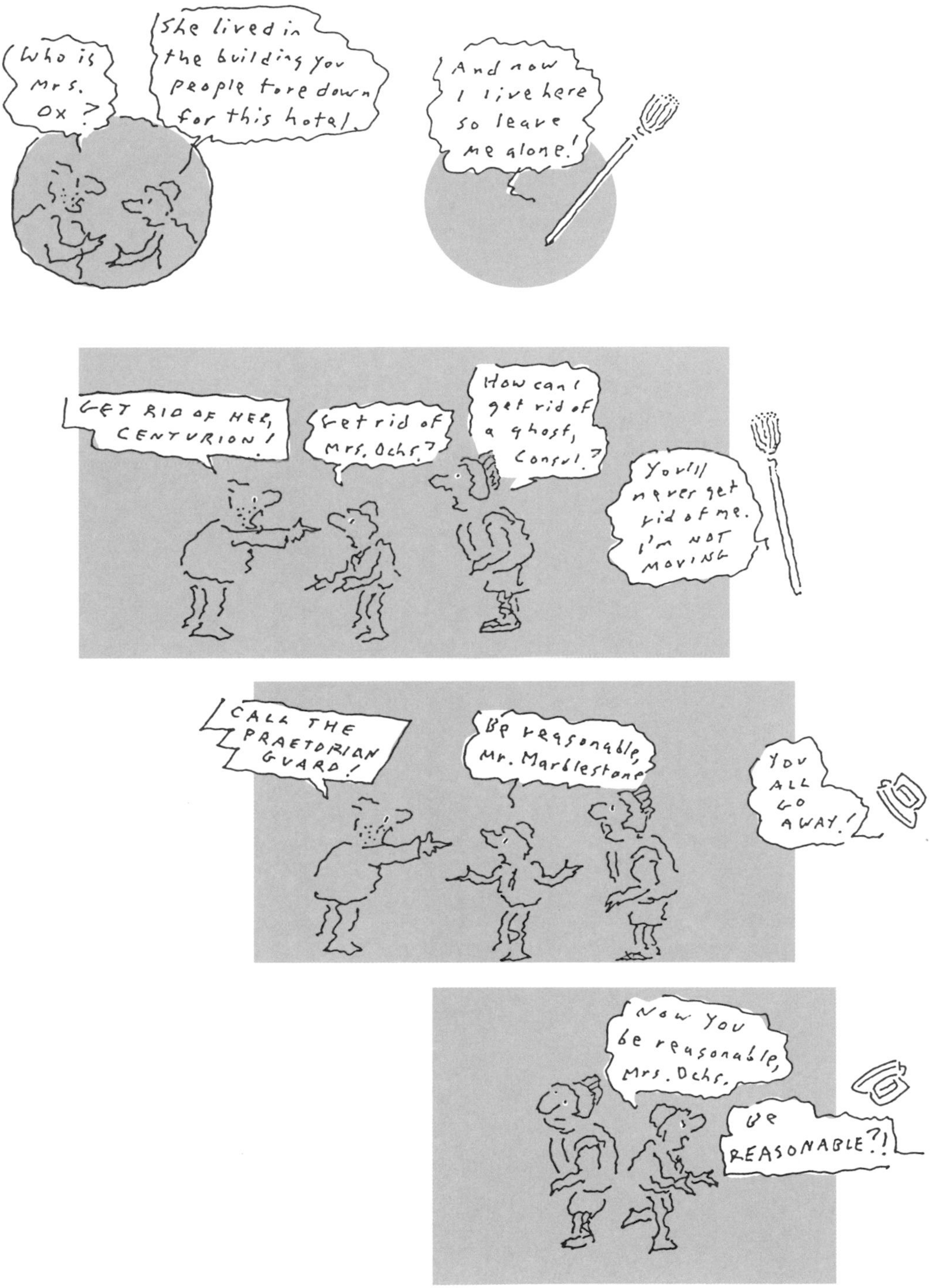
Who is Mrs. Ox?
She lived in the building you people tore down for this hotel.
And now I live here so leave me alone!
GET RID OF HER, CENTURION!
Get rid of Mrs. Ochs?
How can I get rid of a ghost, Consul?
You'll never get rid of me. I'm NOT MOVING
CALL THE PRAETORIAN GUARD!
Be reasonable, Mr. Marblestone
YOU ALL GO AWAY!
Now you be reasonable, Mrs. Ochs.
BE REASONABLE?!

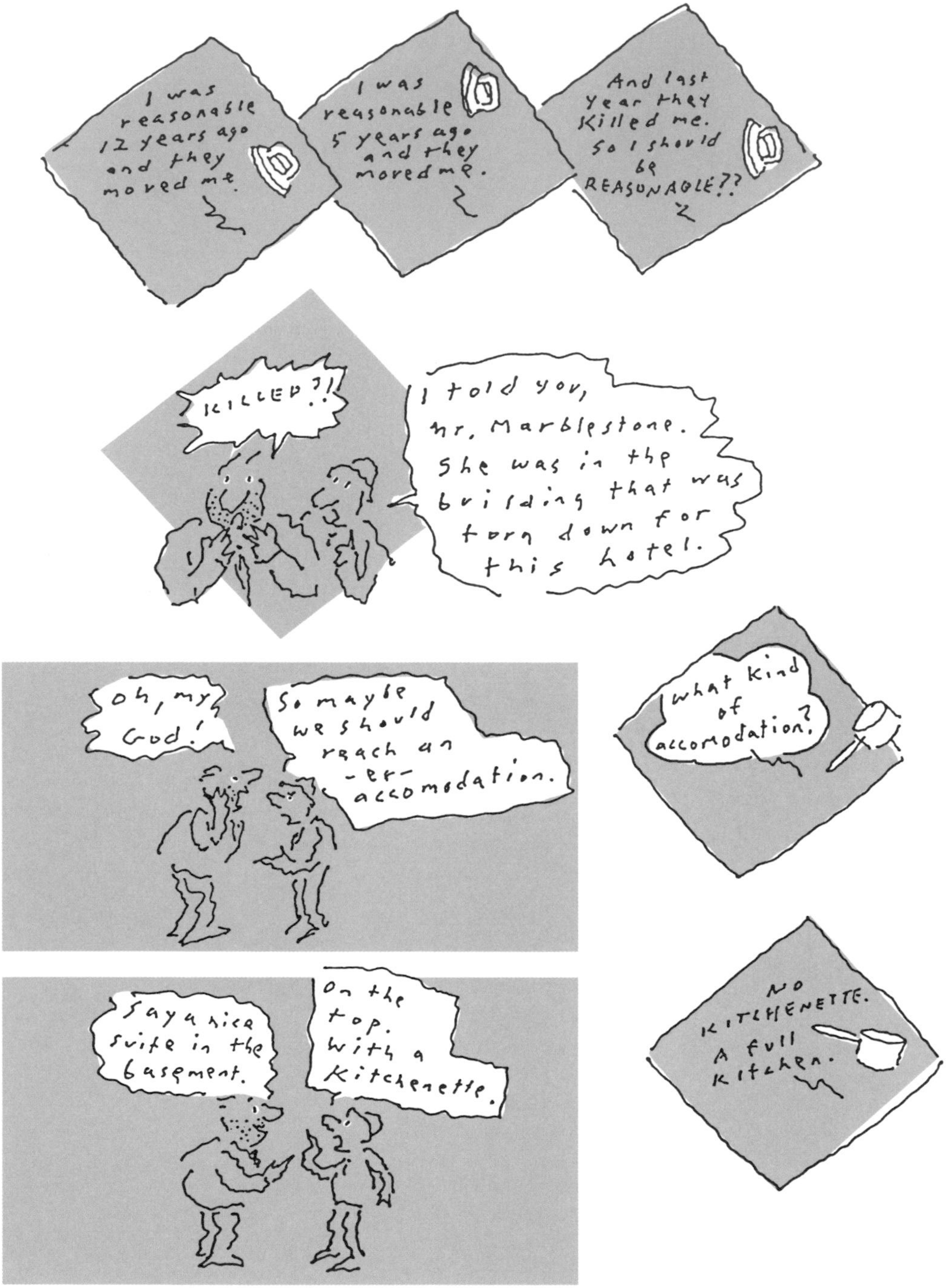
I was reasonable 12 years ago and they moved me.
I was reasonable 5 years ago and they moved me.
And last year they killed me. So I should be REASONABLE??
KILLED?!!
I told you, Mr. Marblestone. She was in the building that was torn down for this hotel.
Oh, my God!
So maybe we should reach an -er- accomodation.
What kind of accomodation?
Say a nice suite in the basement.
On the top. With a kitchenette.
NO KITCHENETTE. A full kitchen.

Absolutely. On a top floor, with a full kitchen.
Alright, Mrs. Ochs?
I want to see it first!
I'll show it to you myself. But..
There's always a but with these people
NO RAPPING, NO TAPPING, NO KNOCKING
NO DISTURBING OUR OTHER GUESTS.

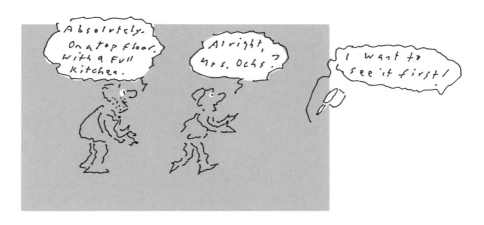

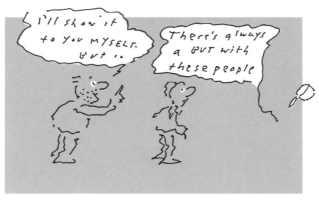

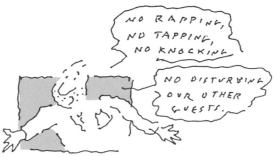

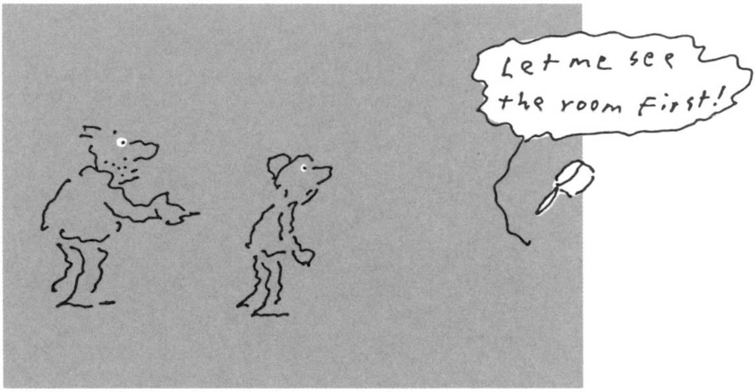
Let me see the room First!

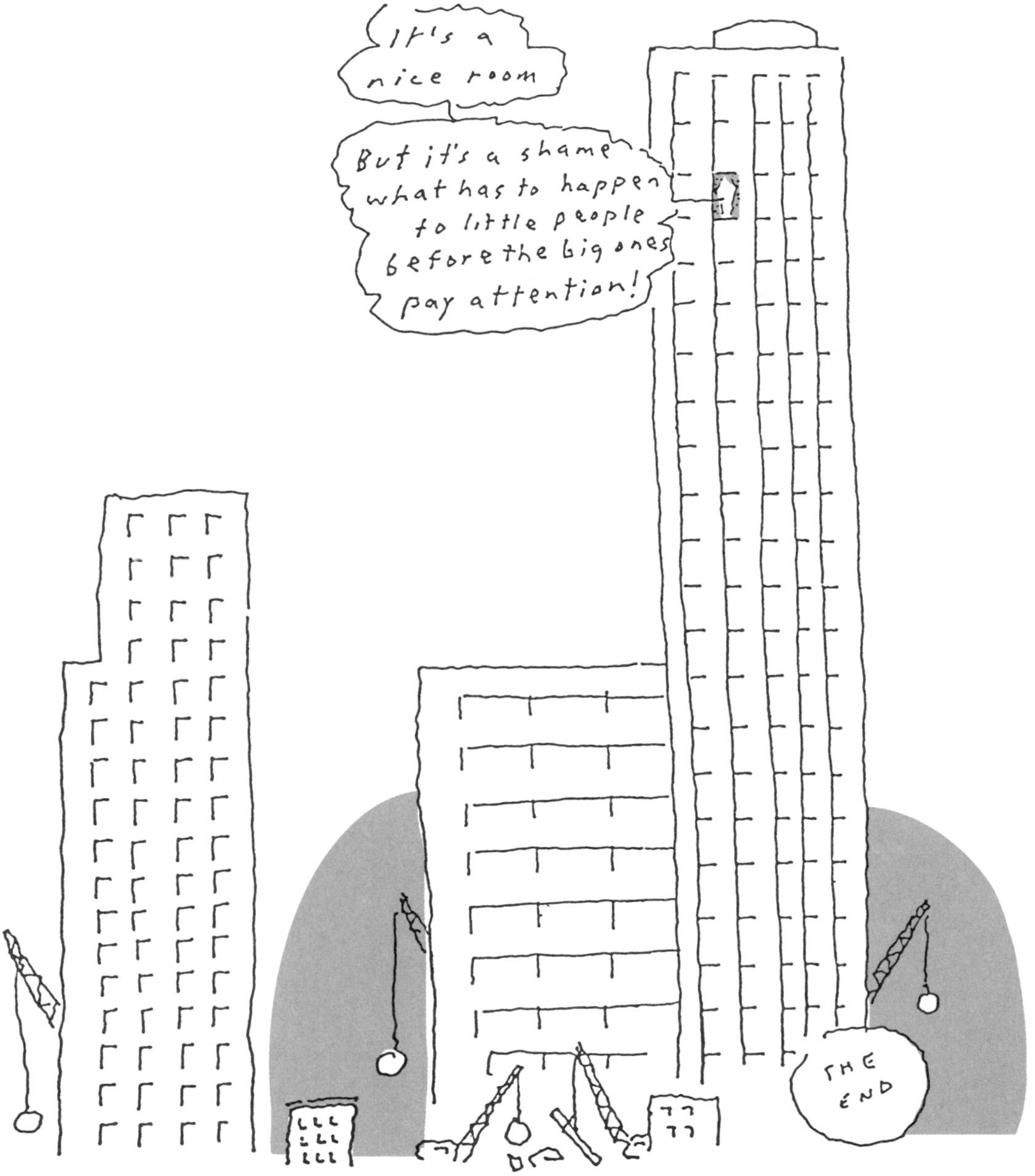
It's a nice room
But it's a shame what has to happen to little people before the big ones pay attention!
THE END

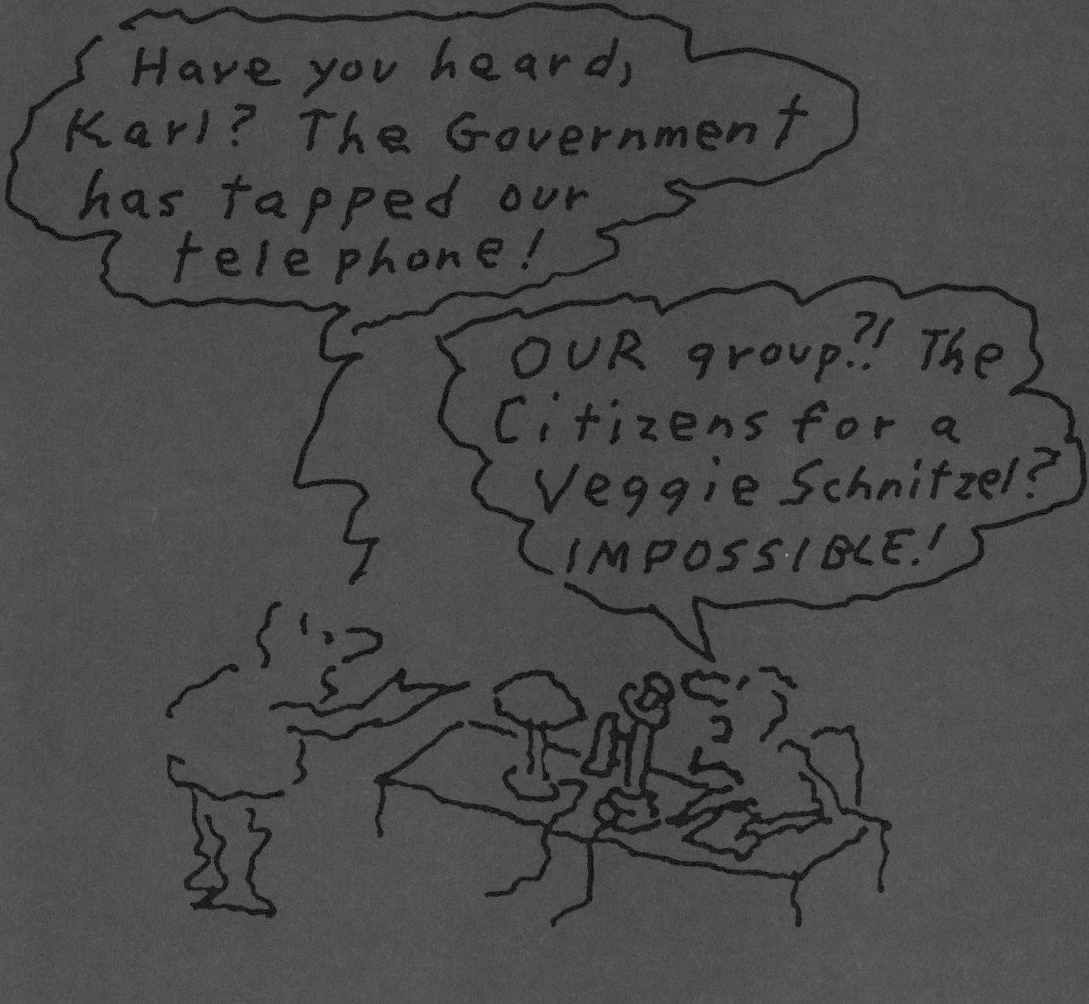
Have you heard, Karl? The Government has tapped our telephone!
OUR group?! The Citizens for a Veggie Schnitzel? IMPOSSIBLE!

T(R)APPED

....

THE NATION, 2006

Last year we learned that our government was illegally tapping organizations as benign as the Quakers. I had to wonder, where would it all lead? Did Germany in the early thirties experience a similar danger sign? Did we, like Germany, ignore it?

T(R)APPED

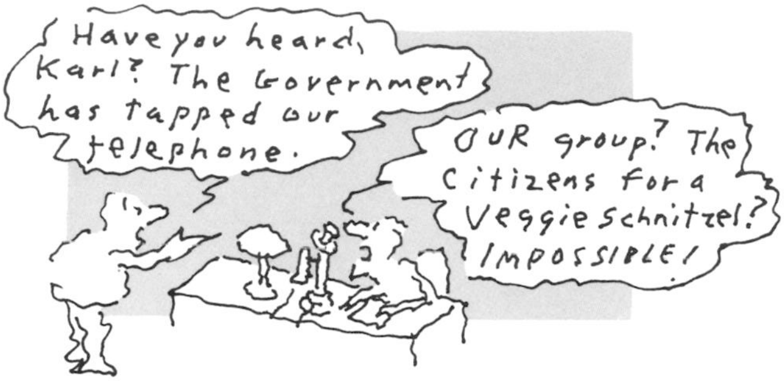
Have you heard, Karl? The Government has tapped our telephone.
OUR group? The Citizens for a Veggie Schnitzel? IMPOSSIBLE!

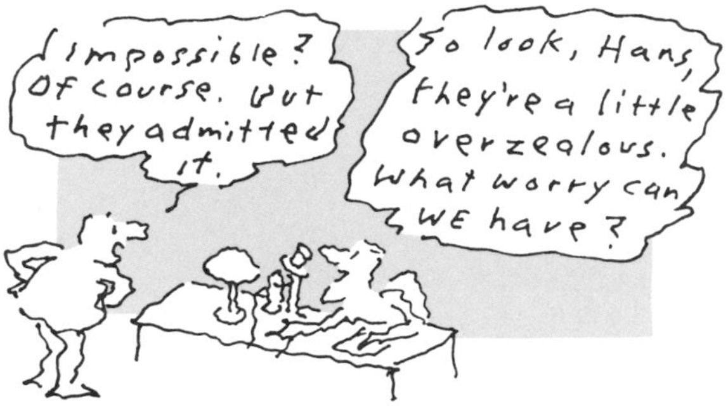
Impossible? Of course. But they admitted it.
So look, Hans, they're a little overzealous. What worry can WE have?

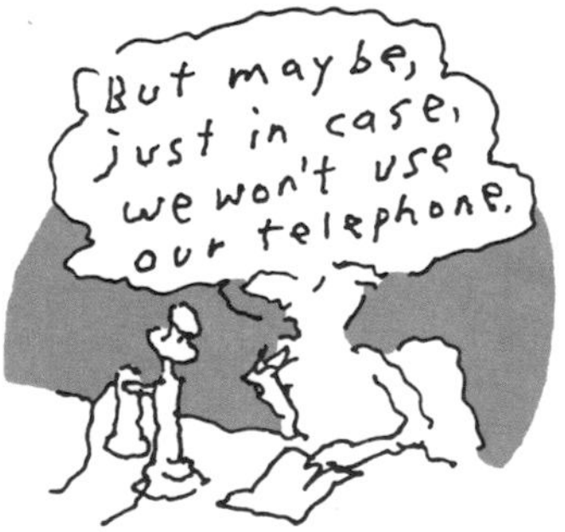
But maybe, just in case, we won't use our telephone.

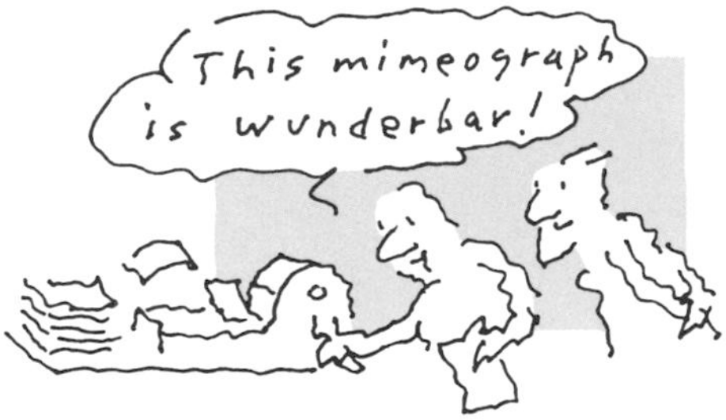
This mimeograph is wunderbar!

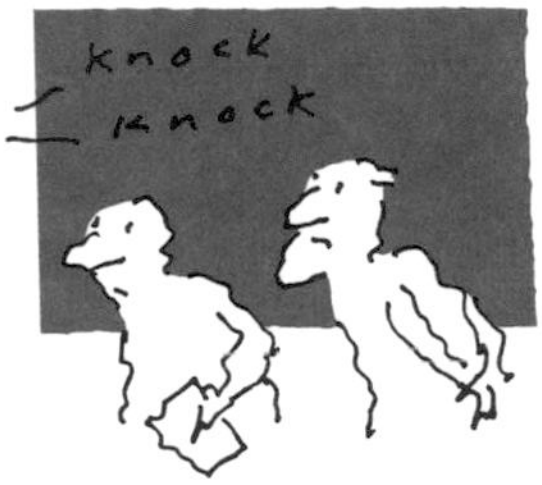
knock
knock

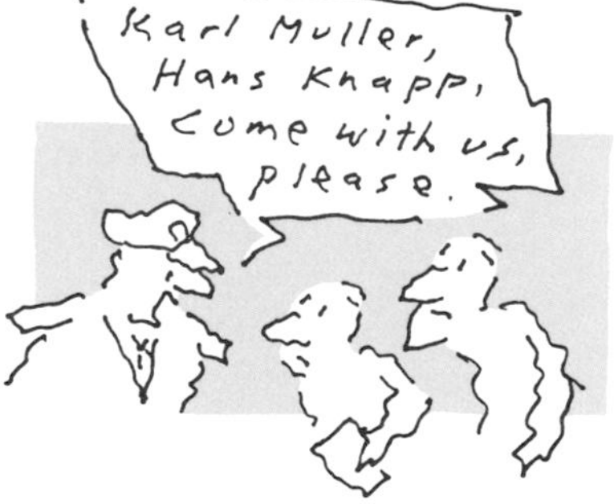
Karl Muller, Hans Knapp, come with us, please.

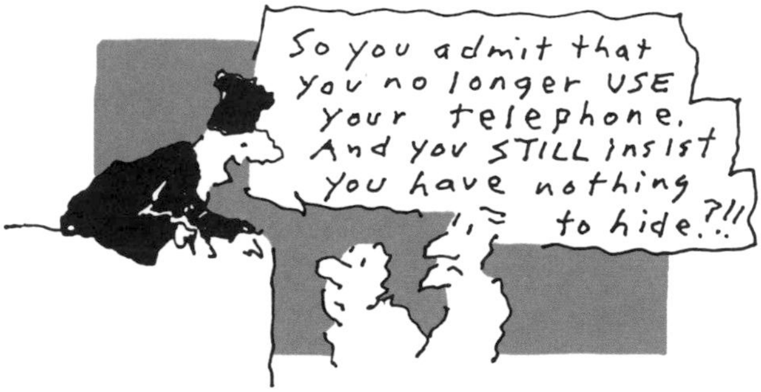
So you admit that you no longer USE your telephone. And you STILL insist you have nothing to hide?!!

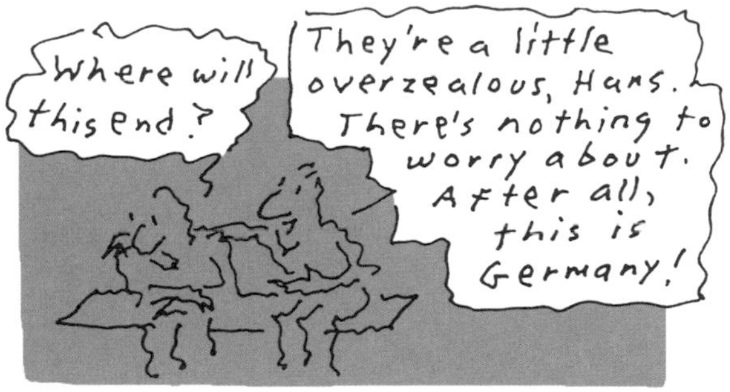
Where will this end?
They're a little overzealous, Hans. There's nothing to worry about. After all, this is Germany!

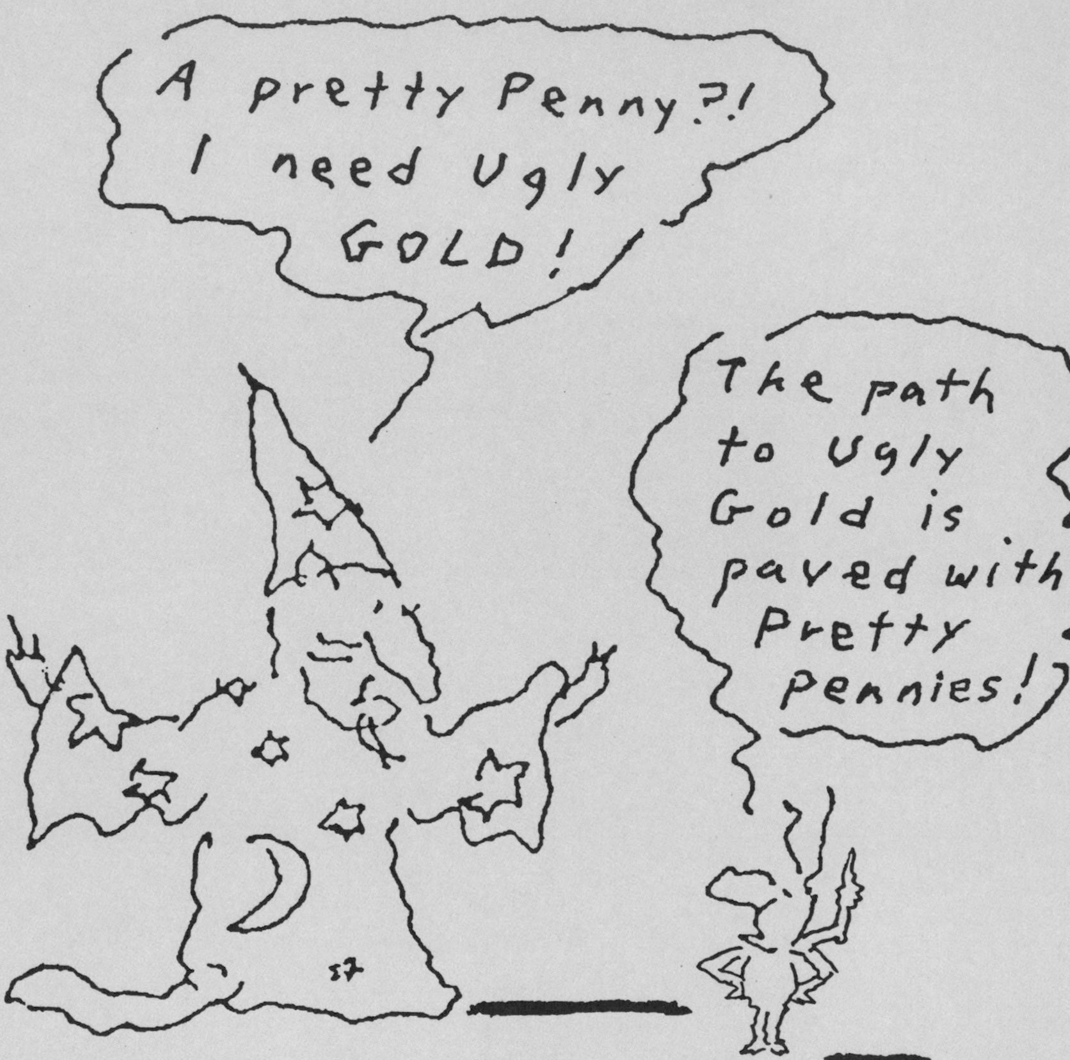
A pretty Penny?! I need Ugly GOLD!
The path to Ugly Gold is paved with Pretty pennies!

UNPUBLISHED, 1972

In 1972, I decided to try my hand at a comic strip. I developed *Magicat*, based on a character proposed by the astrologer, Jeane Dixon. I added a sidekick to the cat, a cockroach named Cornelius (every Laurel needs a Hardy, every Abbot a Costello). The comic strip never found a publisher, but at the time I didn't care. I like it now.

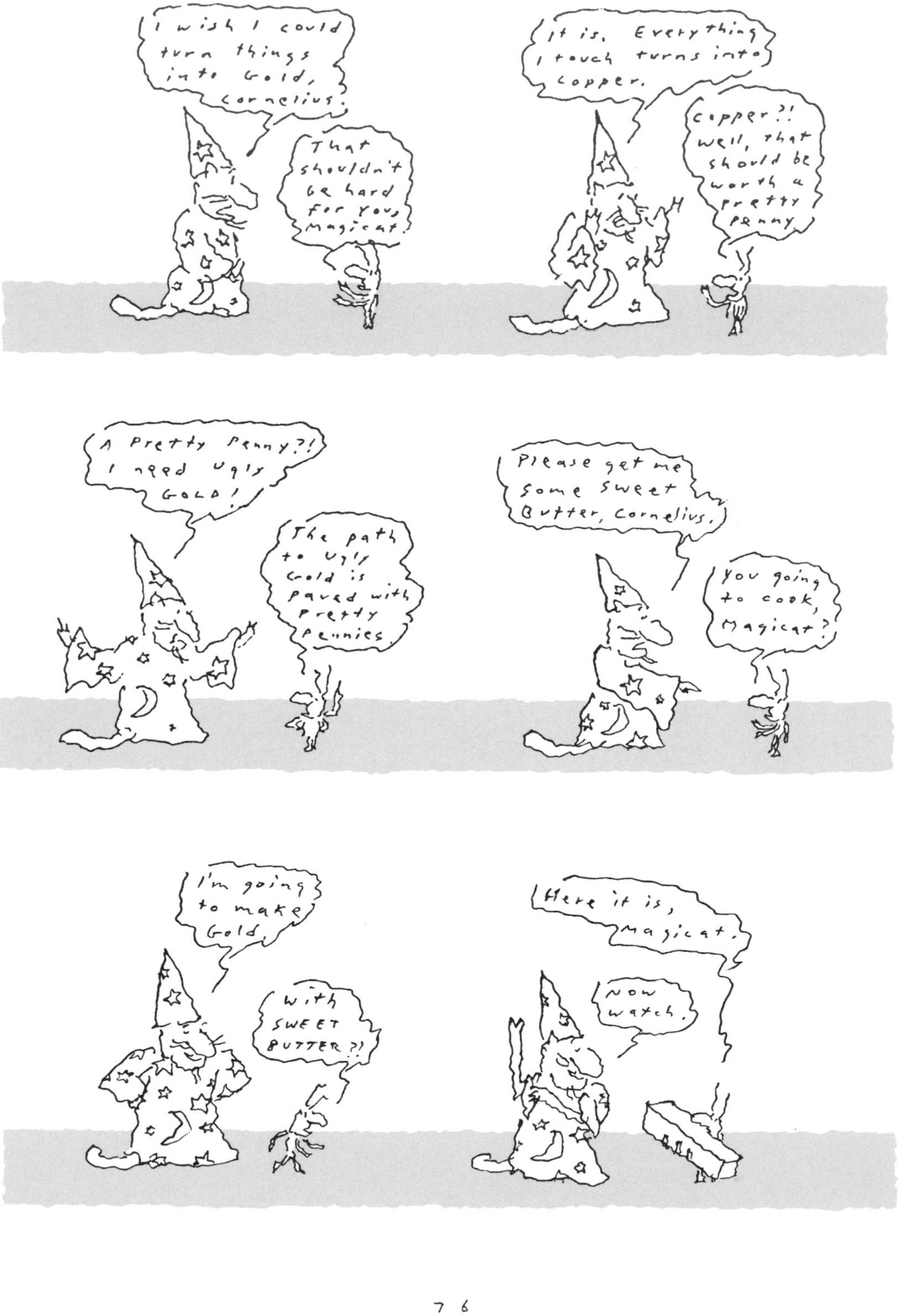
I wish I could turn things into Gold, Cornelius.
That shouldn't be hard for you, Magicat.
It is. Everything I touch turns into copper.
Copper?! Well, that should be worth a pretty penny.
A Pretty Penny?! I need Ugly Gold!
The path to Ugly Gold is paved with pretty pennies.
Please get me some Sweet Butter, Cornelius.
You going to cook, Magicat?
I'm going to make Gold.
With SWEET BUTTER?!
Here it is, Magicat.
Now watch.

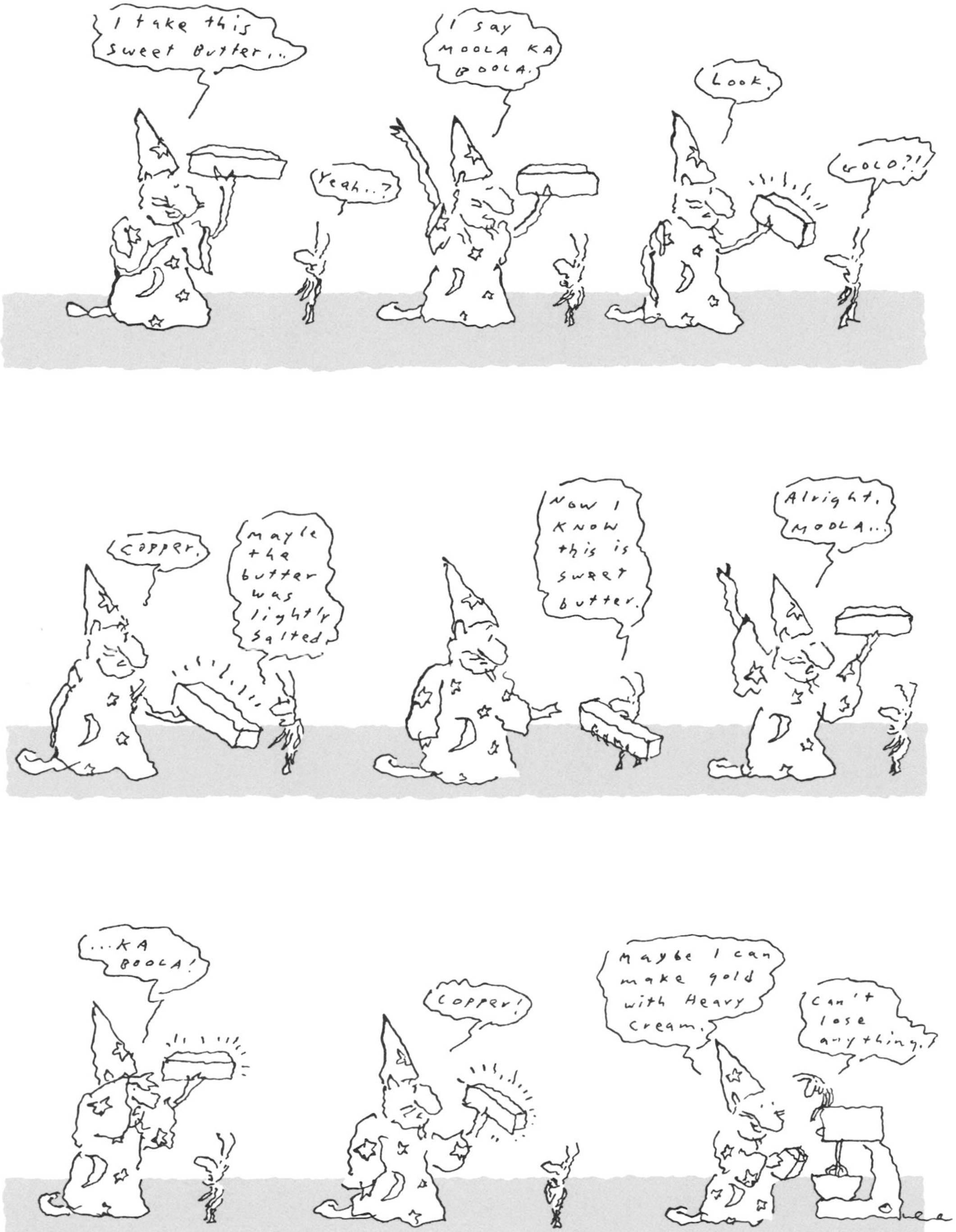
I take this sweet Butter...
Yeah..?
I say MOOLA KA BOOLA.
Look.
GOLD?!
Copper.
mayle the butter was lightly salted.
Now I KNOW this is sweet butter.
Alright. MOOLA...
...KA BOOLA!
Copper!
Maybe I can make gold with Heavy cream.
Can't lose anything.

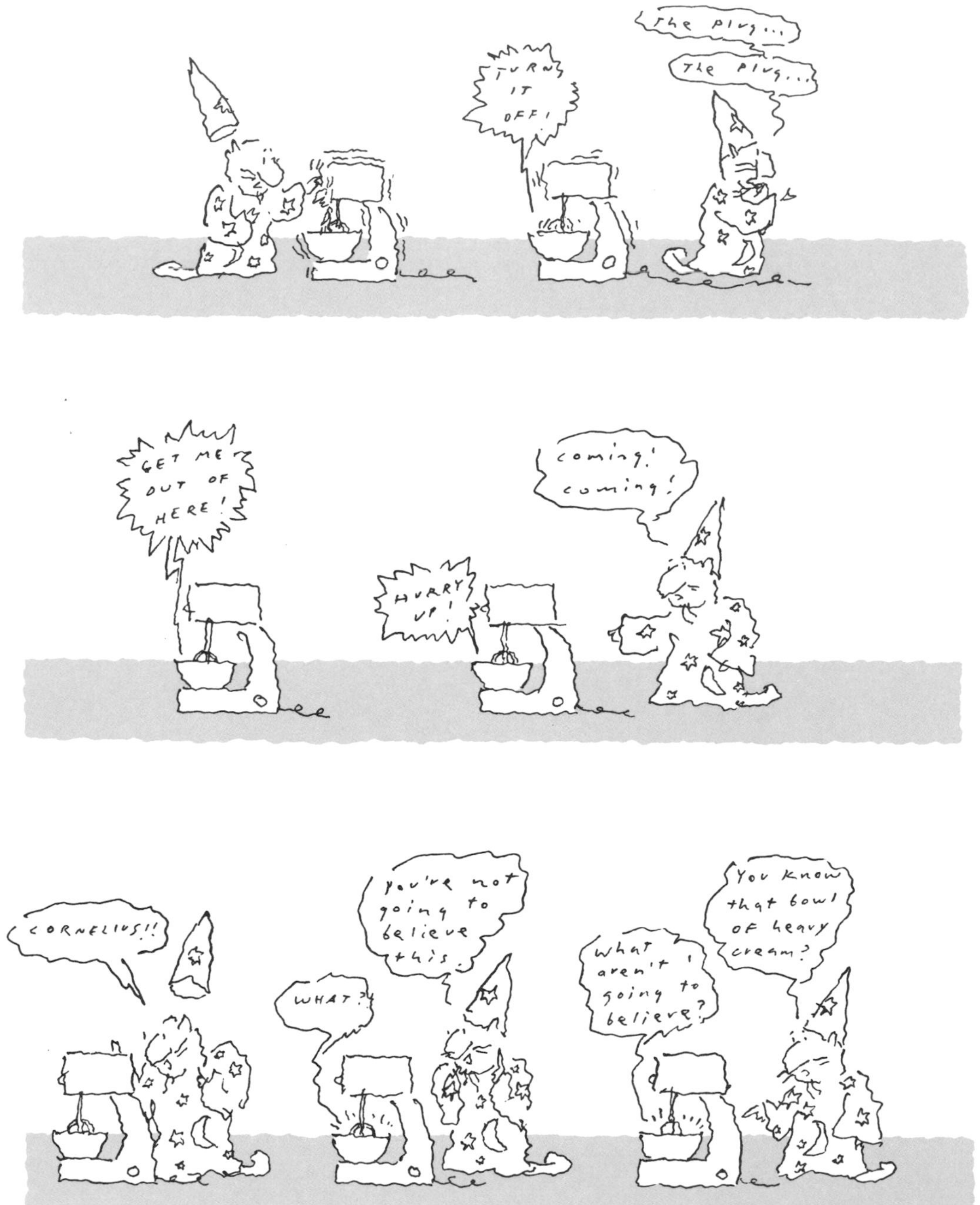

TURN IT OFF!
The plug...
The plug...
GET ME OUT OF HERE!
HURRY UP!
coming! coming!
CORNELIUS!!
WHAT?
you're not going to believe this.
what aren't I going to believe?
You know that bowl of heavy cream?

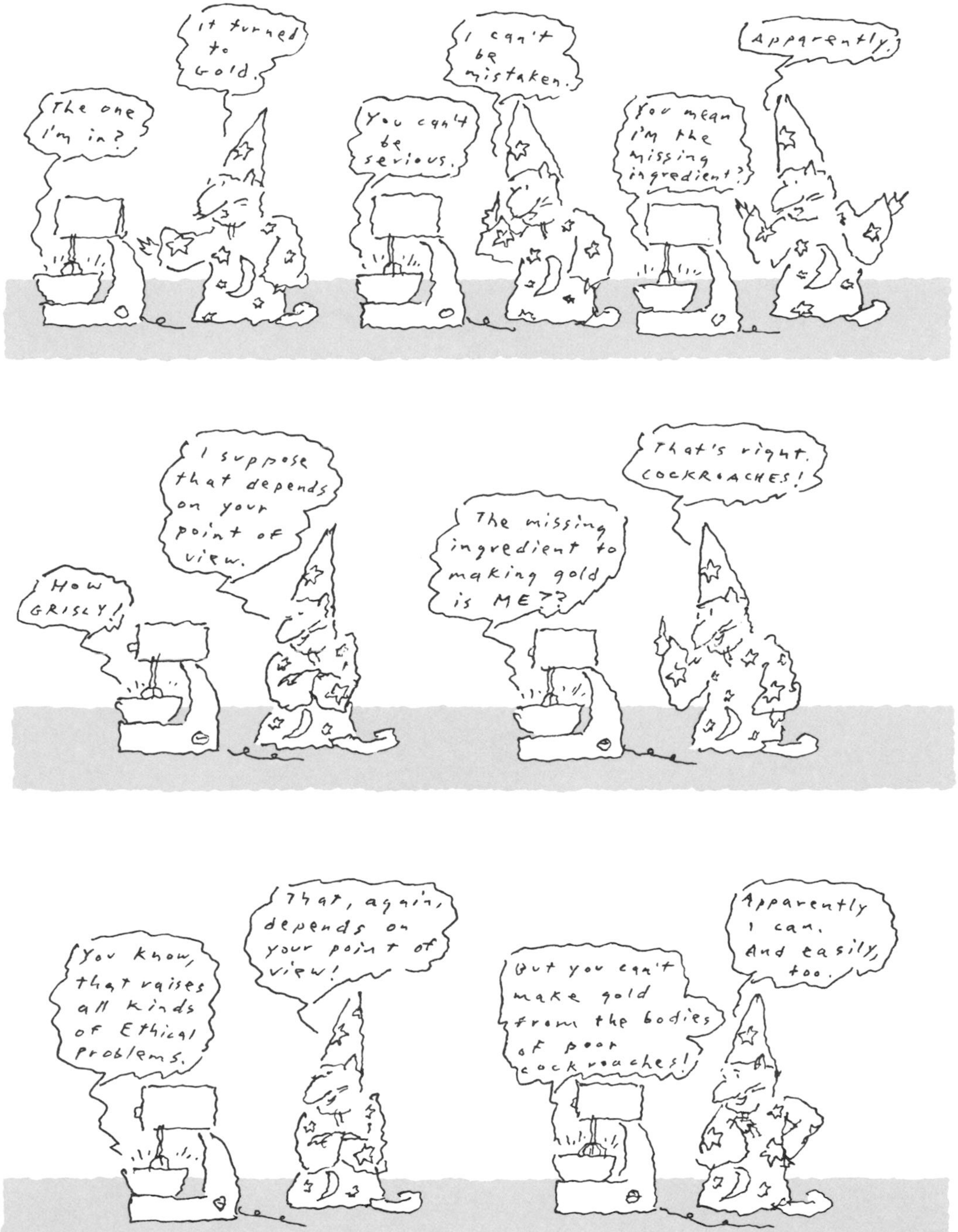
The one I'm in?
it turned to Gold.
You can't be serious.
I can't be mistaken.
You mean I'm the missing ingredient?
Apparently.
HOW GRISLY!
I suppose that depends on your point of view.
The missing ingredient to making gold is ME??
That's right. COCKROACHES!
You know, that raises all kinds of Ethical problems.
That, again, depends on your point of view!
But you can't make gold from the bodies of poor cockroaches!
Apparently I can. And easily, too.

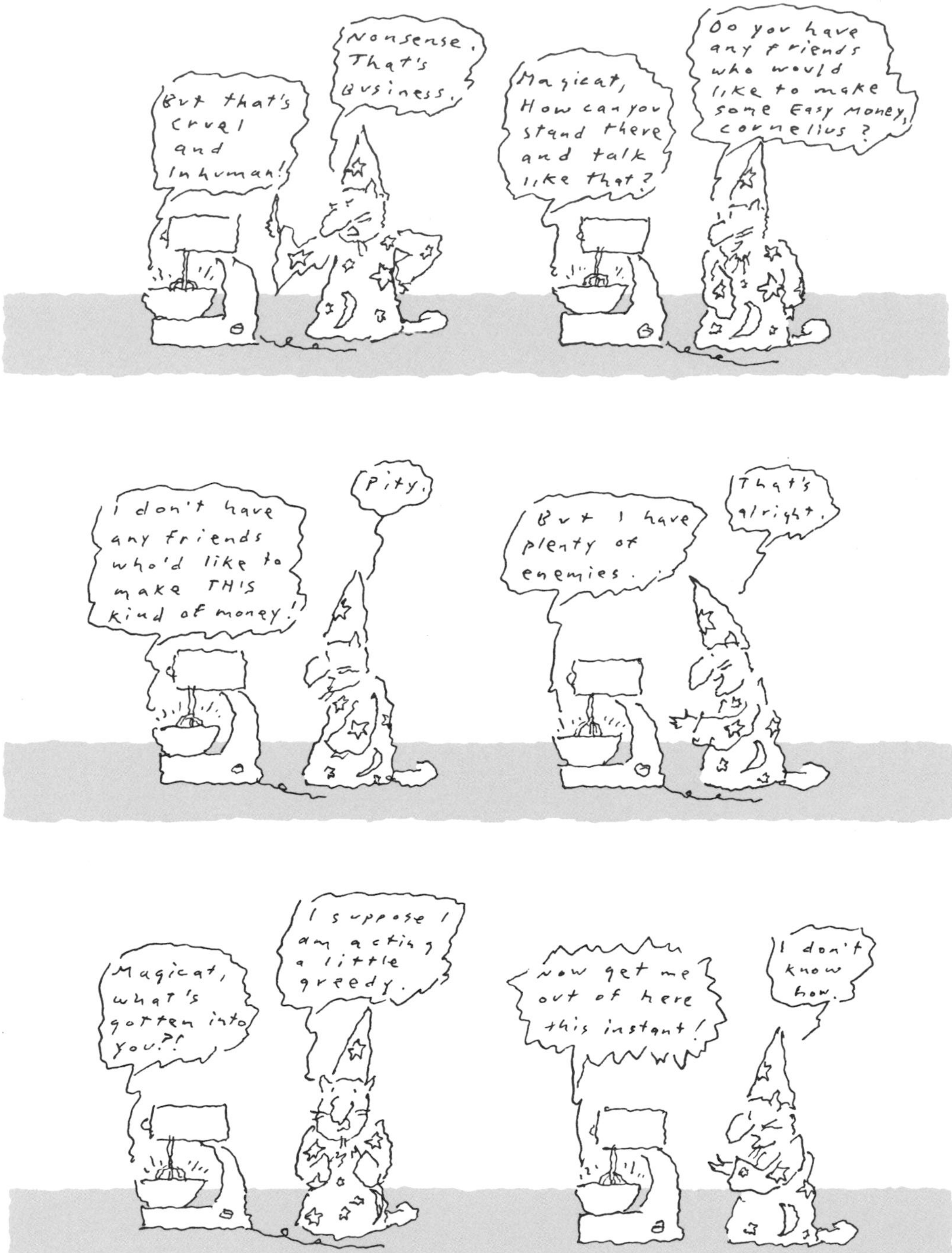
But that's cruel and Inhuman!
Nonsense. That's Business.
Magicat, How can you stand there and talk like that?
Do you have any friends who would like to make some Easy money, cornelius?
I don't have any friends who'd like to make THIS kind of money!
Pity.
But I have plenty of enemies.
That's alright.
Magicat, what's gotten into you?!
I suppose I am acting a little greedy.
Now get me out of here this instant!
I don't know how.

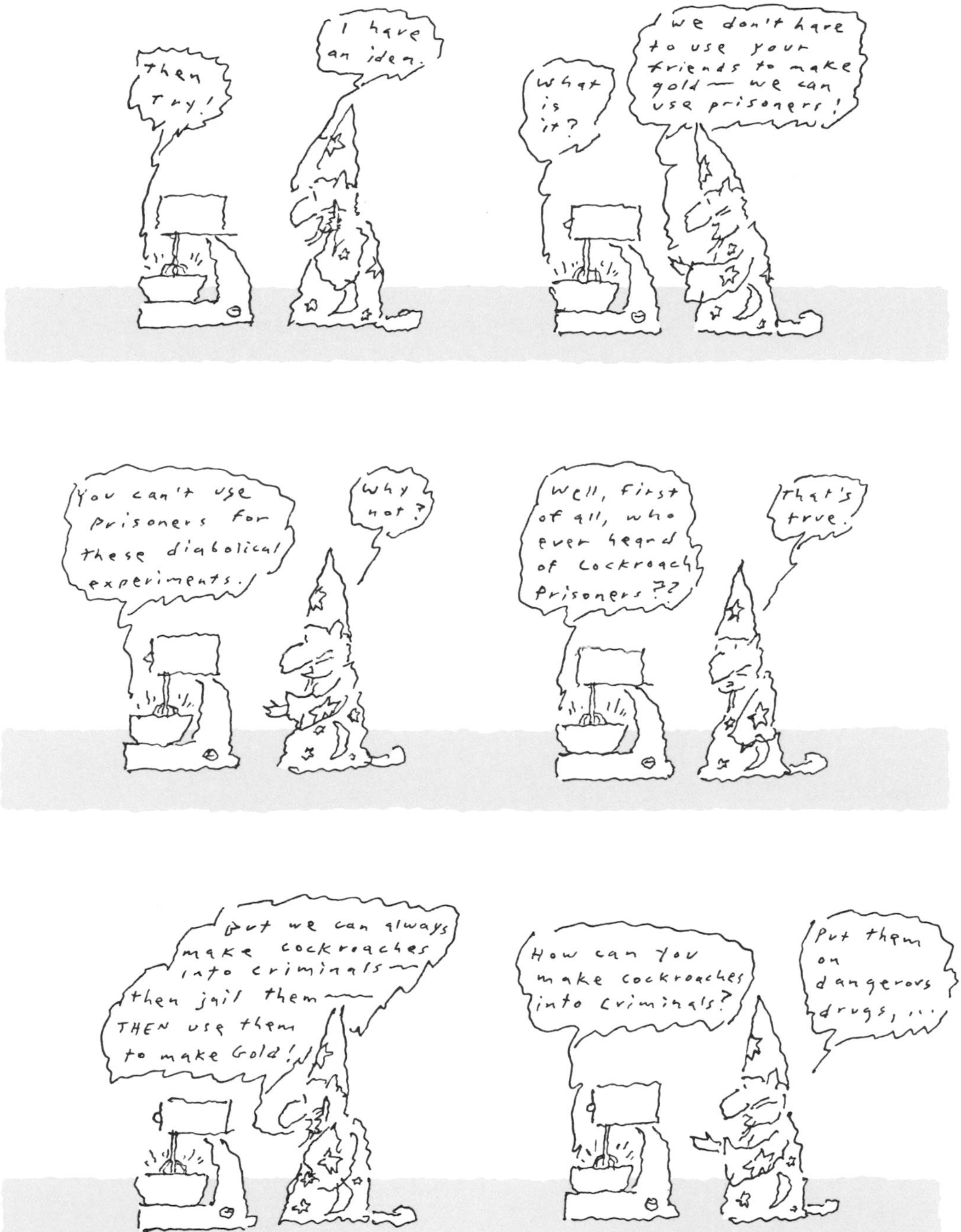
Then try!
I have an idea.
What is it?
We don't have to use your friends to make gold — we can use prisoners!
You can't use prisoners for these diabolical experiments.
Why not?
Well, first of all, who ever heard of cockroach prisoners??
That's true.
But we can always make cockroaches into criminals — then jail them — THEN use them to make Gold!
How can you make cockroaches into criminals?
Put them on dangerous drugs, ...

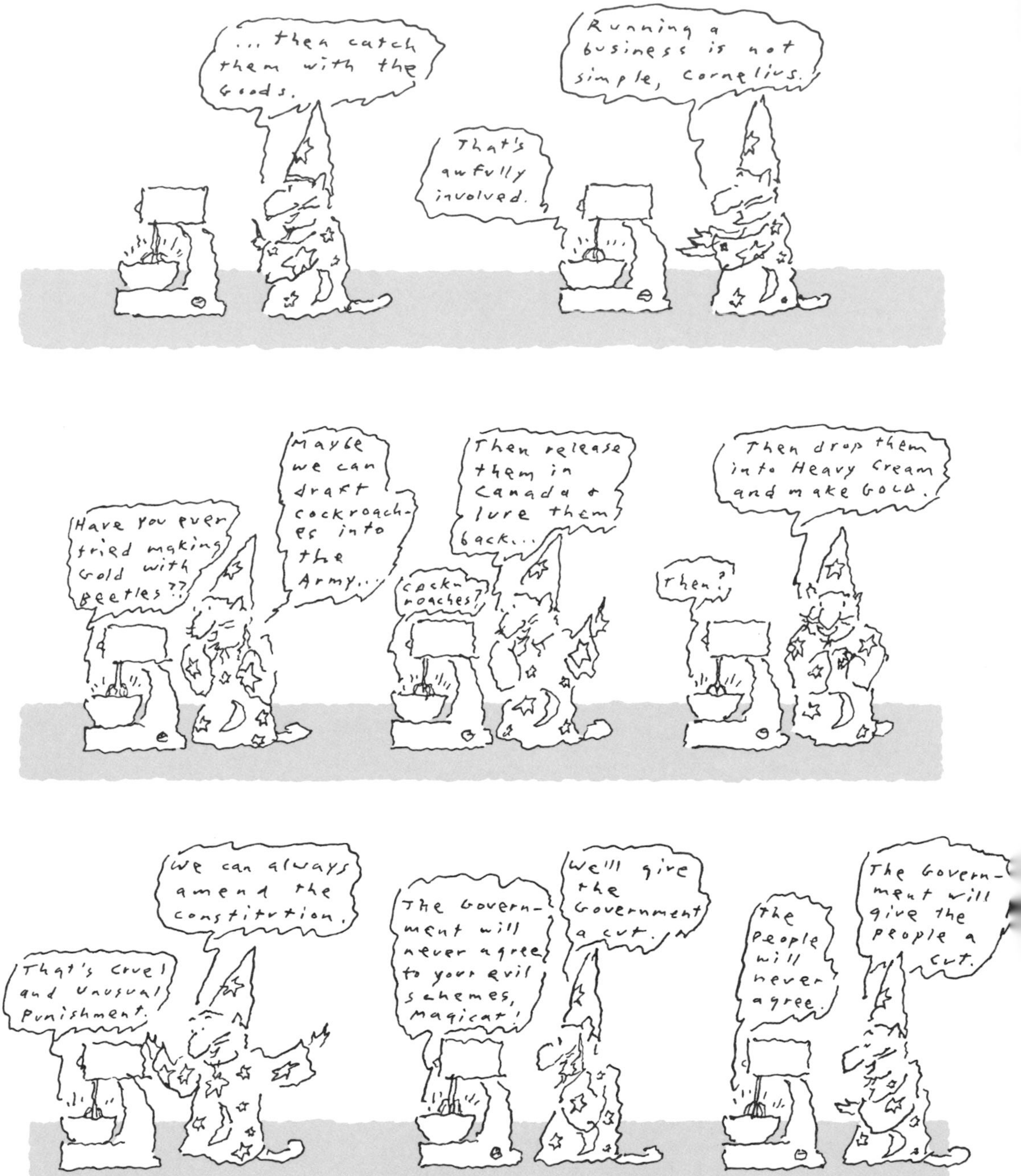
...then catch them with the Goods.
That's awfully involved.
Running a business is not simple, Cornelius.
Have you ever tried making Gold with Beetles??
Maybe we can draft cockroaches into the Army...
Cockroaches?
Then release them in Canada & lure them back...
Then?
Then drop them into Heavy Cream and make Gold.
That's cruel and unusual Punishment.
We can always amend the constitution.
The Government will never agree to your evil schemes, magicat!
We'll give the Government a cut.
The People will never agree.
The Government will give the people a cut.

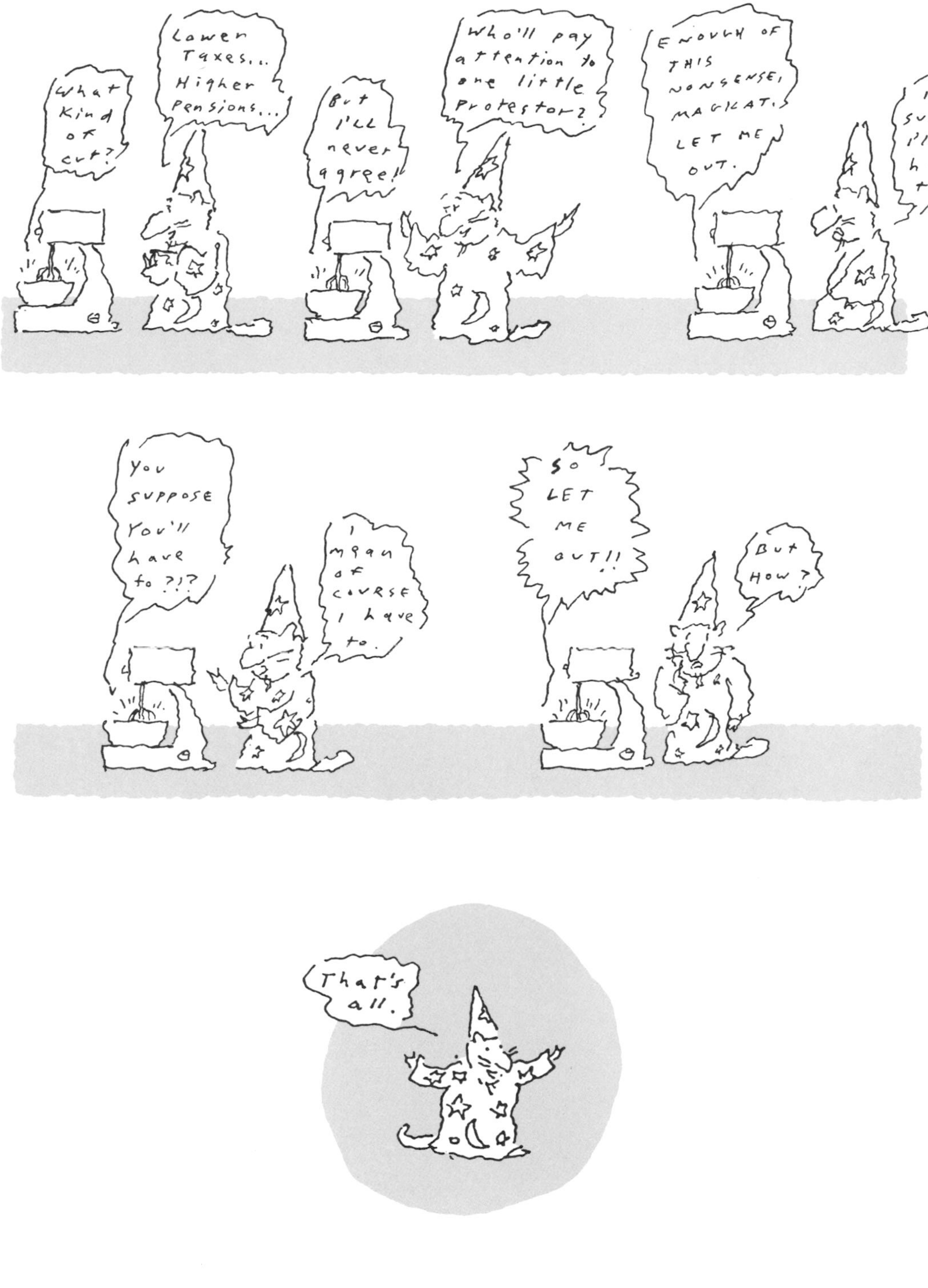
What kind of cut?
Lower Taxes... Higher Pensions...
But I'll never agree!
Who'll pay attention to one little protestor?
ENOUGH OF THIS NONSENSE, MAGICAT. LET ME OUT.
I suppose I'll have to.
You suppose you'll have to?!?
I mean of course I have to.
SO LET ME OUT!!
But HOW?
That's all.

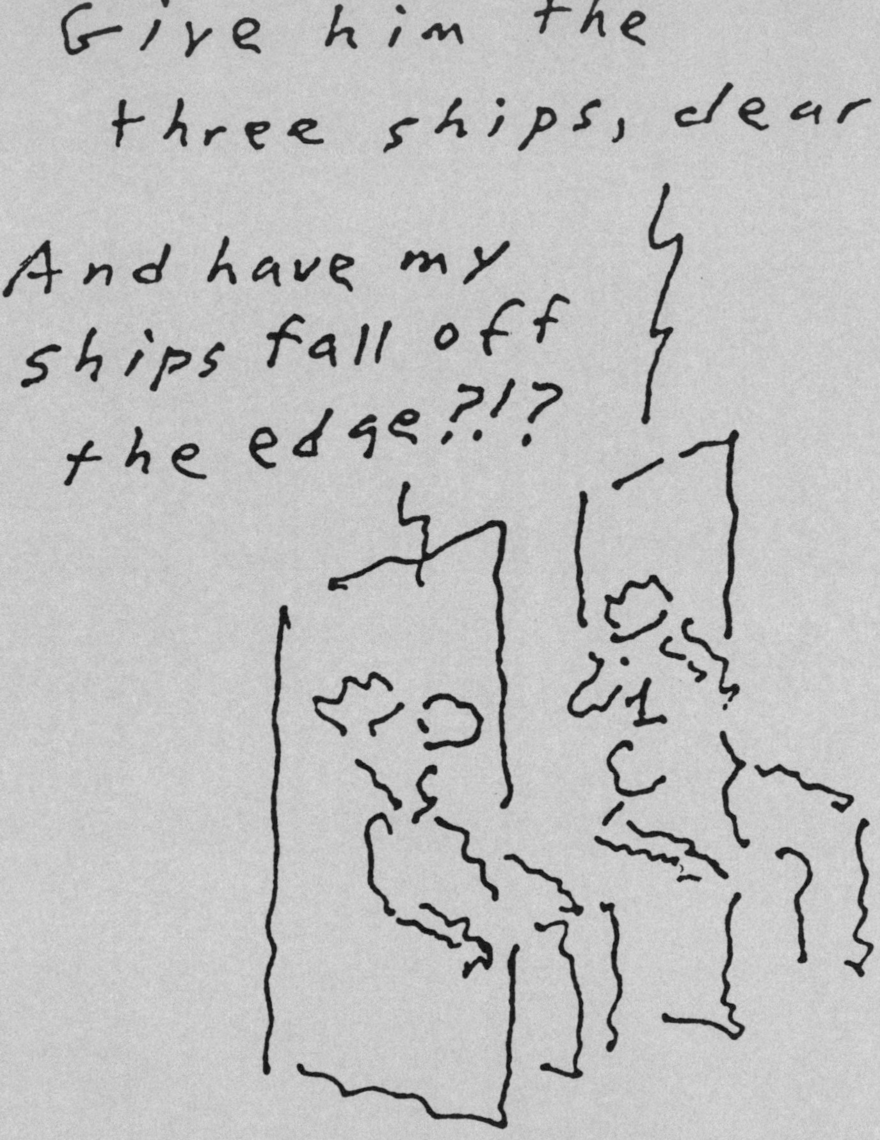
Give him the three ships, dear
And have my ships fall off the edge?!?

The
New
World

UNPUBLISHED, 1992

The 500th Anniversary of Columbus' landing in
America was the occasion for scores of heavy-
breathing revisionist critiques (some of which
were downright silly. One writer claimed that
Columbus was a rotten sailor. He may have been
a rotten human being, but it was no mean trick
to have sailed three small ships safely across the
Atlantic Ocean). My contribution to the holiday
was this piece of froth. It may have been an an-
tidote to all the scholarly claptrap that was published.

The New World

What do you mean, "The earth isn't flat?!"
It's round!

Is he out of his mind?
Here's an egg
The King isn't hungry, señor Columbus. He just ate.

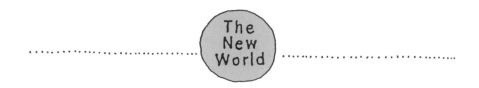

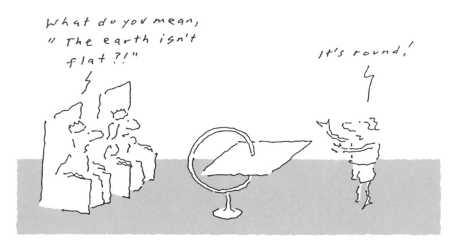

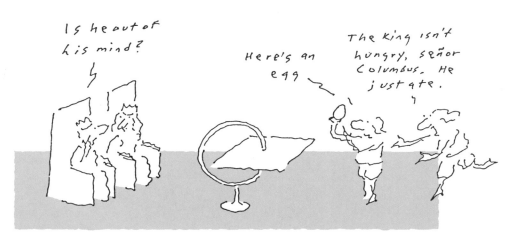

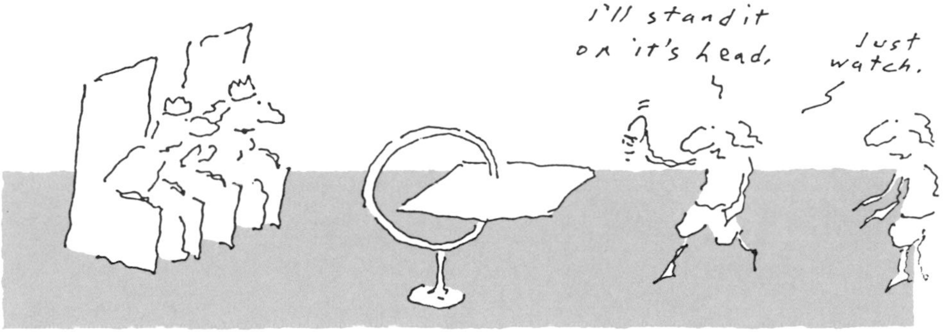
I'll standit on it's head.
Just watch.

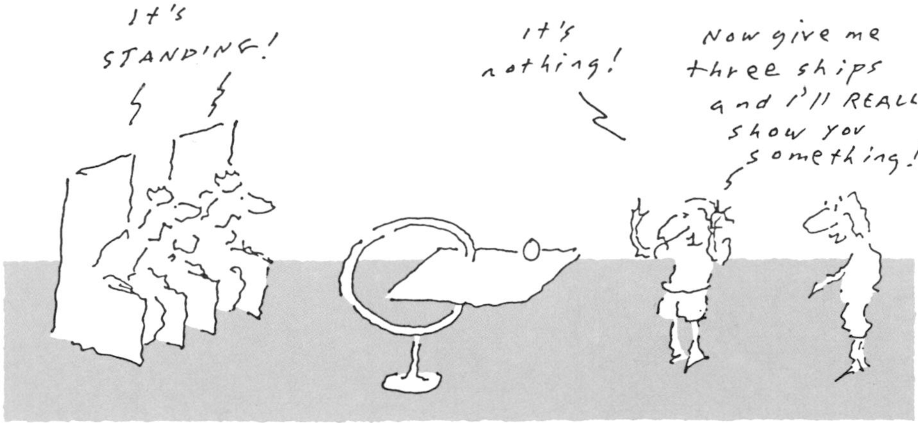
It's STANDING!
It's nothing!
Now give me three ships and I'll REALLY show you something!

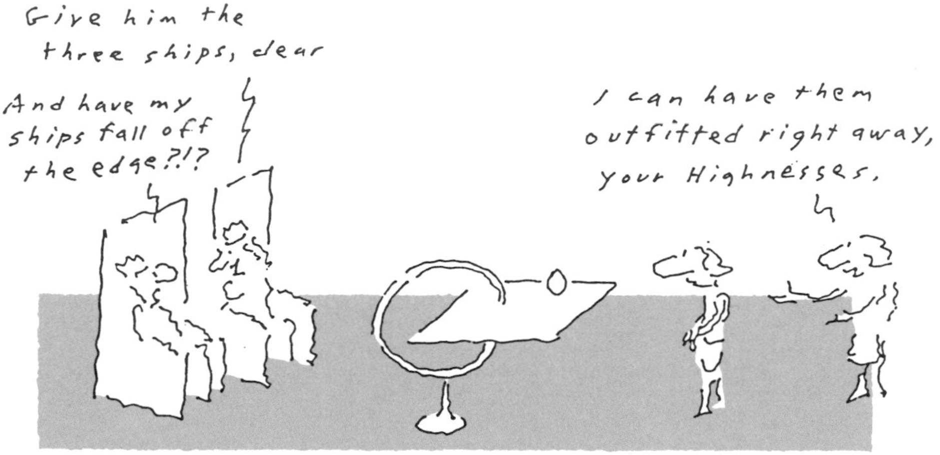
Give him the three ships, dear
And have my ships fall off the edge?!?
I can have them outfitted right away, your Highnesses.

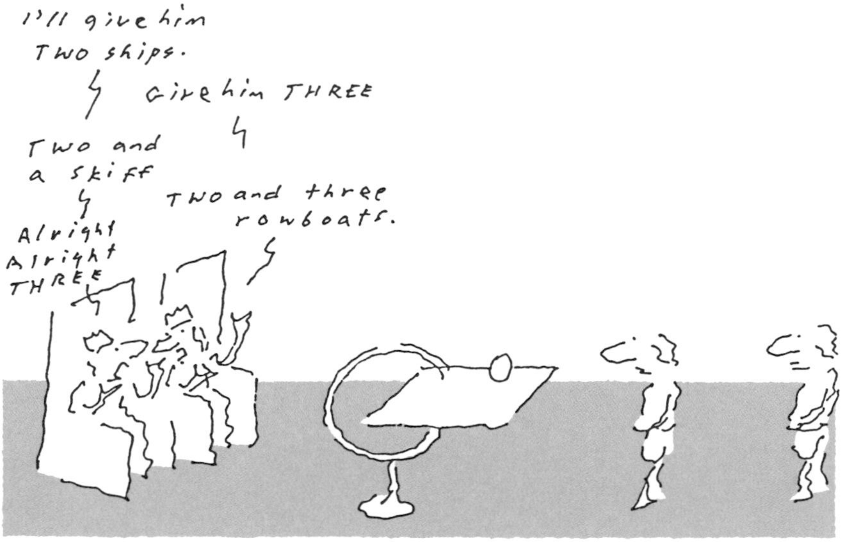
I'll give him TWO ships.
Give him THREE
Two and a skiff
TWO and three rowboats.
Alright Alright THREE

MANY
MONTHS
LATER

It's
Columbus
to see you,
Your Highnesses,

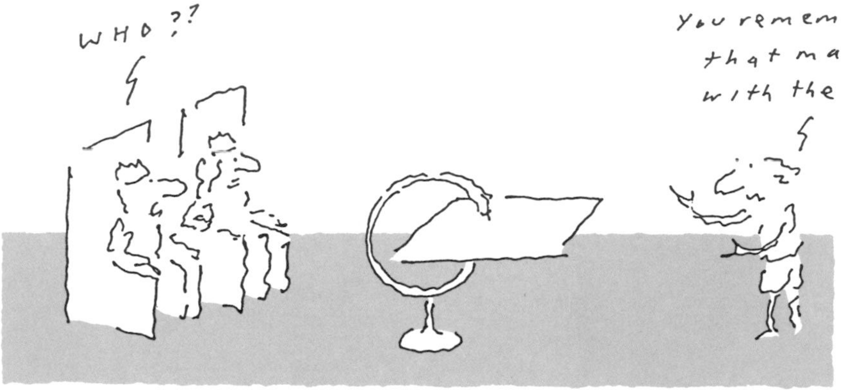
WHO ??
You remember, that man with the egg!

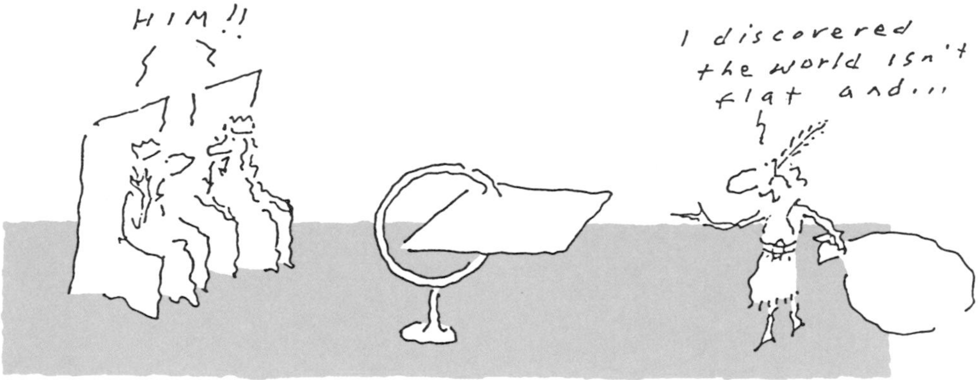
HIM !!
I discovered the world isn't flat and...

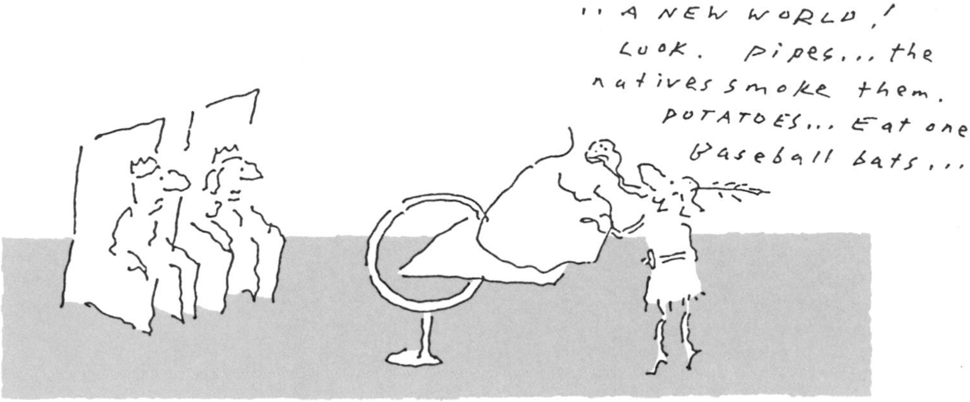
''A NEW WORLD,! LOOK. Pipes... the natives smoke them. POTATOES... Eat one. Baseball bats...

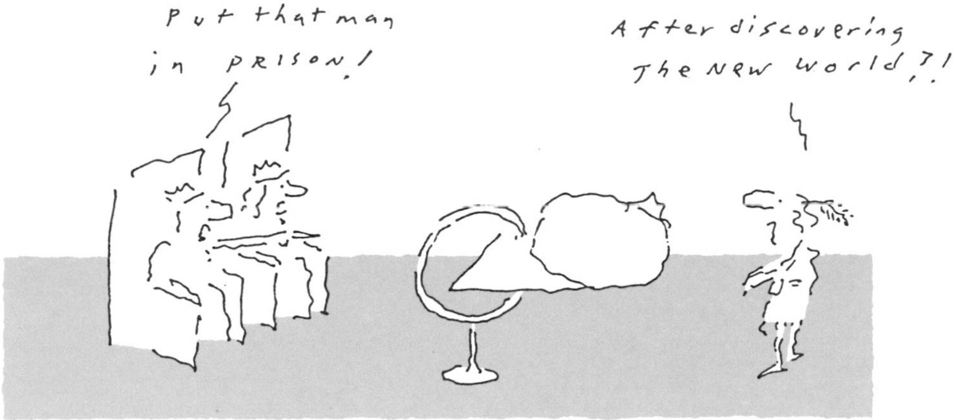
Put that man in PRISON!
After discovering The New World?!

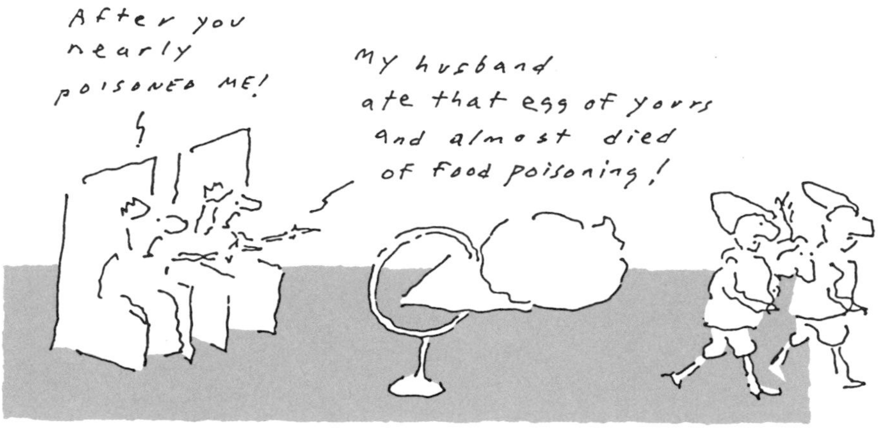
After you nearly poisoned me!
My husband ate that egg of yours and almost died of food poisoning!

He doesn't know anything about food, but I have a feeling that man is on to something important!

FINIS

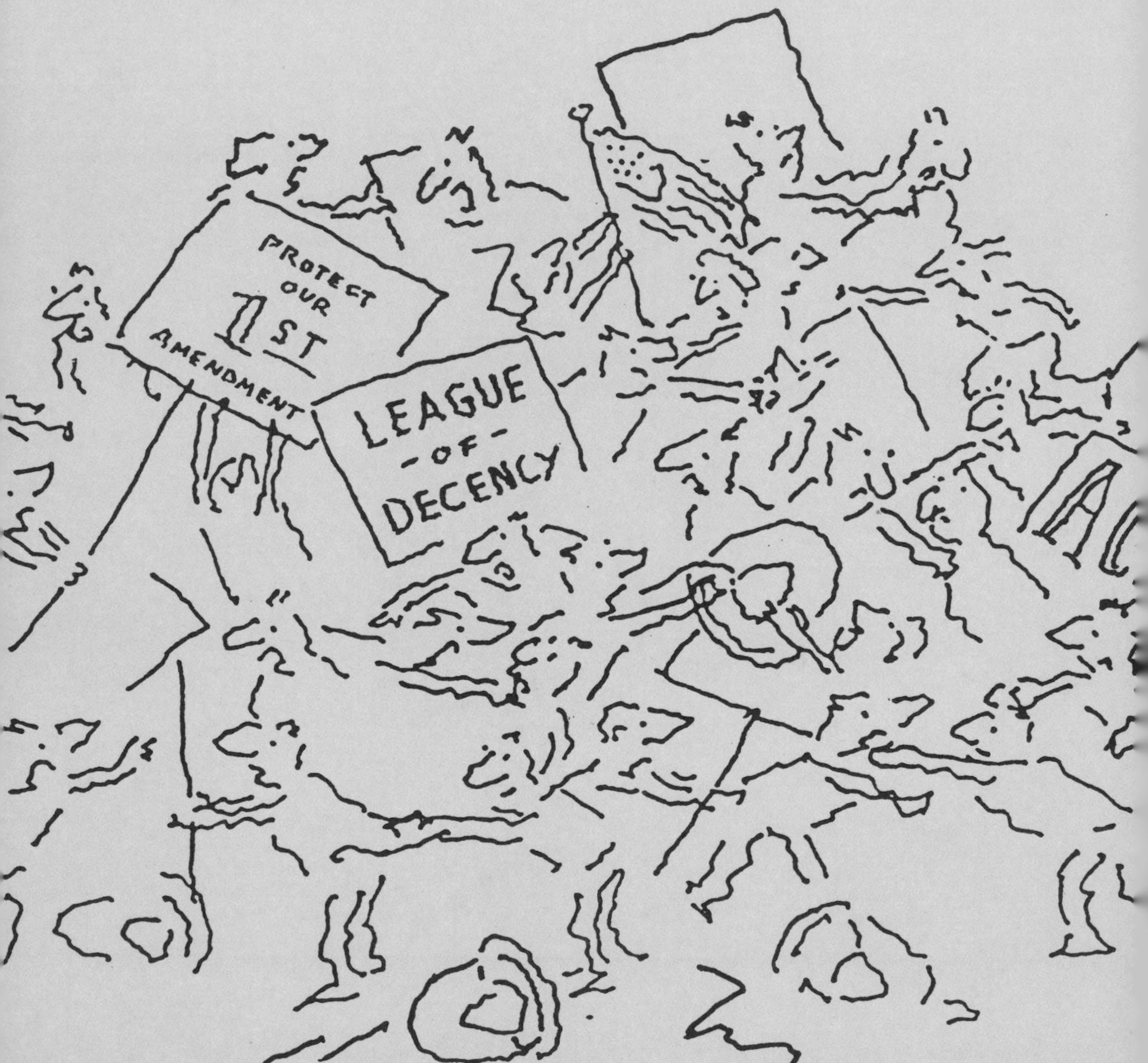
PROTECT OUR 1ST AMENDMENT
LEAGUE -OF- DECENCY

THE GILDED AGE

UNPUBLISHED, 2009

Robert Crumb said it first. "What's the price of shit today?" That was back in the Sixties when it was merely an outrageous thing to say.

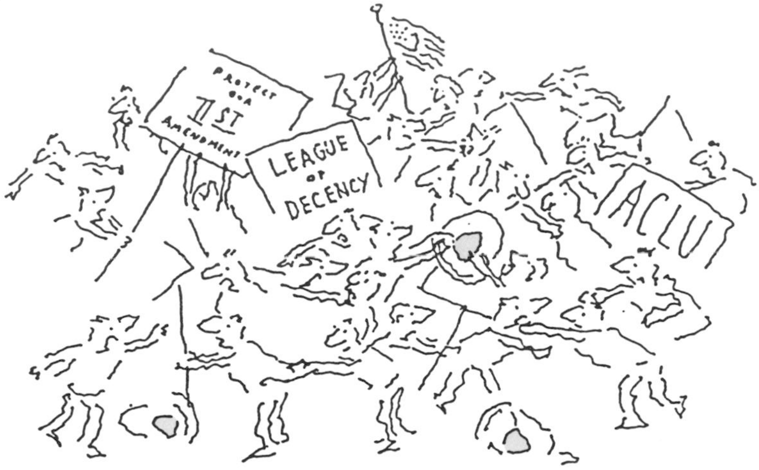
PROTECT OUR 1ST AMENDMENT
LEAGUE OF DECENCY
ACLU

At the opening of the exhibition, a fistfight broke out between protestors and Free Speech advocates.

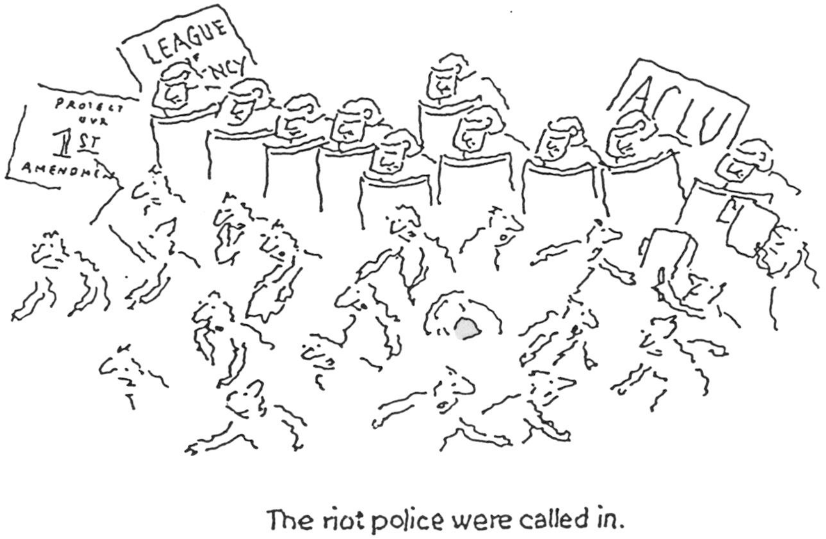
LEAGUE NCY
PROTECT OUR 1ST AMENDMEN
ACLU

The riot police were called in.

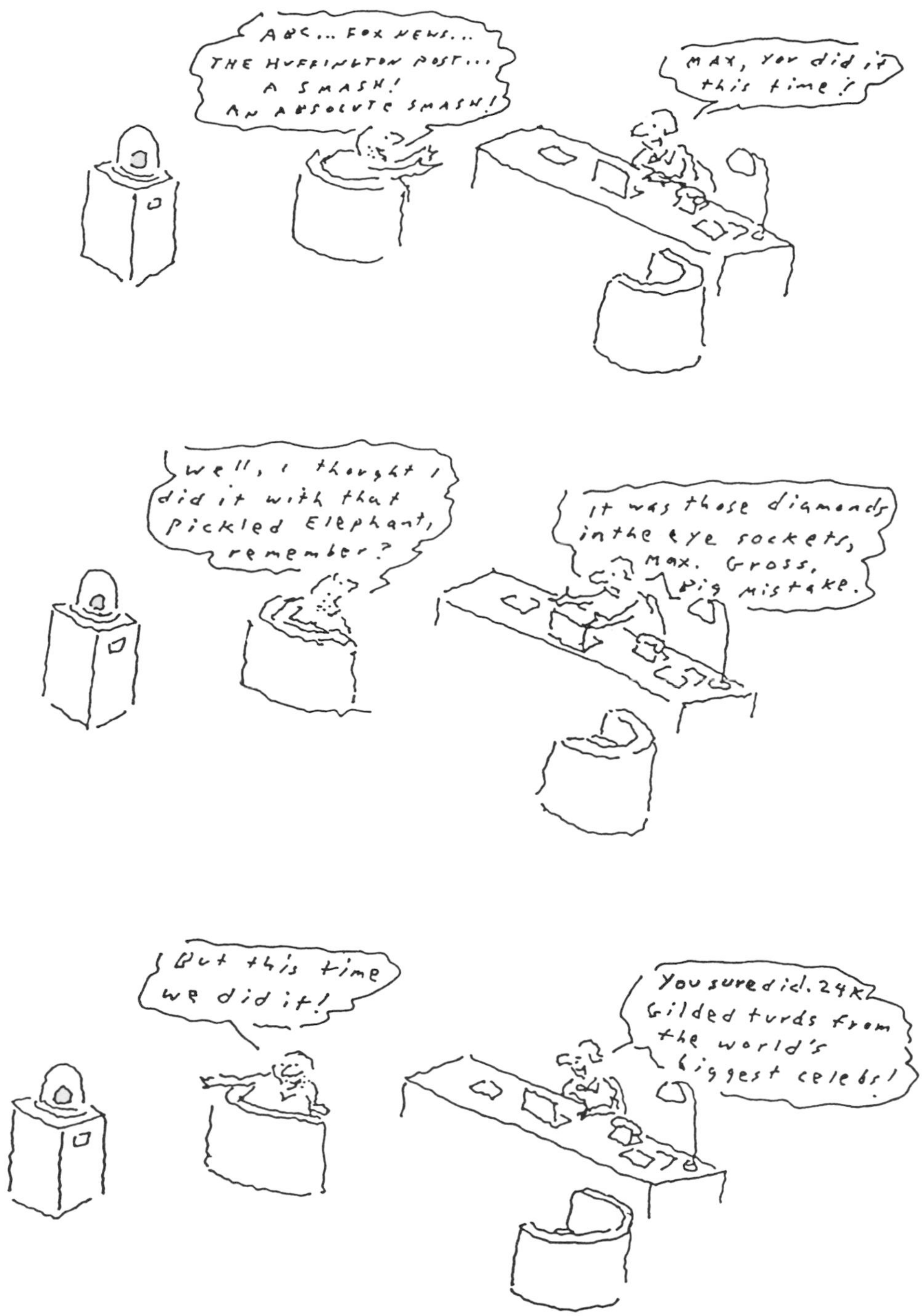
ABC... FOX NEWS... THE HUFFINGTON POST... A SMASH! AN ABSOLUTE SMASH!
MAX, YOU DID IT THIS TIME!
Well, I thought I did it with that pickled Elephant, remember?
It was those diamonds in the eye sockets, Max. Gross, big mistake.
But this time we did it!
You sure did. 24K Gilded turds from the world's biggest celebs!

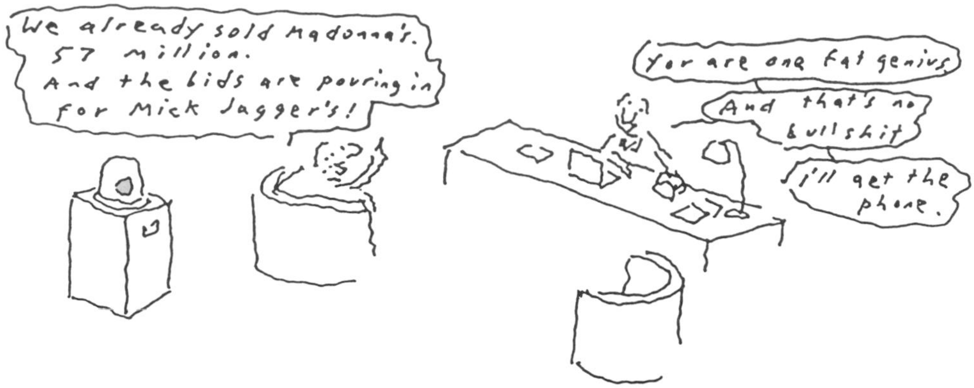
We already sold Madonna's. 57 million. And the bids are pouring in for Mick Jagger's!
You are one fat genius
And that's no bullshit
I'll get the phone.

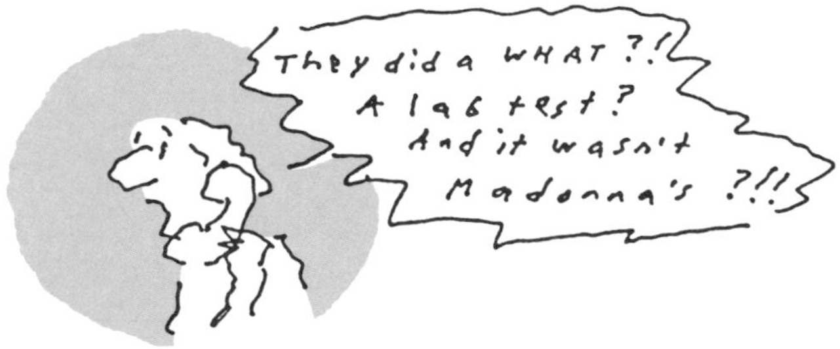
They did a WHAT?! A lab test? And it wasn't Madonna's?!!

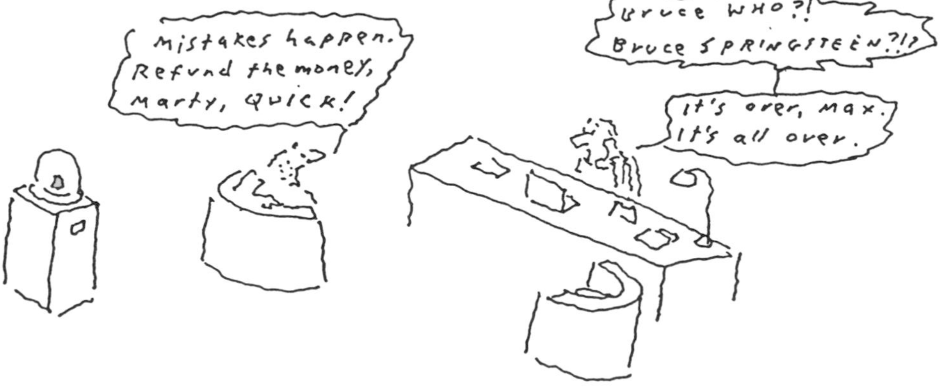
Mistakes happen. Refund the money, Marty, QUICK!
Bruce WHO?! Bruce SPRINGSTEEN?!?
It's over, Max. It's all over.

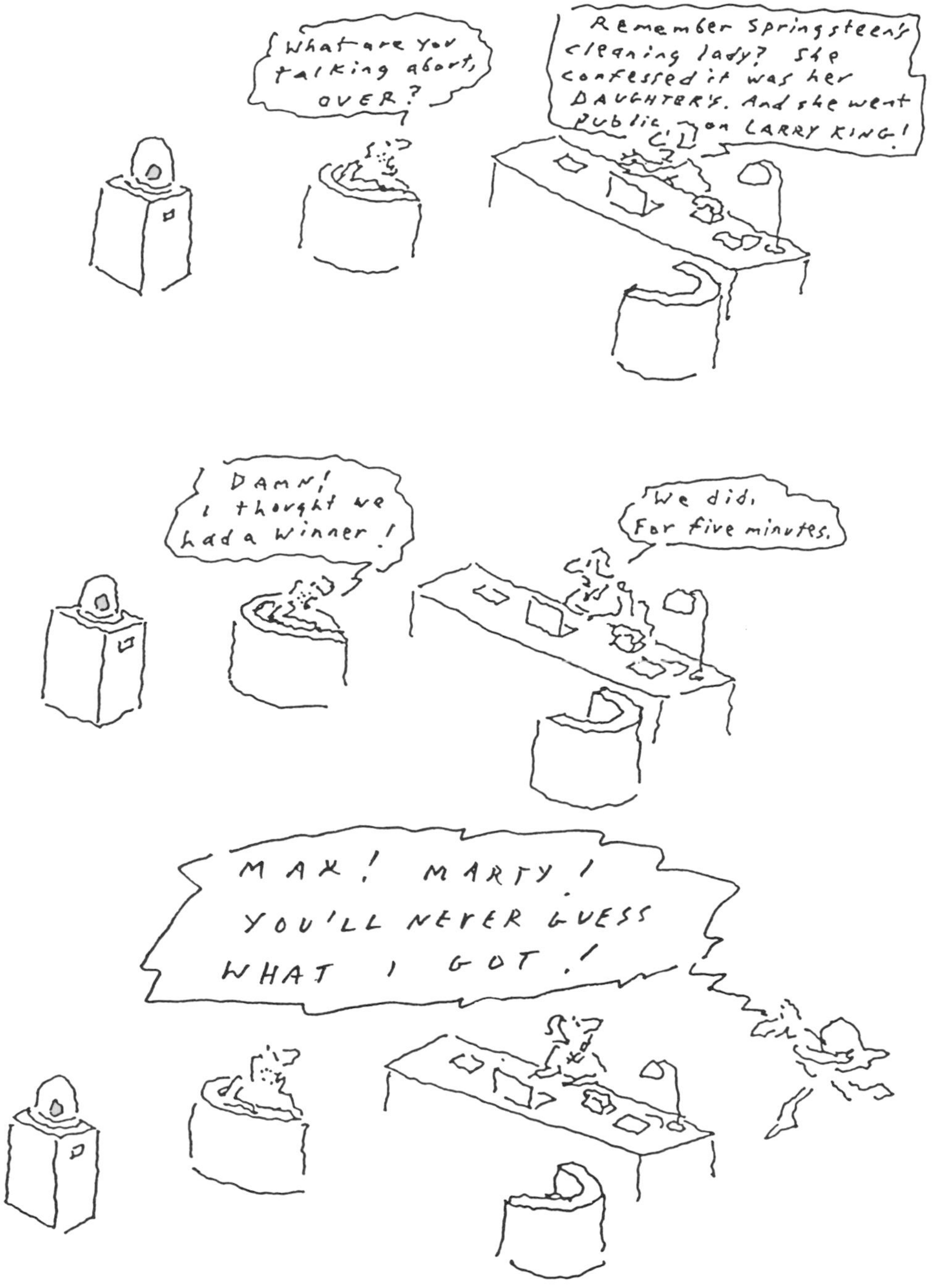
What are you talking about, OVER?
Remember Springsteen's cleaning lady? She confessed it was her DAUGHTER'S. And she went public on LARRY KING!
DAMN! I thought we had a winner!
We did. For five minutes.
MAX! MARTY! YOU'LL NEVER GUESS WHAT I GOT!

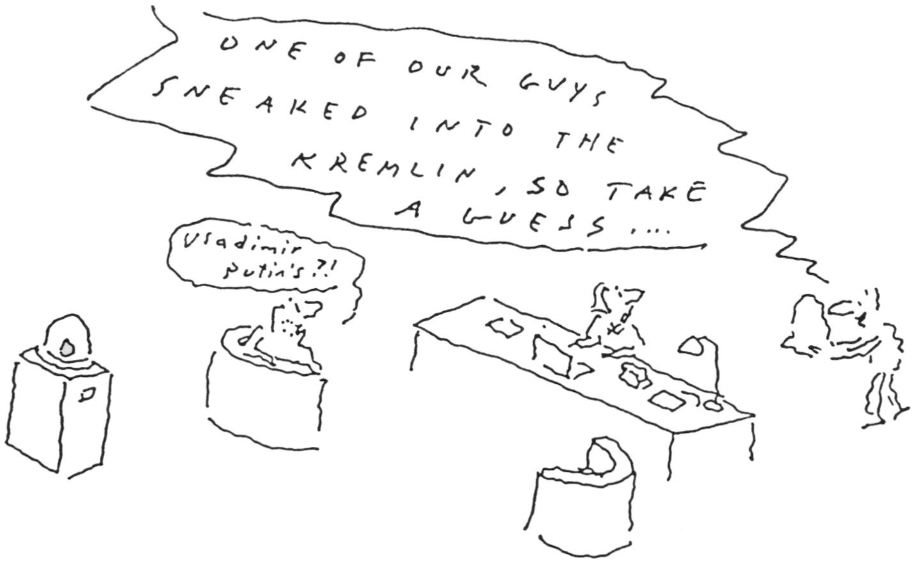
ONE OF OUR GUYS SNEAKED INTO THE KREMLIN, SO TAKE A GUESS....
Vladimir Putin's?!

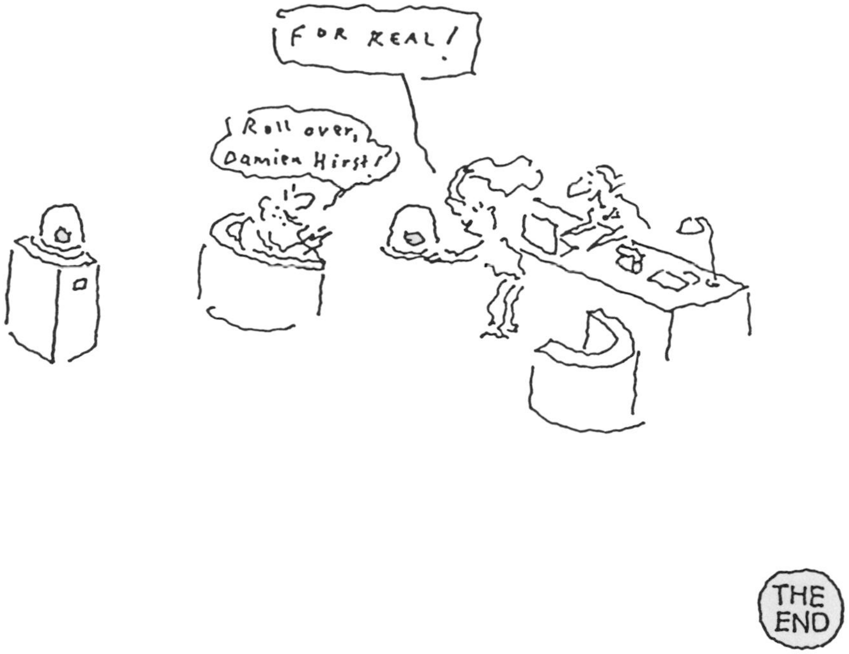
FOR REAL!
Roll over, Damien Hirst!
THE END

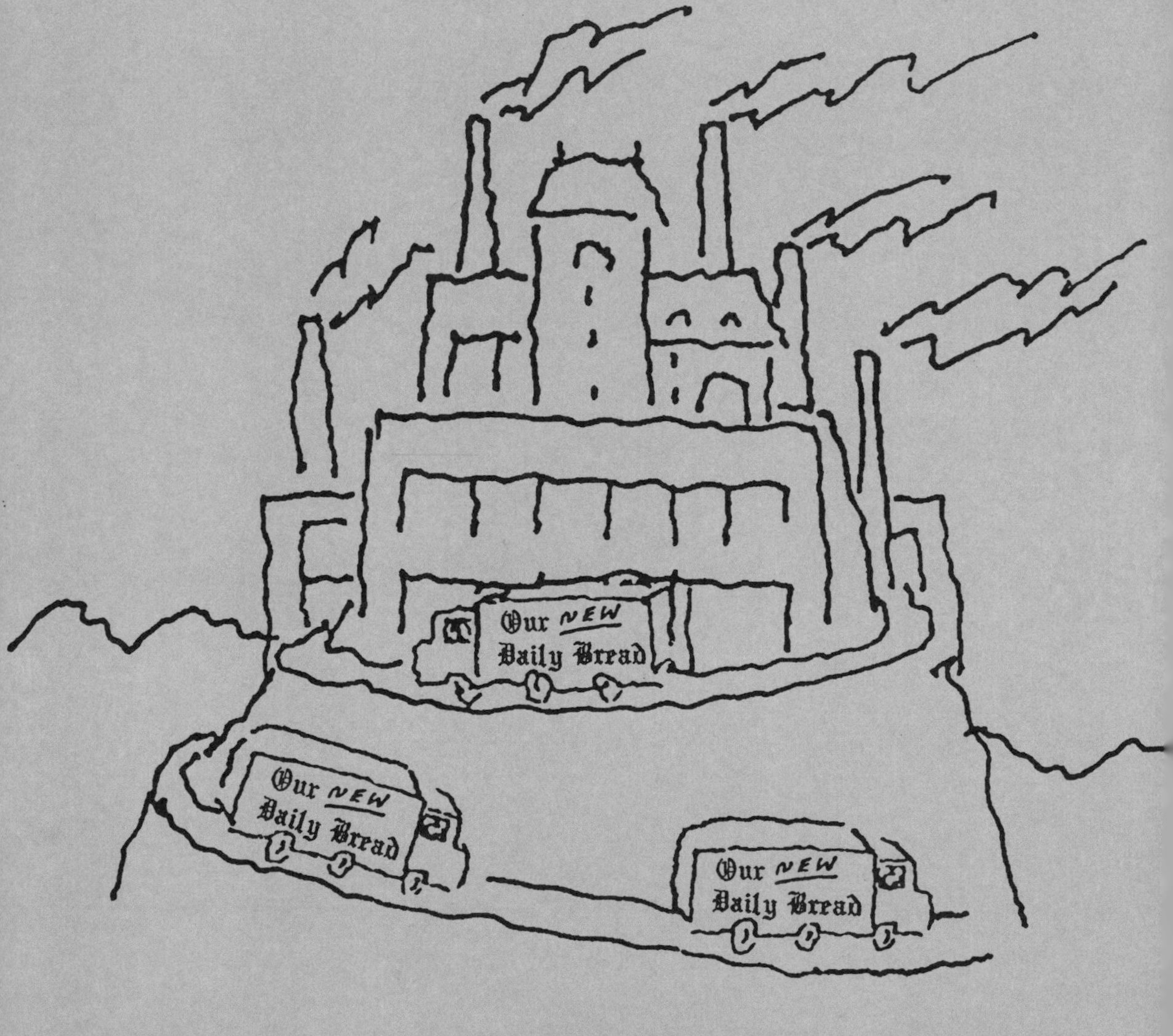
Our NEW Daily Bread
Our NEW Daily Bread
Our NEW Daily Bread

Our Daily Bread

. . . .

NOZONE, 2004

I did this for my son's magazine, *Nozone*. It was a special issue on "Empire." I knew that most people would interpret this politically, so I chose to deal with economic imperialism — the octopus that grabs all the world's little fish.

The novelist, Daniel Quinn, once wrote, "If they give you lined paper, write sideways."

Our Daily Bread

The Abbey of St. Crispus (Apologia, N.Y. 12534) was renowned for its bread.

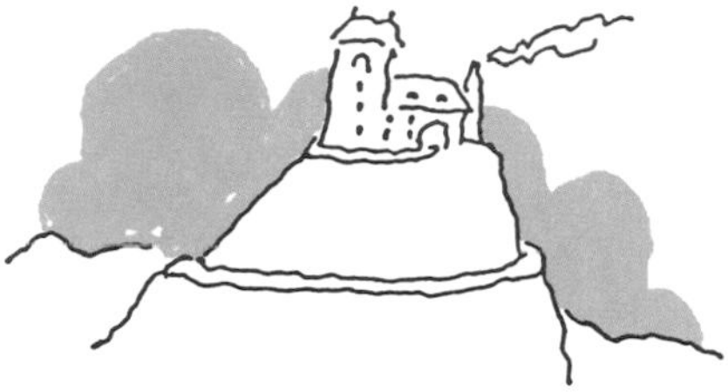

It was baked using a 125-year-old oven and a 260-year-old-formula.

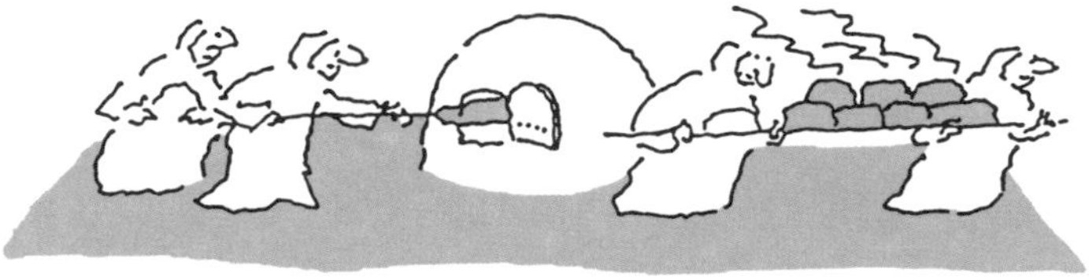

The bread was delivered in a 74-year-old station wagon.

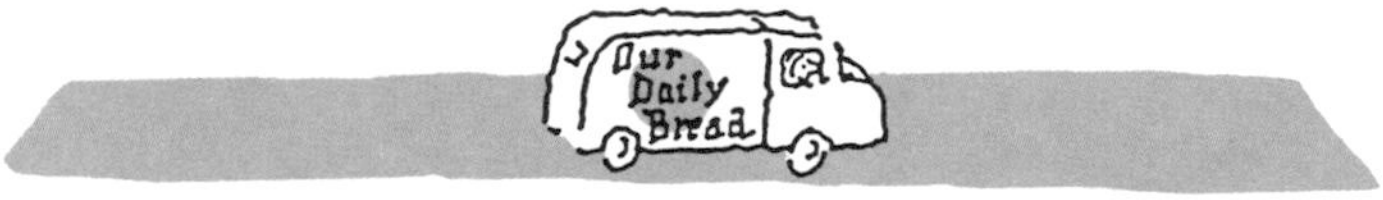
Our Daily Bread

It sometimes broke down.

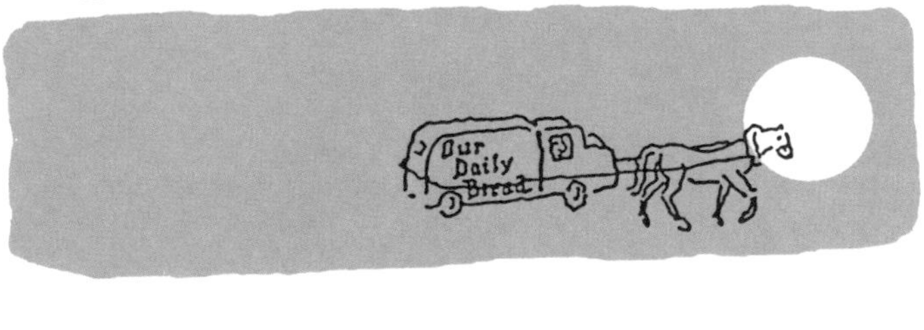
Our Daily Bread

The fame of *Our Daily Bread* spread throughout the Northeast.

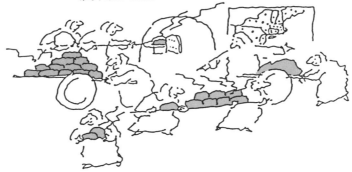

Word of its success soon reached the corporate headquarters of Krassko Kookery.

Make them an offer they can't refuse.
They refused, Mr. Krass.
Double it and throw in two Hummer station wagons.
They still refused, Mr. Krass.
SEND JOEY

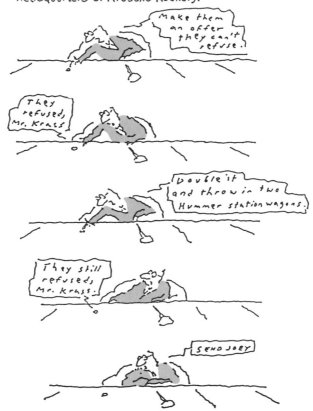

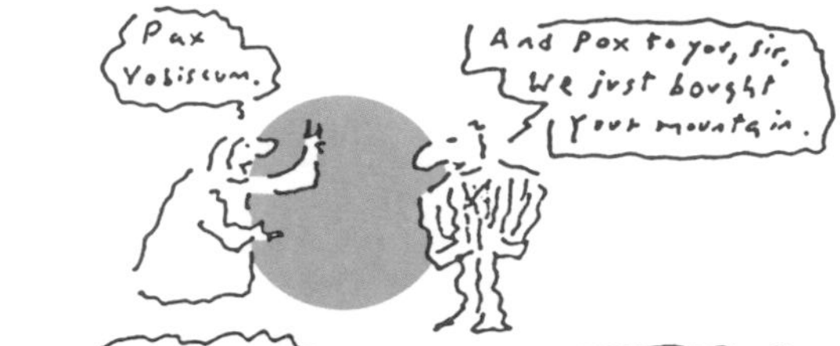
Pax Vobiscum.
And Pox to you, sir, We just bought your mountain.

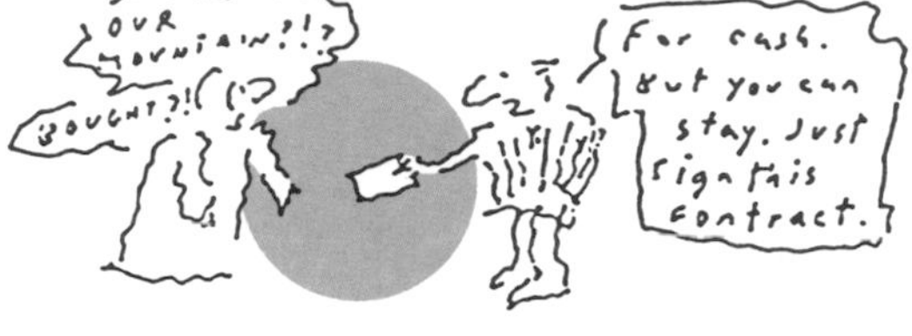
OUR MOUNTAIN?!?
BOUGHT?!
For cash. But you can stay. Just sign this contract.

Nutrition experts from Krassko began making improvements to the bread.

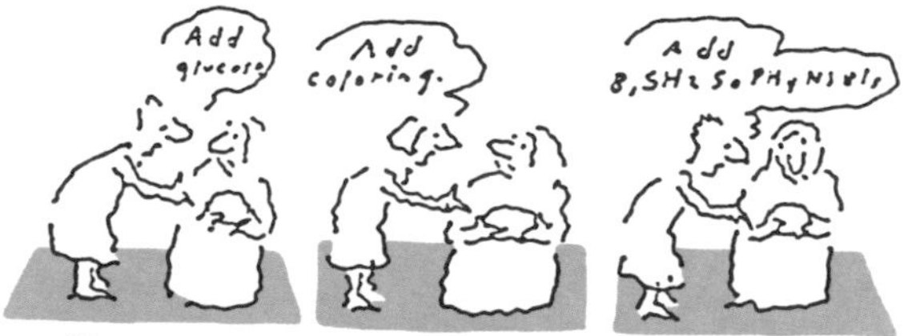
Add glucose
Add coloring.
Add

Merchandising experts followed.

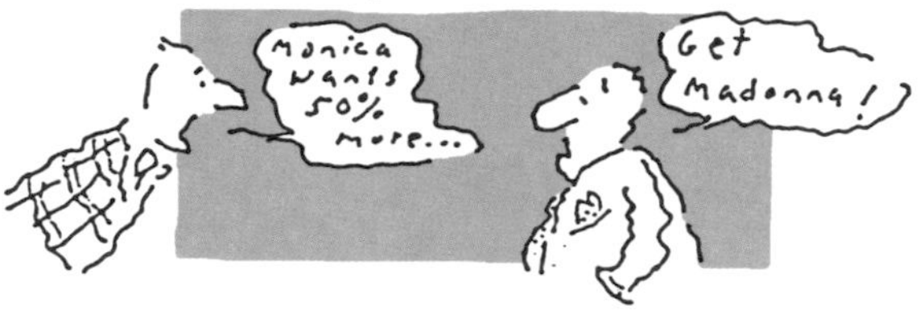
Monica wants 50% more...
Get Madonna!

Within a year *Our Daily Bread* became global.

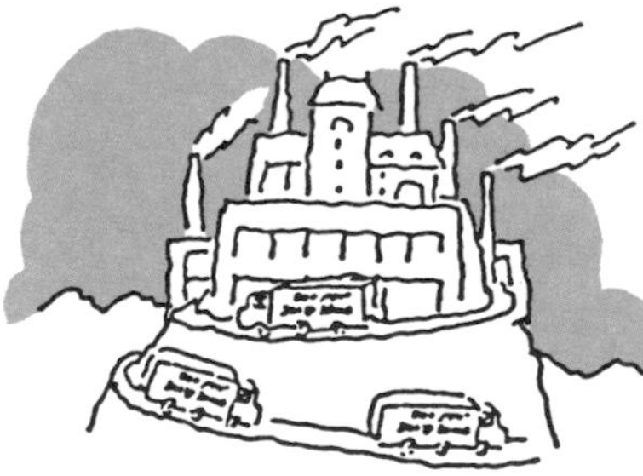

Several younger monks decided to form a new bakery.

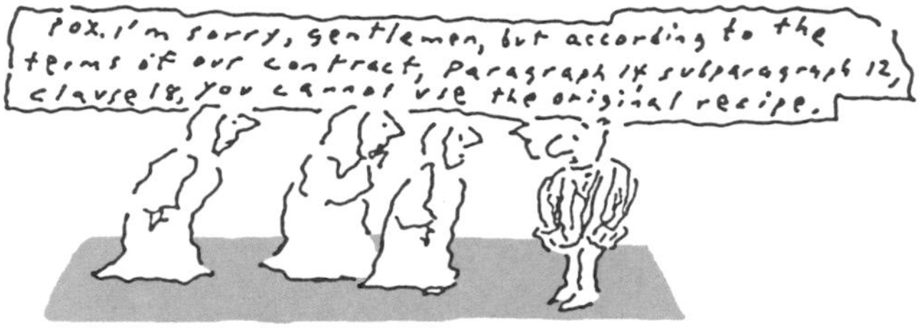
Pox. I'm sorry, gentlemen, but according to the terms of our contract, paragraph 14 subparagraph 12, clause 18, you cannot use the original recipe.

A few tried to bake *Our Daily Bread* in secret.

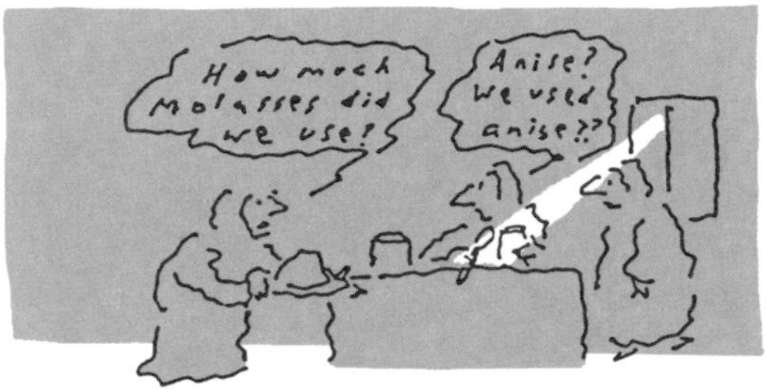
How much molasses did we use?
Anise? We used anise??

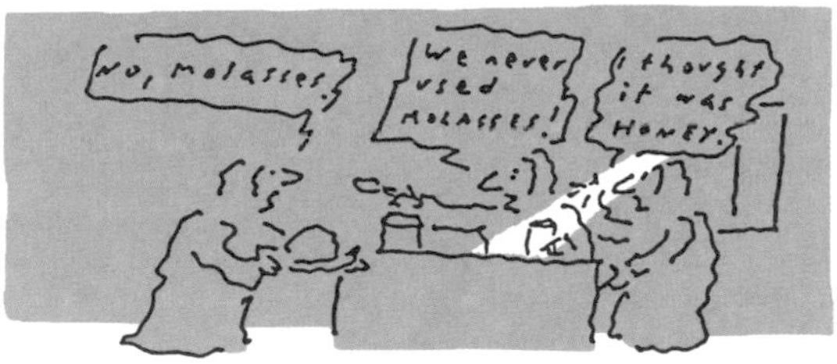
No, molasses.
We never used MOLASSES!
I thought it was HONEY.

Nobody could remember the recipe.

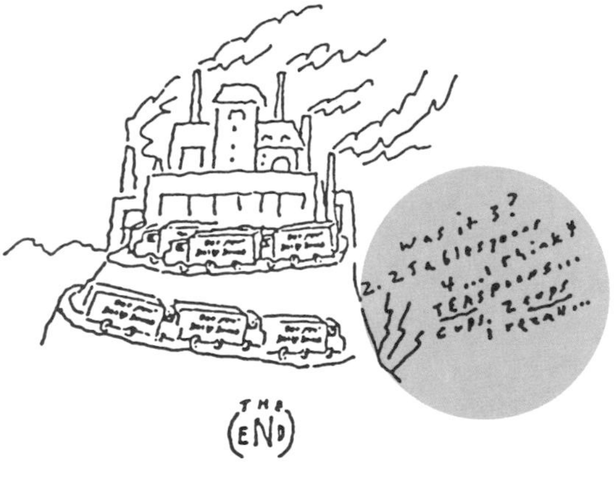
Was it 3?
2. 2 tablespoons
I think 4
4... teaspoons...
TEAS cups, 2 cups
I mean...

THE END

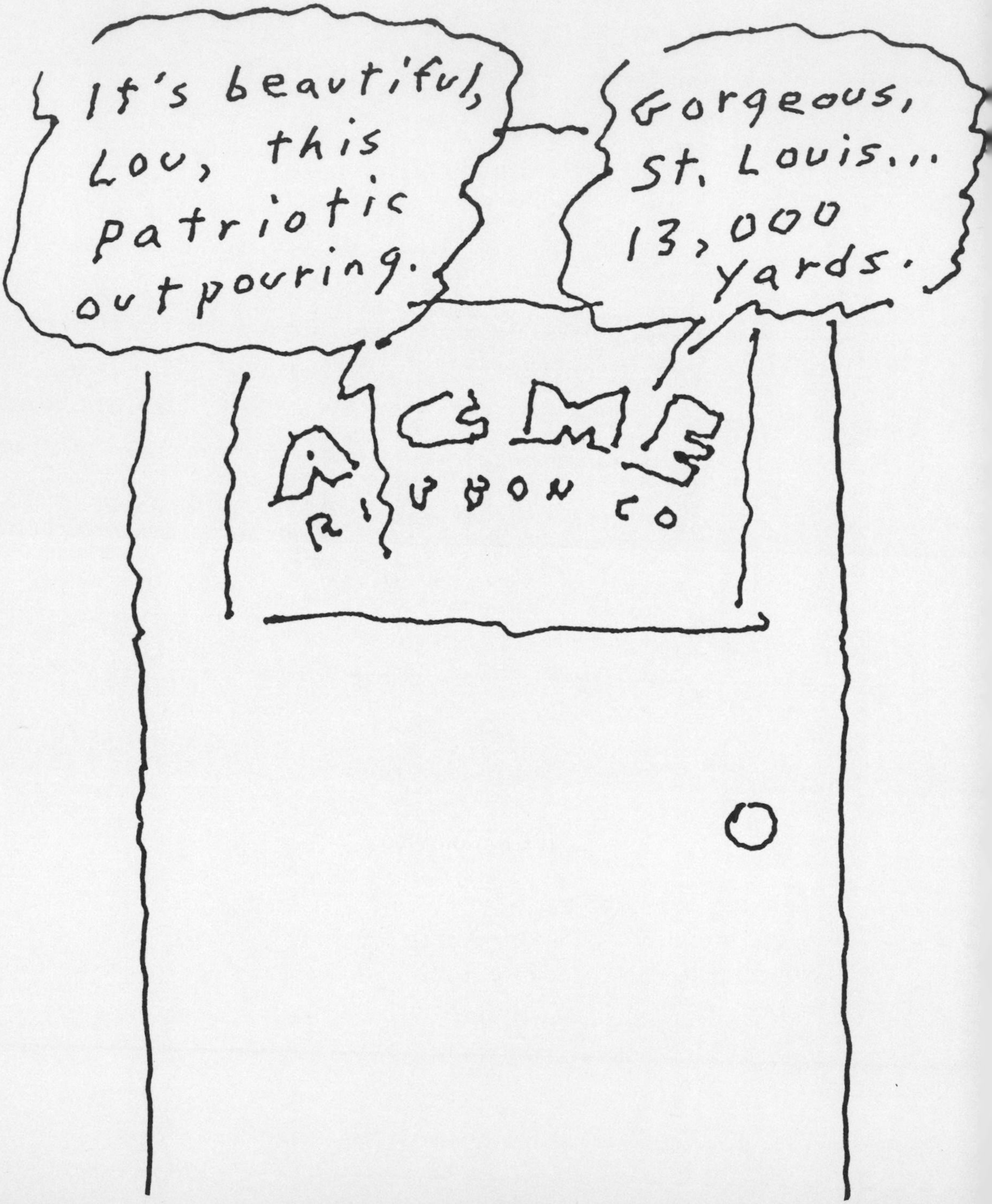
It's beautiful, Lou, this patriotic outpouring.
Gorgeous, St. Louis... 13,000 yards.
ACME
RIBBON CO

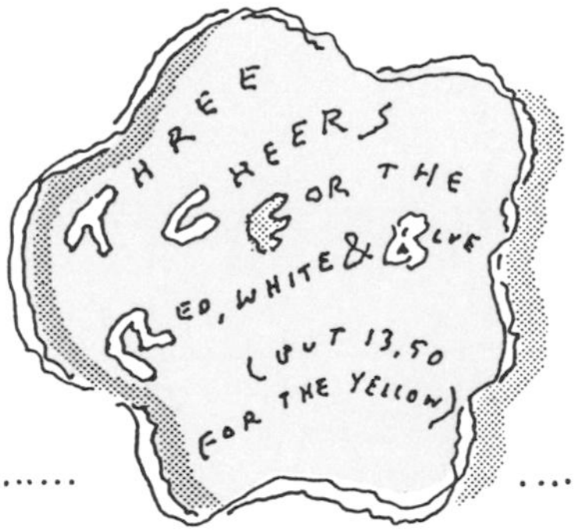
THREE CHEERS FOR THE RED, WHITE & BLUE
(BUT 13.50 FOR THE YELLOW)

THE NATION, 1990

During the 1st Iraq War, yellow ribbons of support were everywhere. There was one even on a venerable oak near my country house (as if nature was supporting our war!). At the time I saw the Iraq War as questionable. I still do.

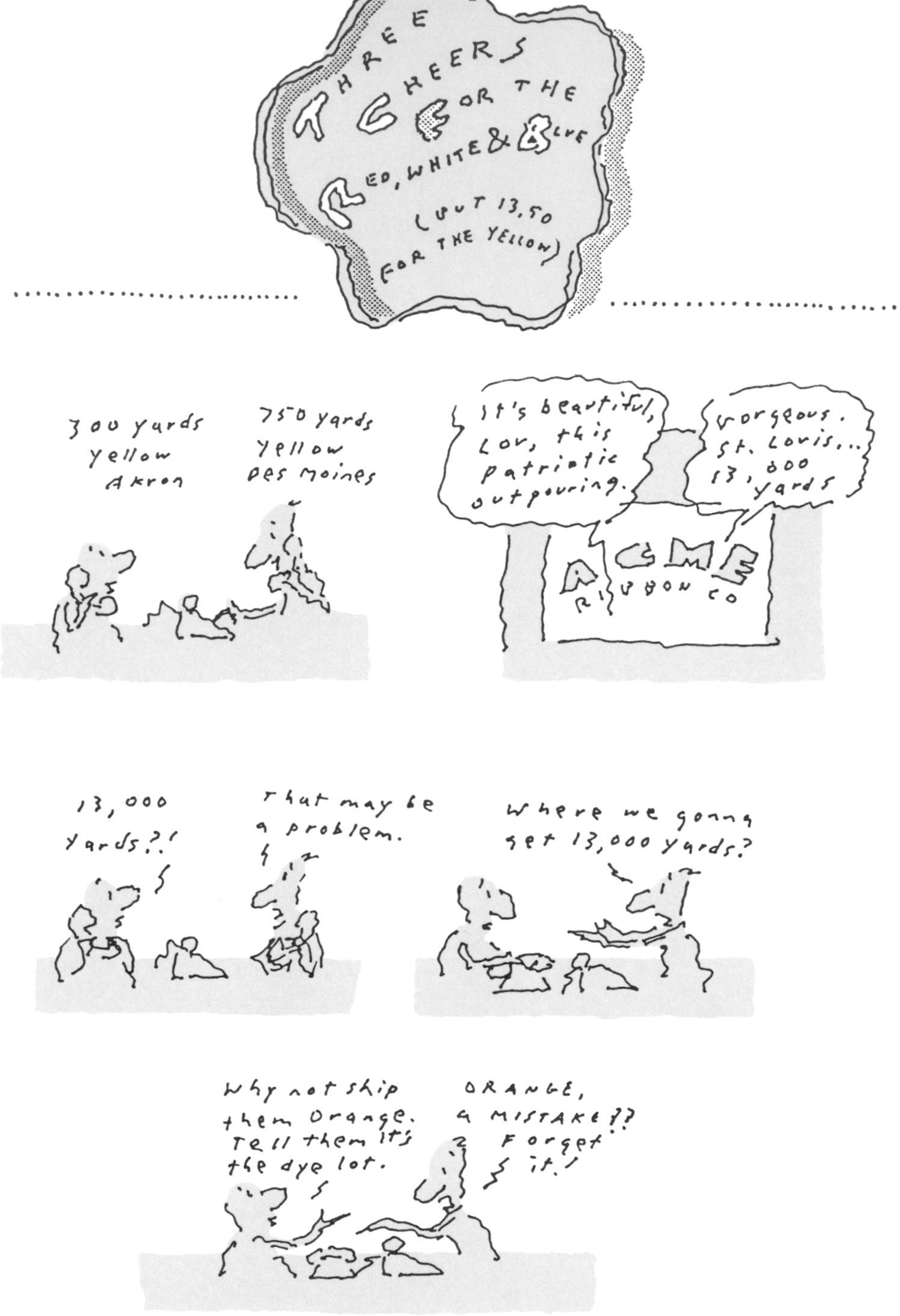
THREE CHEERS FOR THE RED, WHITE & BLUE
(BUT 13.50 FOR THE YELLOW)
300 yards yellow Akron
750 yards yellow Des Moines
It's beautiful, Lou, this patriotic outpouring.
Gorgeous. St. Louis... 13,000 yards
ACME RIBBON CO
13,000 yards?!
That may be a problem.
Where we gonna get 13,000 yards?
Why not ship them Orange. Tell them it's the dye lot.
ORANGE, A MISTAKE?? Forget it!

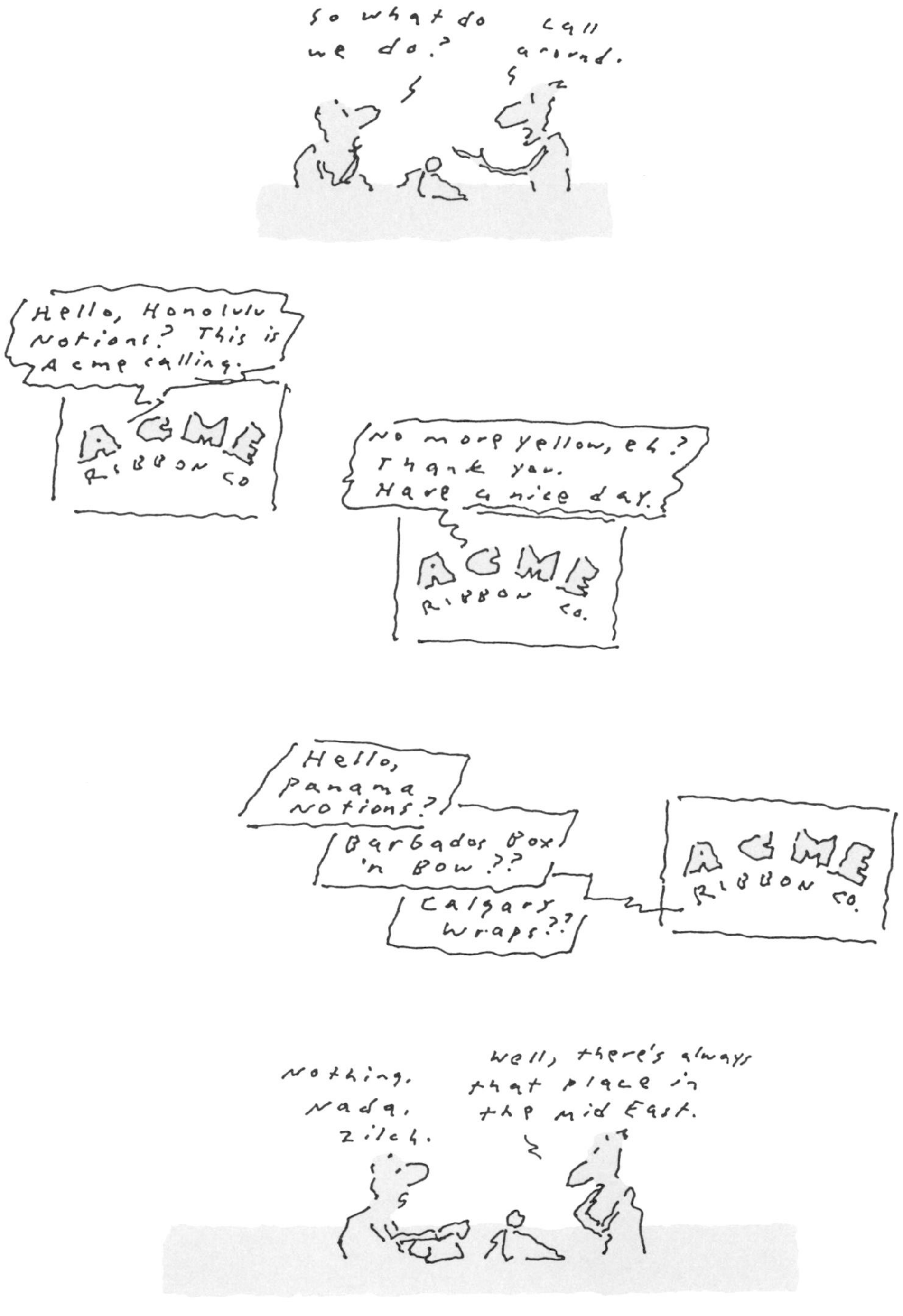
So what do we do?
Call around.
Hello, Honolulu Notions? This is Acme calling.
ACME RIBBON CO
No more yellow, eh? Thank you. Have a nice day.
ACME RIBBON CO.
Hello, Panama Notions?
Barbados Box 'n Bow??
Calgary Wraps??
ACME RIBBON CO.
Nothing. Nada. Zilch.
Well, there's always that place in the mid East.

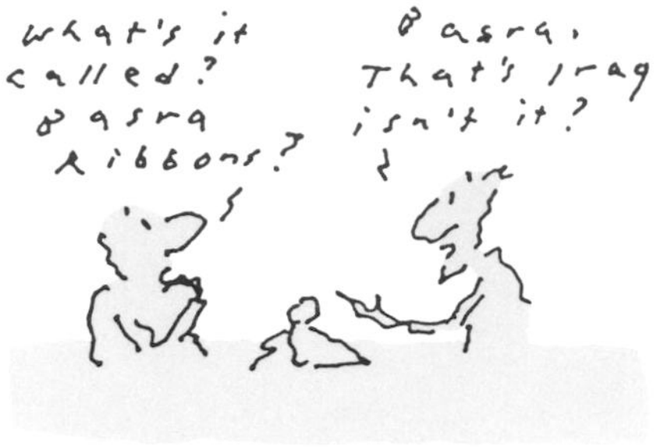
What's it called? Basra Ribbons?
Basra. That's Iraq isn't it?

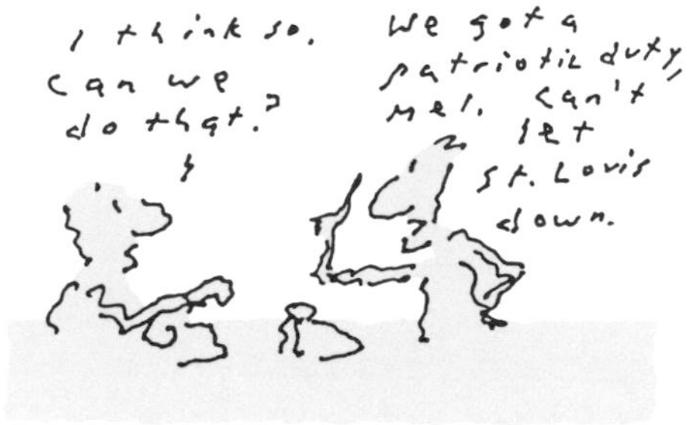
I think so. Can we do that?
We got a patriotic duty, Mel. Can't let St. Louis down.

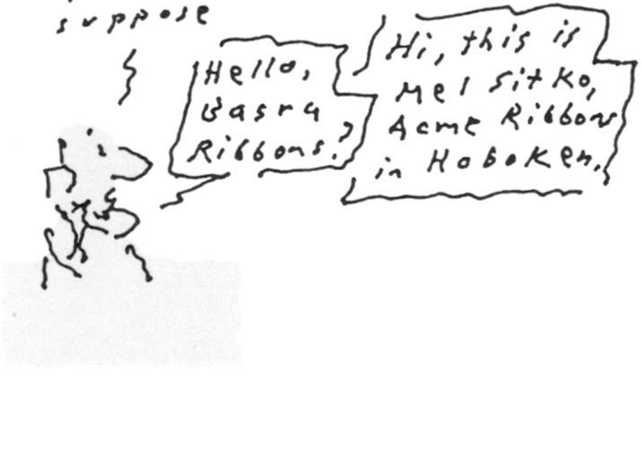
I suppose
Hello, Basra Ribbons?
Hi, this is Mel Sitko, Acme Ribbons in Hoboken.

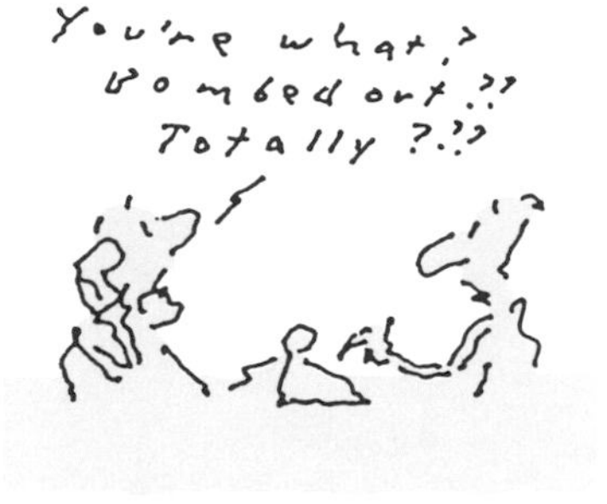
You're what?
Bombed out?!?
Totally?!?

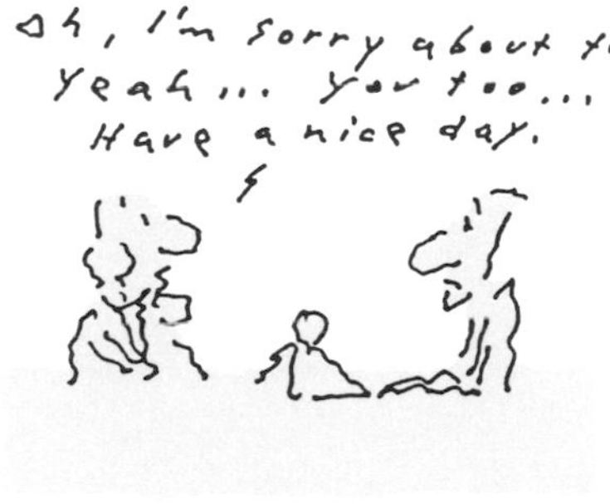
Oh, I'm sorry about that.
Yeah... You too...
Have a nice day.

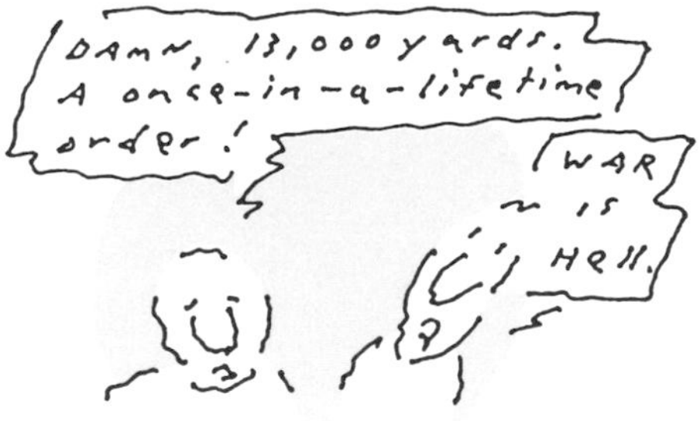
DAMN, 13,000 yards.
A once-in-a-lifetime
order!
WAR
is
Hell.

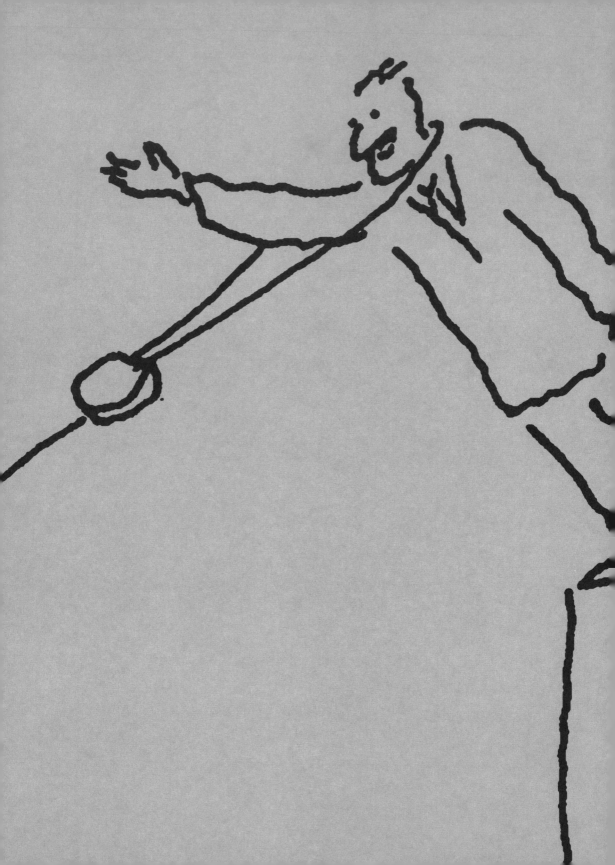

Nobody Loves
a Liberator

· ·

THE NEW YORK TIMES, 2004

When the statue of Saddam Hussein
was toppled in 2003, I wasn't sure
that our troubles were over. How
right I was!

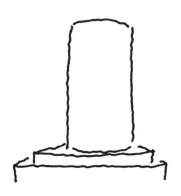

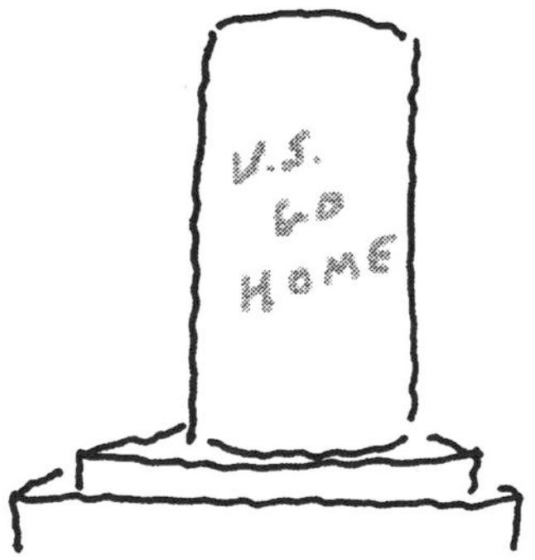
U.S.
GO
HOME

w sechman

Please don't interrupt.
Look, language is meant
to communicate.

RIGHT ON.

And type has to
COMMUNICATE
WHAT'S (AROUND) US.

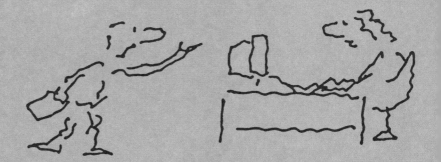

Nobody can read
this type.

You want
boring, I'll give you
boring.

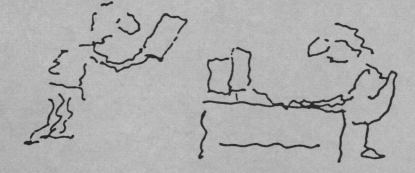

PLAIN TALK

A.I.G.A. JOURNAL, 1997

In retrospect, I think I was too clever by half for having done this. After all, readability is as important as appearance. I can't help thinking that this piece may have offended such classic (and brilliant) designers like Henry Wolf who despised the "new typography."

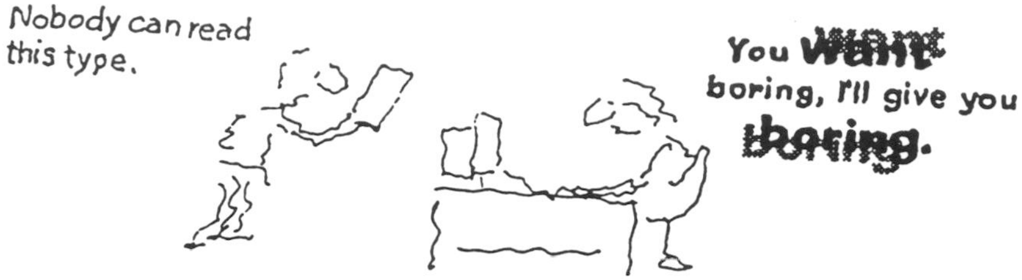
Nobody can read this type.
You want boring, I'll give you boring.

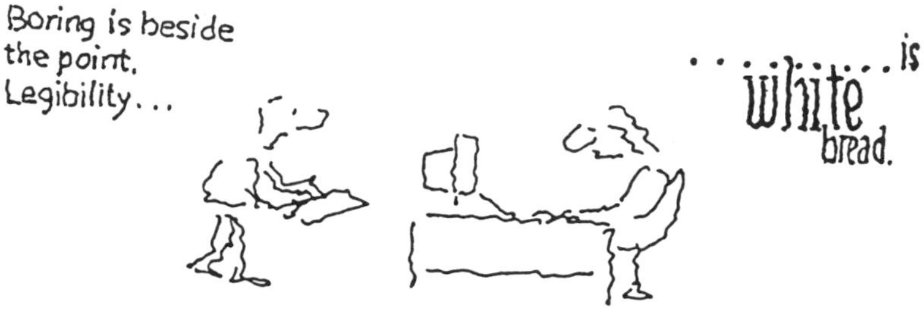
Boring is beside the point. Legibility...
........is white bread.

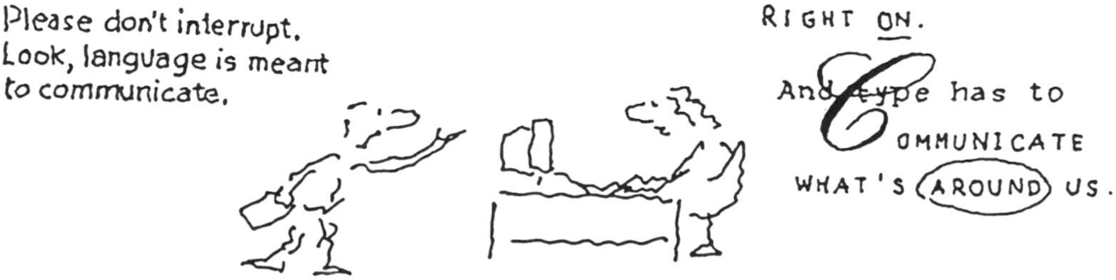
Please don't interrupt. Look, language is meant to communicate.
RIGHT ON.
And type has to COMMUNICATE WHAT'S AROUND US.

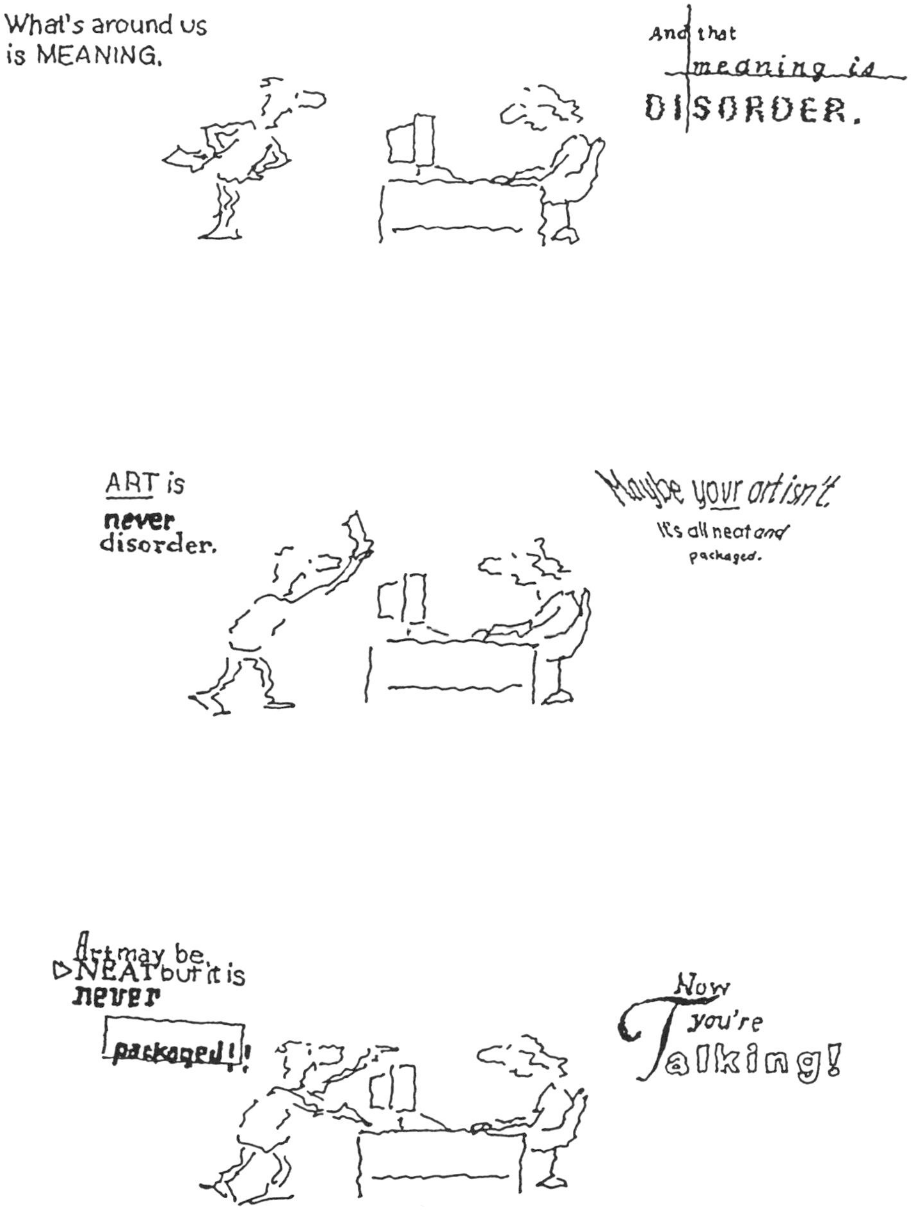
What's around us is MEANING.
And that meaning is DISORDER.
ART is never disorder.
Maybe your art isn't.
It's all neat and packaged.
Art may be NEAT but it is never packaged!!
Now you're Talking!

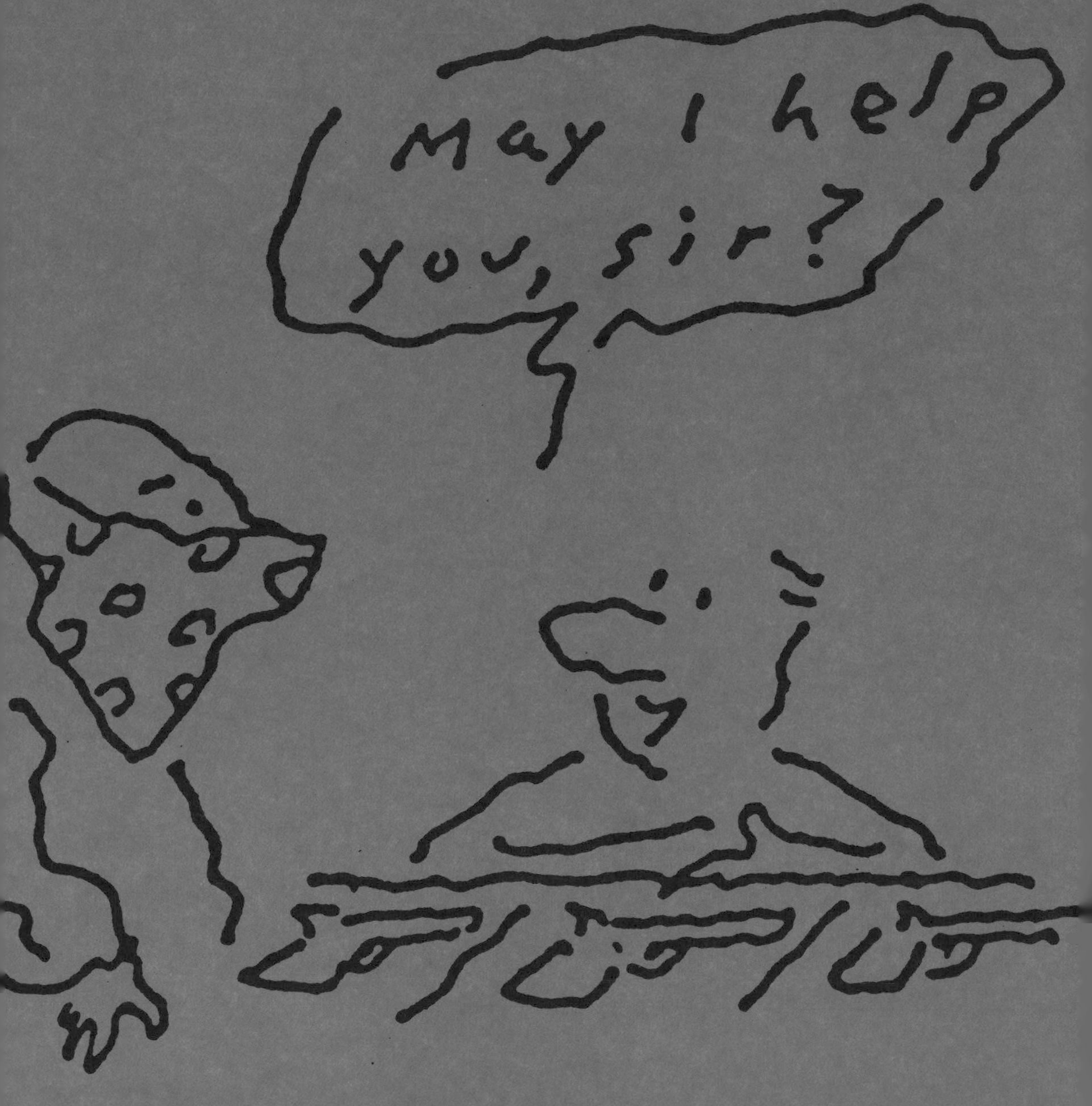
May I help you, sir?

Saturday Night Special

THE NEW YORK TIMES, 1972

It's amazing, isn't it, how we tend to justify all sorts of questionable or nefarious dealings with a shrug-of-the-shoulder, "We have to earn a living."

Saturday Night Special

May I help you, sir?
I'd like a 22.
I've got a lovely model here for 92.50
I'll take it.
Alrighty, that will be 98.27 with tax.

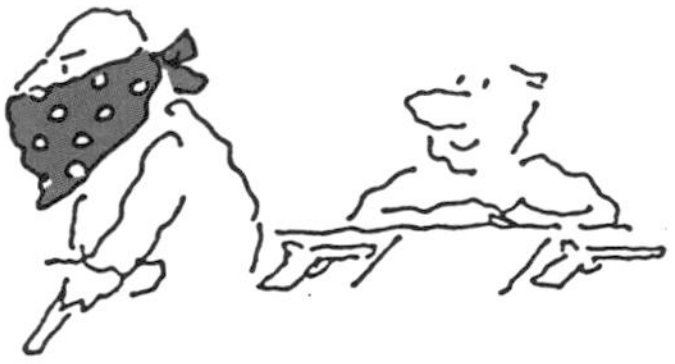

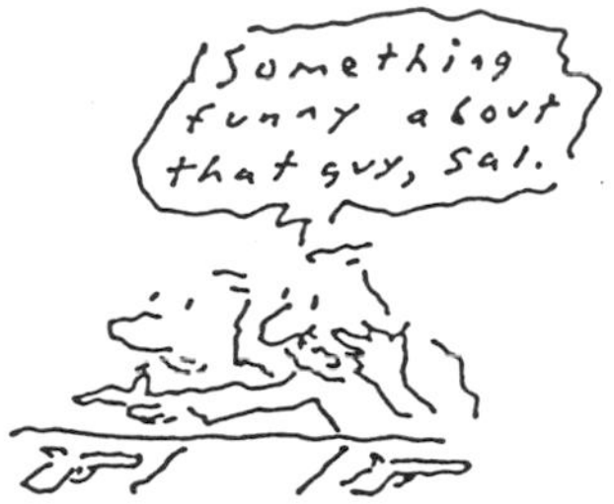
Something funny about that guy, Sal.

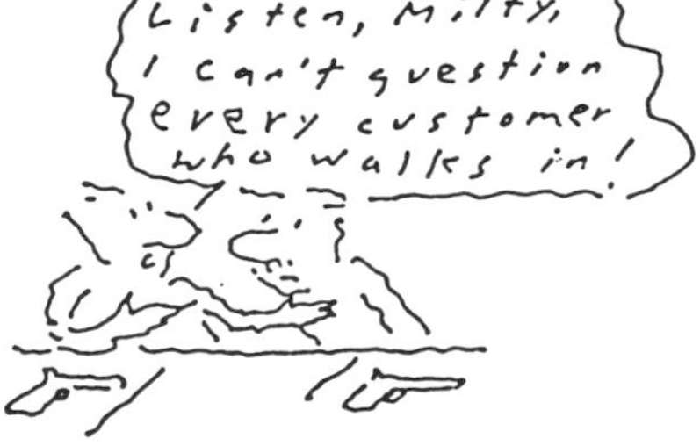
Listen, Milty, I can't question every customer who walks in!

I'll give you 250, Fussbelt!
Keep tal
275, not a florin more.
I can't hear you,

Nothing

························· ···· ·· ······ ······· ·· ·· ······· ·· ·· ··· ··· ·· ·· ······· ··

STORY MAGAZINE, 1996

Why not do a graphic sequence for a magazine
that printed short stories? I did this, and the
magazine's cover artist (me) accepted it. If the
language occasionally smacks of Virginia Woolf,
that's because she's a favorite author of mine.

Nothing

"Listen, it's just a tulip," his wife said.

"A tulip?! You call a coral-colored specimen with pink tips 'just a tulip'?!"

Pieter Fussbelt was indignant because he had just paid 200 florins for the flower, having mortgaged his family farm to raise the downpayment.

"I can't believe," thought Fussbelt's wife, shaking her head emphatically, "that in this so-called Age of Reason a man would spend 200 florins on a flower! What is this world coming to?"

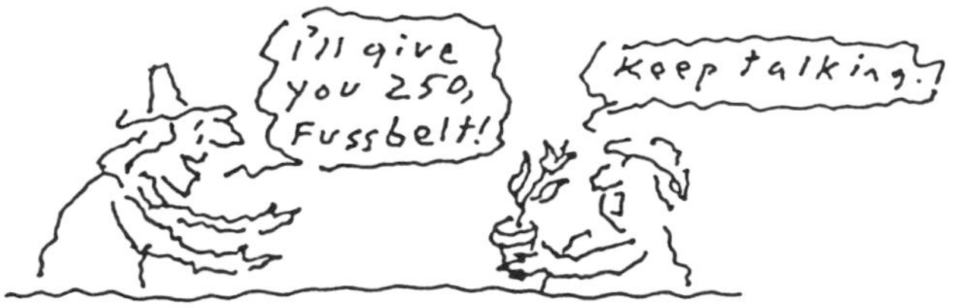

I'll give you 250, Fussbelt!
Keep talking.

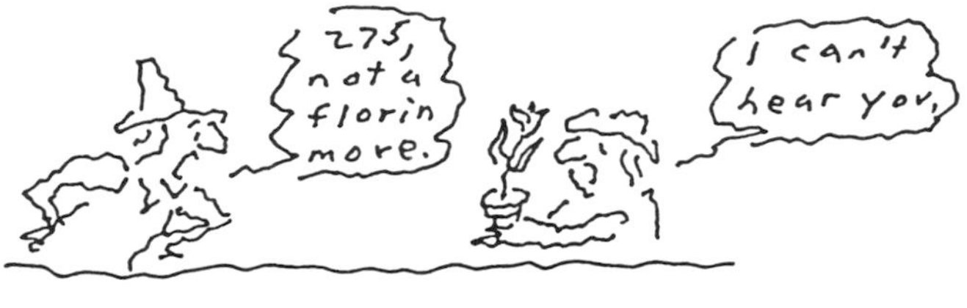

275, not a florin more.
I can't hear you,

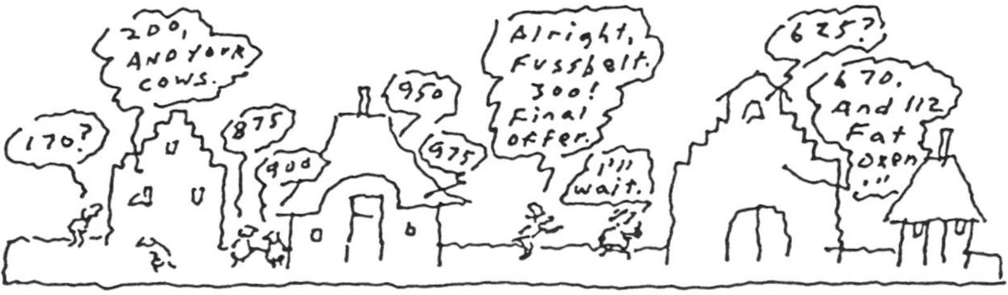

170?
200, AND YORK COWS.
875
900
950
975
Alright, Fussbelt. 300! Final offer.
I'll wait.
625?
670. And 112 Fat Oxen ..."

The entire town of Gelmensdoorf, it seemed, was gripped in a speculative fever, frantically dealing in tulips. Carpenters, coachmen, chimney sweeps, councillors, all travelled daily to Amsterdam, the center of the tulip trade.

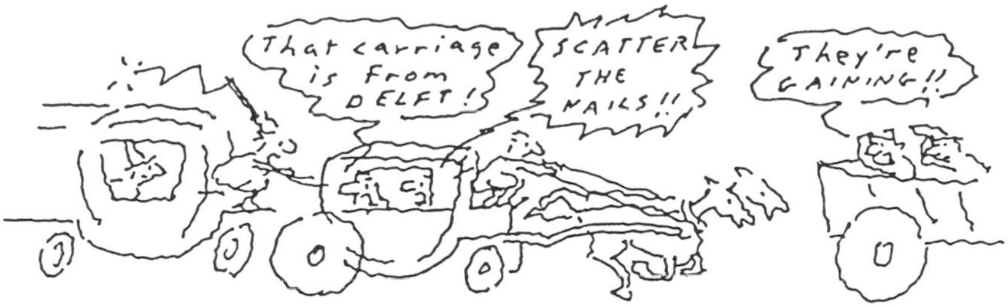
That carriage is from DELFT!
SCATTER THE NAILS!!
They're GAINING!!

That year, quite unexpectedly, the weather turned. What had been a mild autumn, with chestnut trees still holding their leaves in October, and ducks swimming lazily in the ponds—what had been so mild that Gelmensdoorfers even shed their habitual felt hats and high leather boots—suddenly changed. Overnight, a family of ducks found themselves frozen in the Gelmensdoorf canal, their wings poised in the act of flying. Tulips by the hundreds perished in their window boxes.

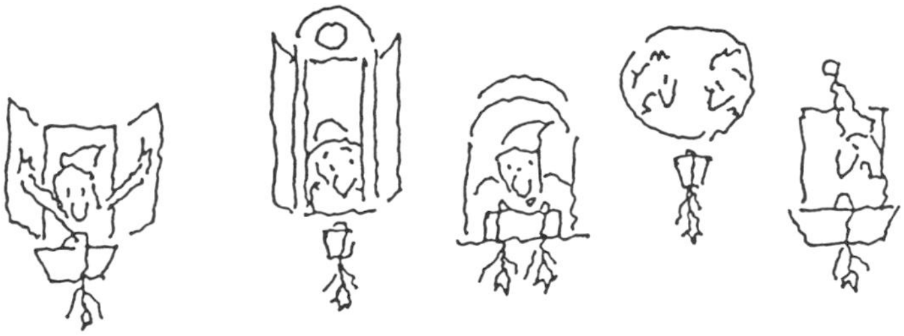

Fussbelt's tulip, however, had been kept inside, safe from any envious eyes and larcenous hands—and, as it happened, the murderous frost. In order to keep his precious specimen alive, Fussbelt felled the trees around his farm for firewood. When the woods disappeared, he burned his furniture.

OUR BED!
We'll sleep on the floor.

One evening, after Fussbelt and his wife had retired for the night, a spark leapt from the fireplace to a curtain. The curtain ignited a shutter. The shutter ignited a wall. The wall ignited the roof beams. By dawn, the house had burned to the ground. Nothing remained.

"Nothing!" cried Fussbelt's wife. "Now we have nothing. No home, no clothes, no food . . ."

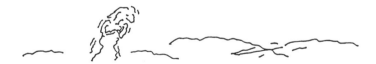

"What do you mean 'nothing'?!" exclaimed Fussbelt. "Remember that ring of mine? Well look," he said, "look what I got for it. This purple beauty! Is this what you call 'nothing'?!'"

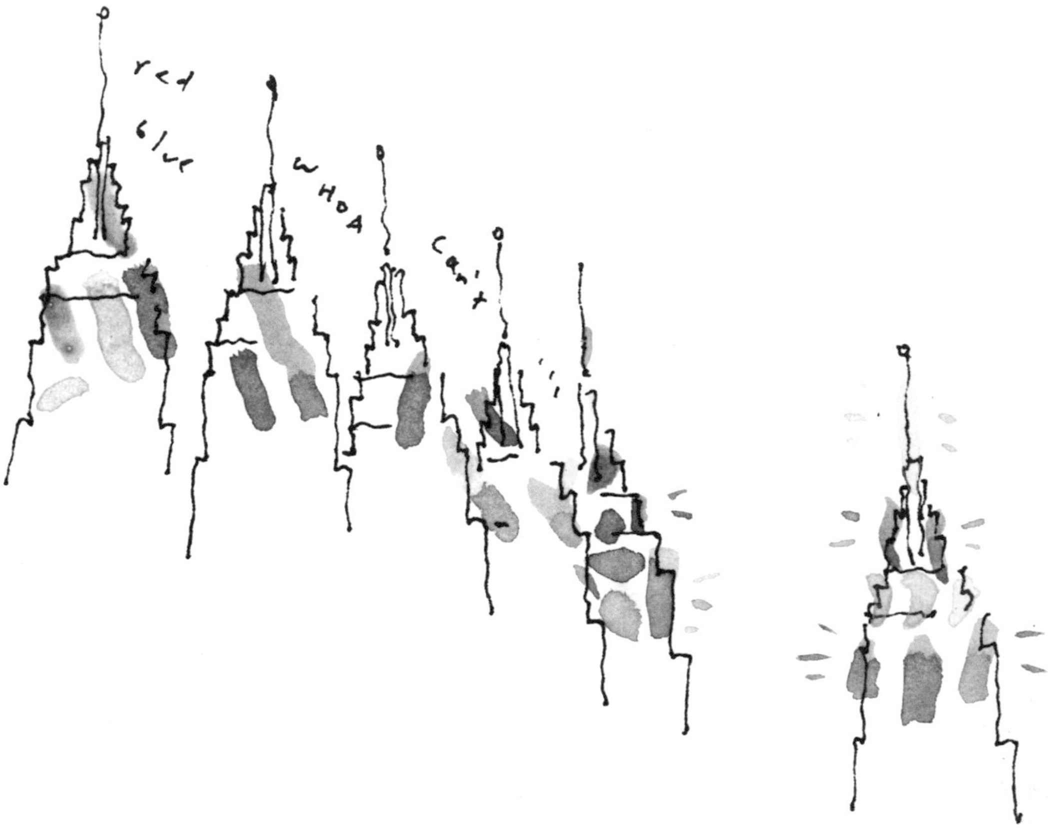
red
blue
WHOA
can't

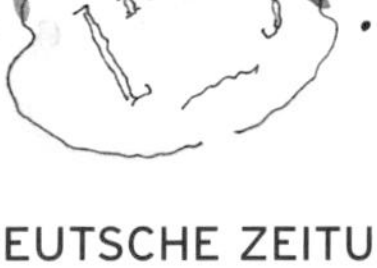
CHRISTMAS

SUDDEUTSCHE ZEITUNG, 1992

This was done during the short-lived recession of the early Nineties. It was rejected by *The New Yorker*, but a variation of it was published in Germany's *Suddeutsche Zeitung*.

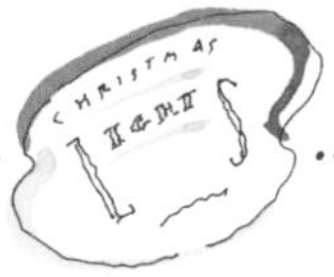
CHRISTMAS

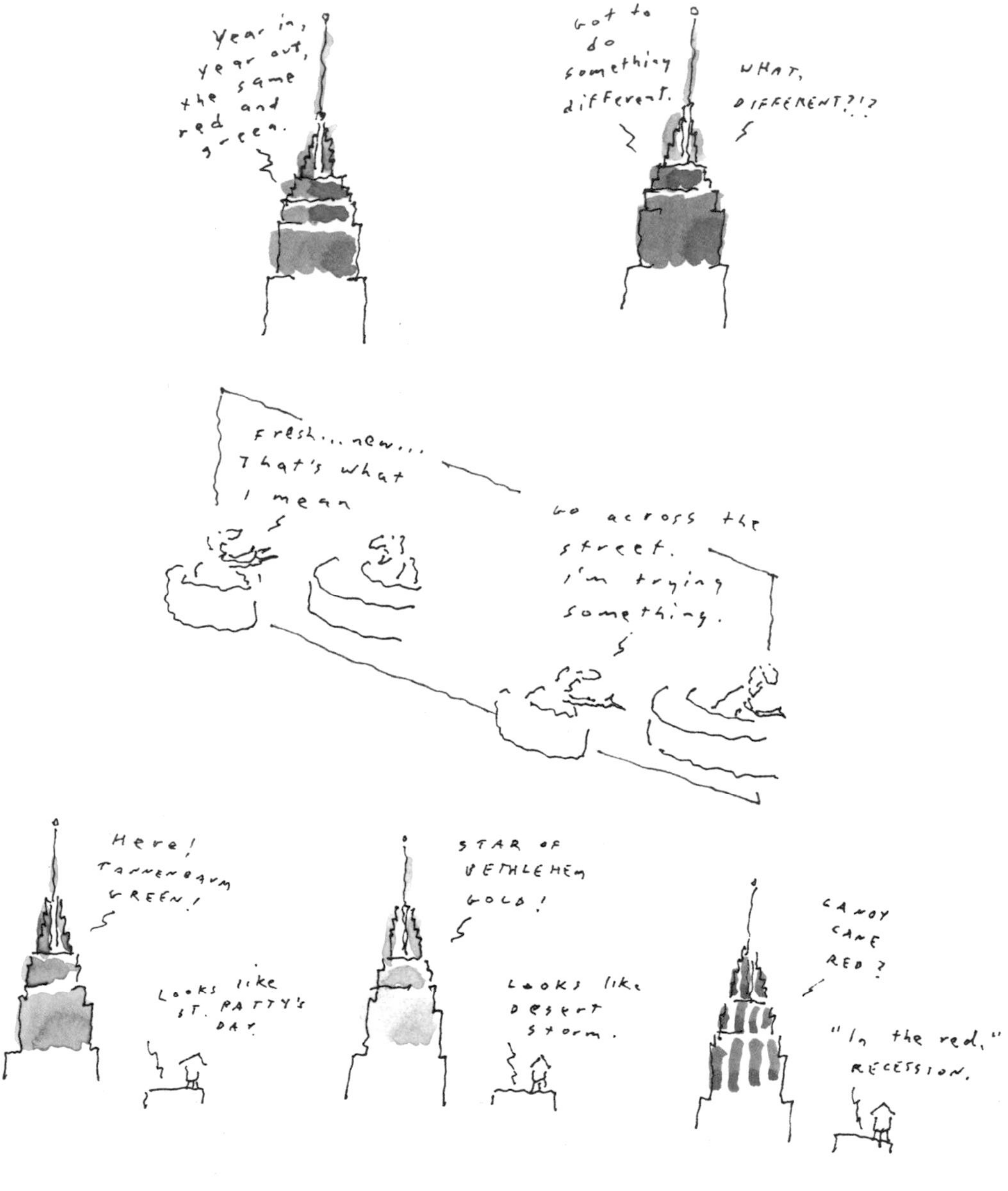
Year in, year out, the same red and green.
Got to do something different.
WHAT, DIFFERENT?!?
Fresh... new... That's what I mean
Go across the street. I'm trying something.
Here! TANNENBAUM GREEN!
Looks like ST. PATTY'S DAY.
STAR OF BETHLEHEM GOLD!
Looks like Desert Storm.
CANDY CANE RED?
"In the red," RECESSION.

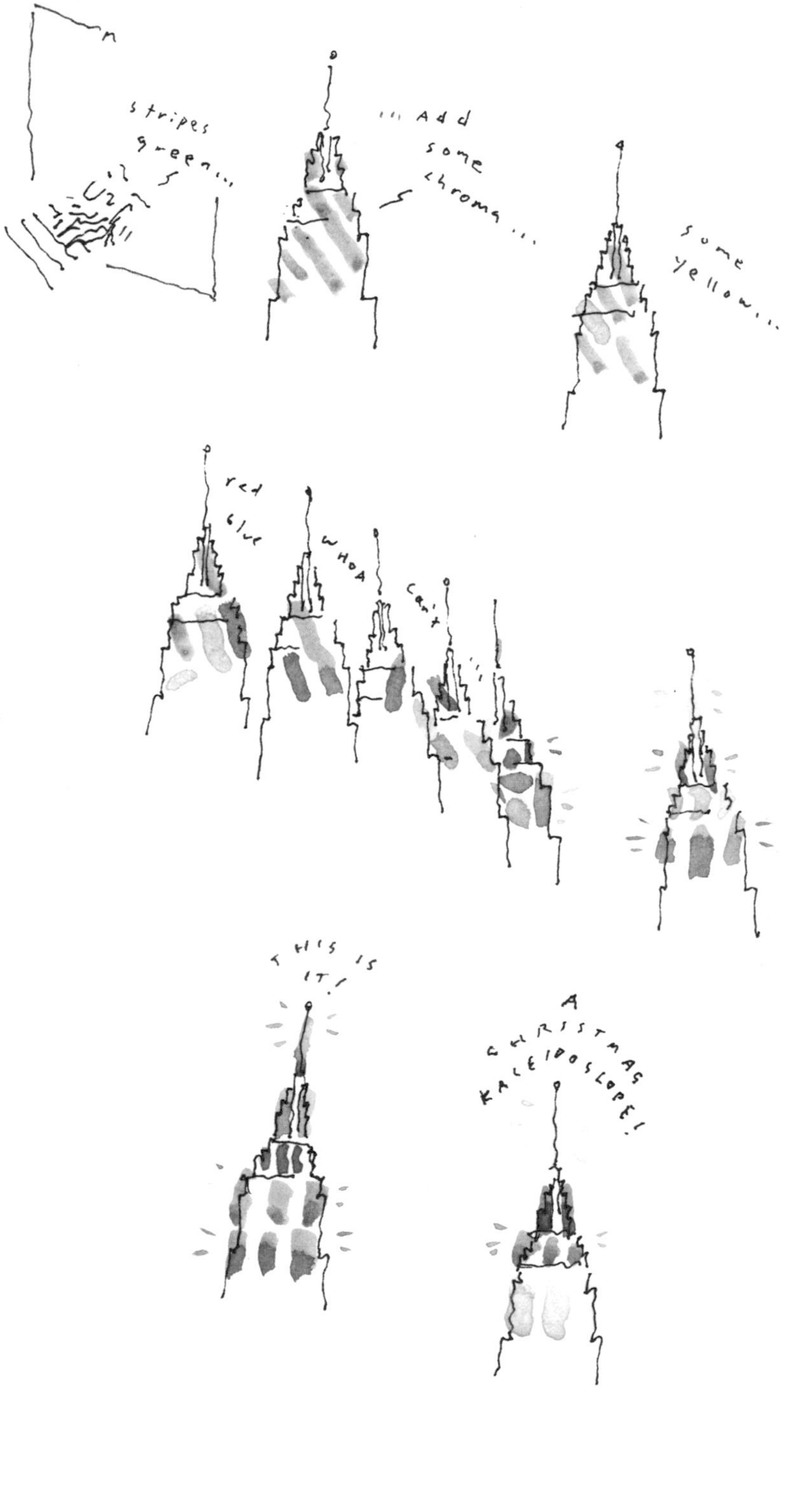
stripes green...
...Add some chroma...
some yellow...
red
blue
WHOA
can't
THIS IS IT!
A CHRISTMAS KALEIDOSCOPE!

PFFT...
well, at least we're saving money.
Energy, too
very economical.
very ECOLOGICAL

VERY
21 ST.
CENTURY!

I KNEW
WE'D COME UP
WITH
SOMETHING.

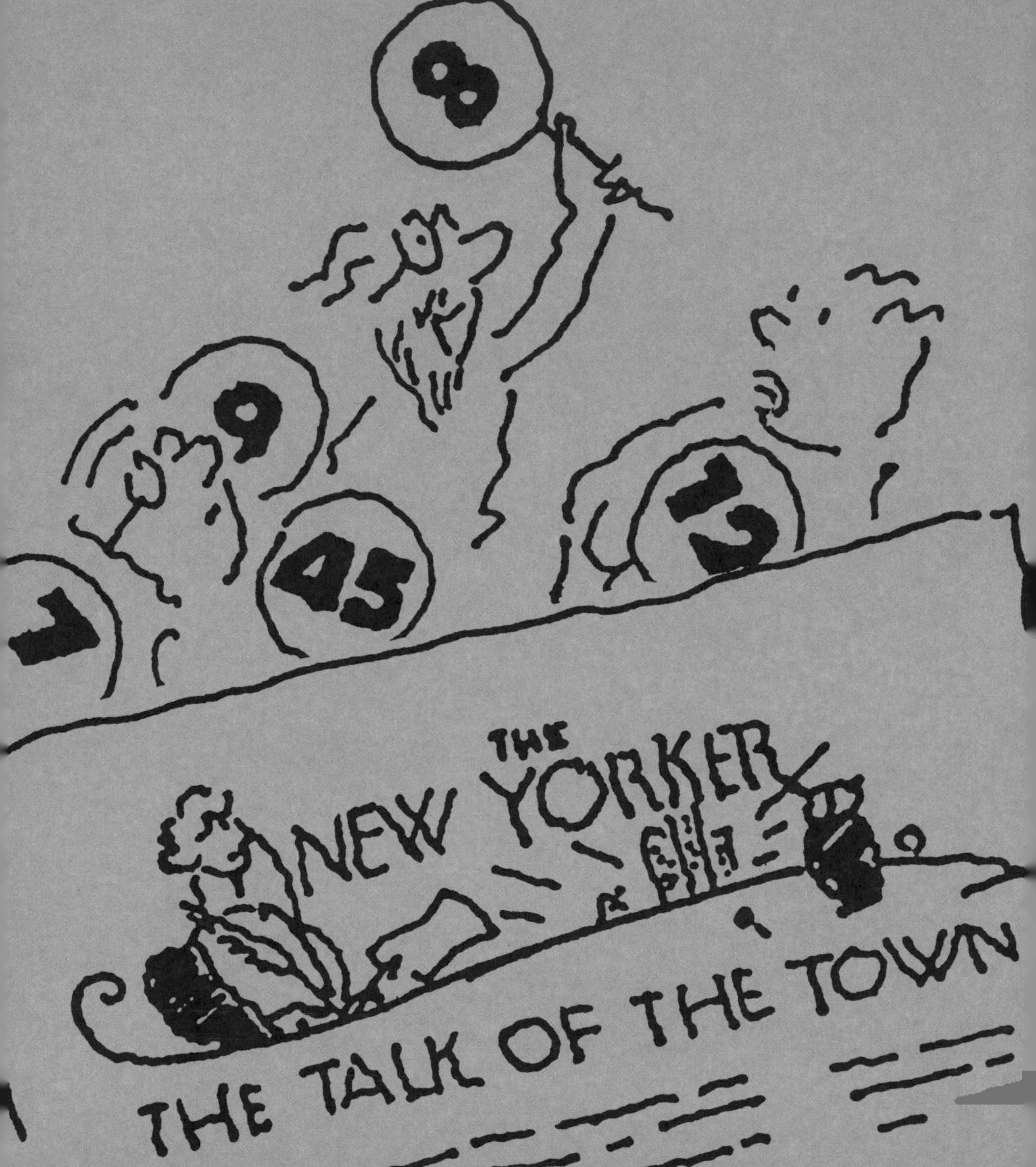
8
9
45
THE NEW YORKER
THE TALK OF THE TOWN

T OLSTOY'S PE N

THE NEW YORK TIMES BOOK REVIEW, 2002

In the last few years, auction prices for ephemera have gone through the roof. For example, a poster for the Universal Pictures film, *The Mummy*, sold last year for $435,500. That got me to thinking, what might a person pay for something like, say, the pen of a famous author?

T<small>OLSTOY'S</small> P<small>E</small>N

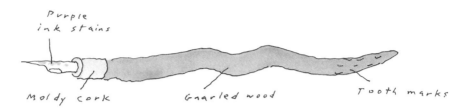

Purple ink stains

Moldy cork

Gnarled wood

Tooth marks

I t was a simple pen of Russian pine, slightly gnarled in the middle, the end pitted with the master's tooth marks. With its point of Georgian steel, Count Leo Tolstoy had penned his immortal, *War and Peace*.

S otheby's pre-sale estimate was $12,000-15,000, but early bidding indicated that the final sales price would go far higher.

A t 80, Spielberg dropped his paddle. At 130, Newhouse lowered his ...

L eaving Bill Gates to win Tolstoy's pen at $135,000, a world record for an author's writing instrument.

THE NEW YORKER
THE TALK OF THE TOWN

A month later, *The New Yorker* revealed that the tooth marks were really those of Tolstoy's young servant, lovely Anna Krupkiskaya.

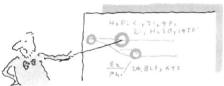

Sotheby's claimed that the residue of purple ink clearly proved the pen's provenance.

That winter, while the controversy raged, the pen (Tolstoy's? Anna Krupkiskaya's??) remained mounted above Bill Gates's fireplace.

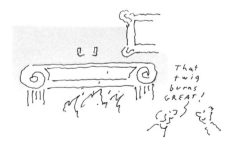

That twig burns GREAT!

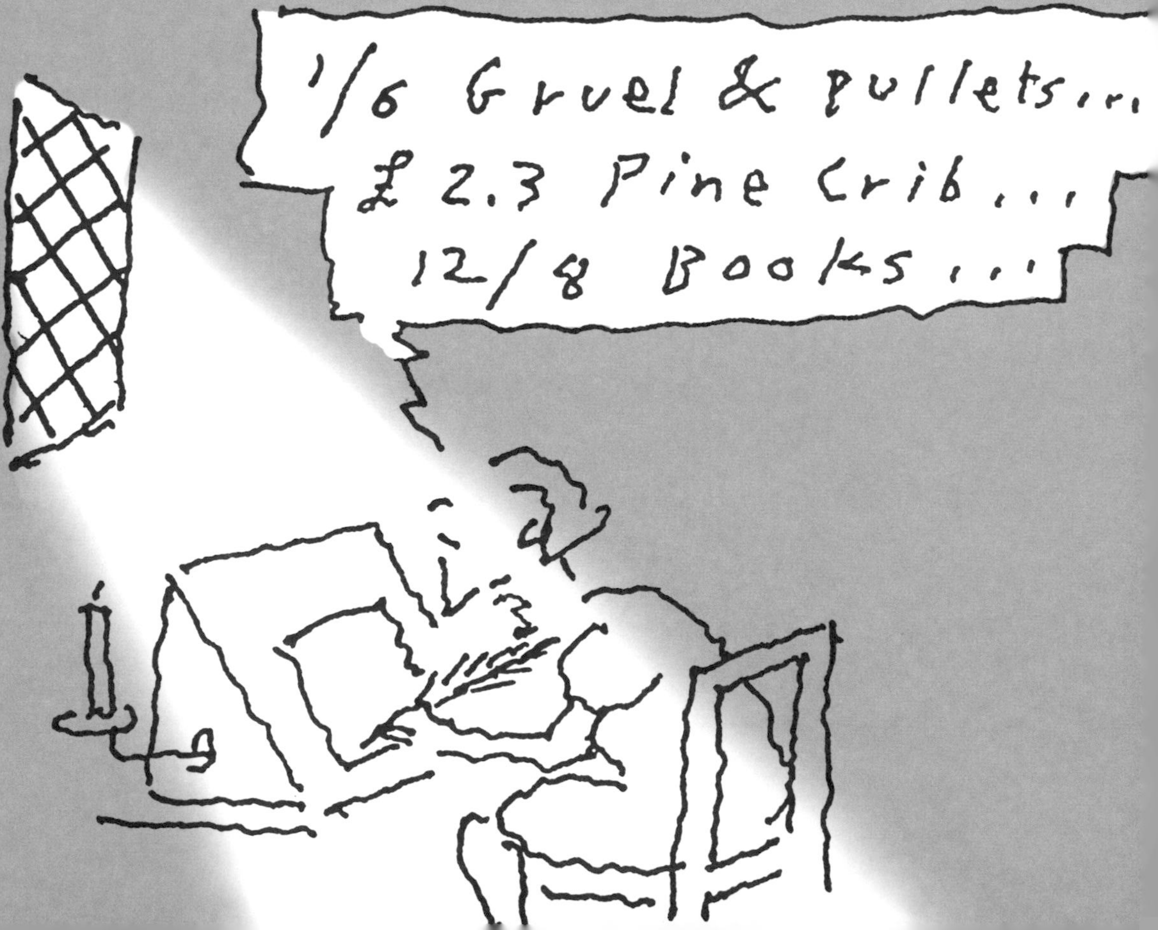
1/6 Gruel & pullets...
£2.3 Pine Crib...
12/8 Books...

ARS BREVIS VITA LONGA

....

THE NEW YORK TIMES BOOK REVIEW, 2002

Shakespeare's father, John, died a bankrupt, stripped of his high office as an alderman. In this story I made him into Polonius. (It's possible that old Polonius, killed by young Hamlet, was Shakespeare's father figure).

Fortunately for posterity, Shakespeare fulfilled his father's ambition for wealth and a coat of arms by writing plays. He might have gone the route of contemporaries like Ben Jonson who grew wealthy writing masques, a lucrative, if evanescent, dramatic form.

This piece was probably inspired by my love/hate relationship with advertising.

Ars Brevis Vita Longa

1/6 Gruel & pullets...
£2.3 Pine Crib...
12/8 Books...

It was a difficult time for the struggling young playwright, William Shakespeare, married to an older woman with no dowry, a sick child, and twins on the way ←

And here he was, with no work, and a mind bursting with the speech of kings and fools, faeries & princes, Pucks and Moors!

Neither a borrower nor a lender be, son!

Nights were the most difficult. Then his father, who died a bankrupt, would lecture him.

Give every man thy ear but few thy voice.... Beware of entrance to a Quarrel....

So when he was approached by Hawkes & Meltdowne to become a Junior Copywriter at £90 per annum, young Shakespeare gladly accepted the offer!

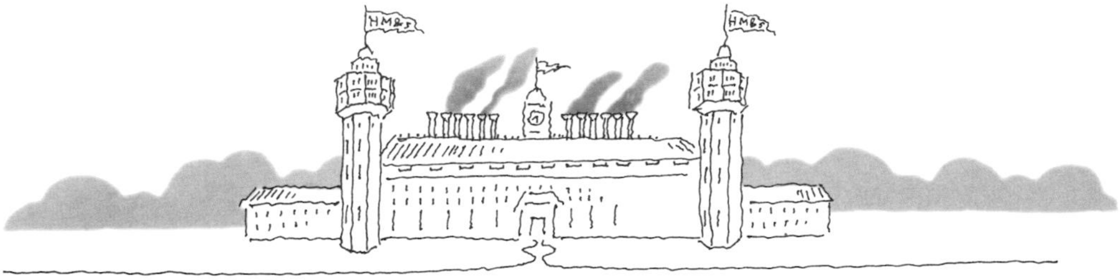

Working on the Globe Theatre and Cock & Bull accounts, he soon caught the attention of old Meltdowne himself. His advancement was rapid — Senior Copywriter, Creative Director and, by 1601, Partner of the newly reorganized Hawkes, Meltdowne & Shakespeare.

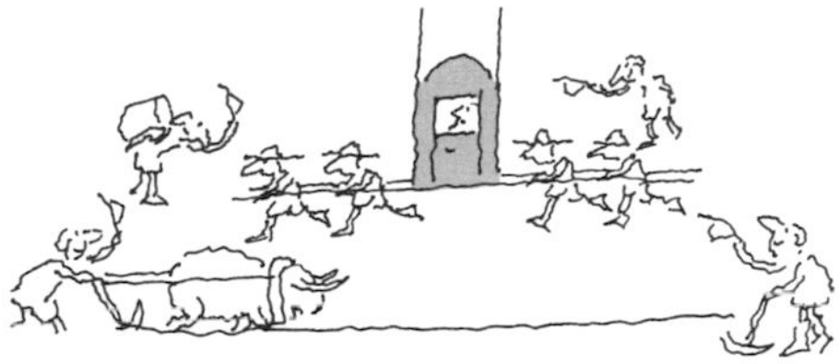

Retiring to his country estate, Great Glibmore, in 1632, Shakespeare attended to the farming of his 2,000 acres.

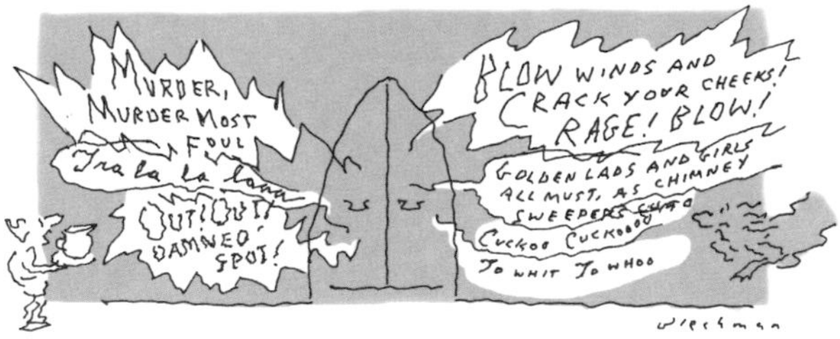

MURDER, MURDER MOST FOUL
OUT! OUT! DAMNED SPOT!
BLOW WINDS AND CRACK YOUR CHEEKS! RAGE! BLOW!
GOLDEN LADS AND GIRLS ALL MUST, AS CHIMNEY SWEEPERS
CUCKOO CUCKOO
TO WHIT TO WHOO

He died at a venerable age, "Quite beside himself," his servants declared.

SHAKESPEARE'S SISTER

THE NEW YORK TIMES BOOK REVIEW, 2004

In *A Room of One's Own*, Virginia Woolf wrote of Shakespeare's imaginary sister, Judith, an "extraordinarily gifted" writer with "the quickest fancy, a gift, like her brother's, for the tune of words." She was soon bent and finally broken by society's indifference and her own self-doubt. My heart went into this story because, like Shakespeare's fictional sister, I also had a consuming dream— for something that has always eluded me: to produce an animated feature.

Shakespeare's Sister

"It is, to speak quite plainly," thought Opinia, "hell. For is not that its definition? An eternal fire that can never be quenched?"

As a girl, the gifted sister of Shakespeare could not enter the Stratford School where Will had learned his spelling, his writing, his logic and his Latin.

She was denied the tools to express thoughts and feelings which burned with such a white-hot intensity.

Her older brother went on to become a celebrated playwright in London,

One evening she ran off to join him.

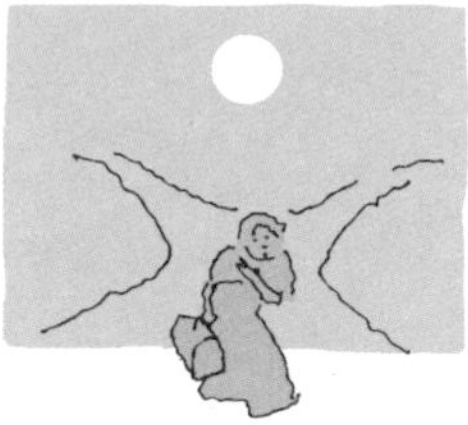

But, midway to London, she stopped at a crossroads.

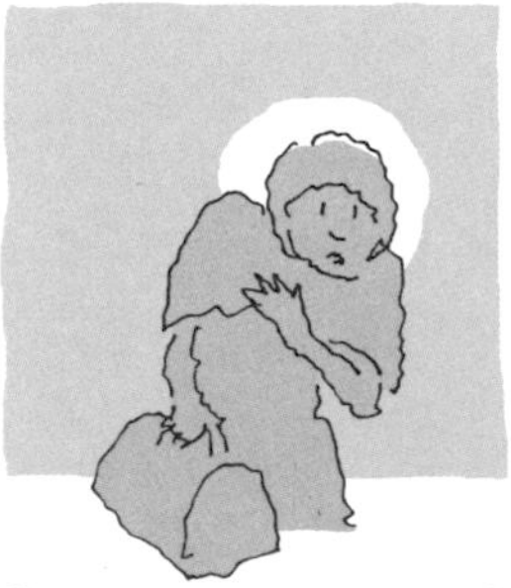

"Can I leave my husband? My children? For a fancy, unproved, unneeded?"

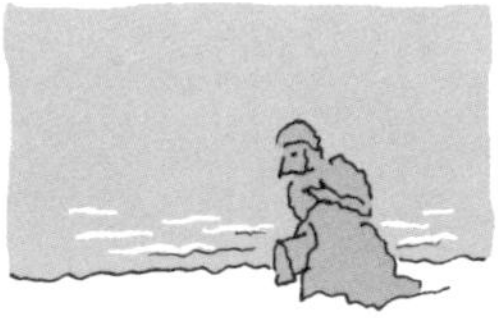

She returned by the river route.

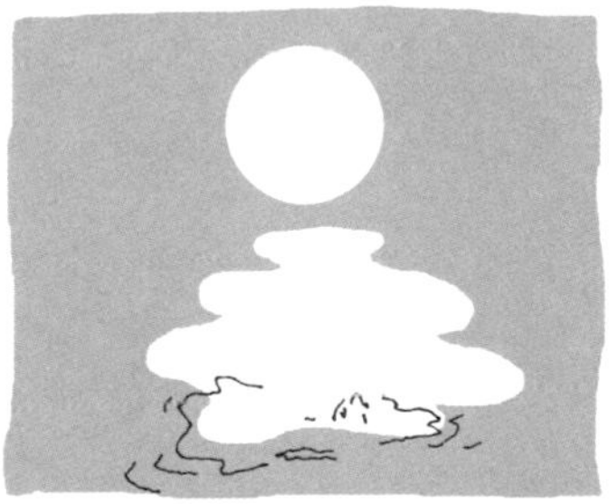

"The fire," she thought, "it must be quenched."

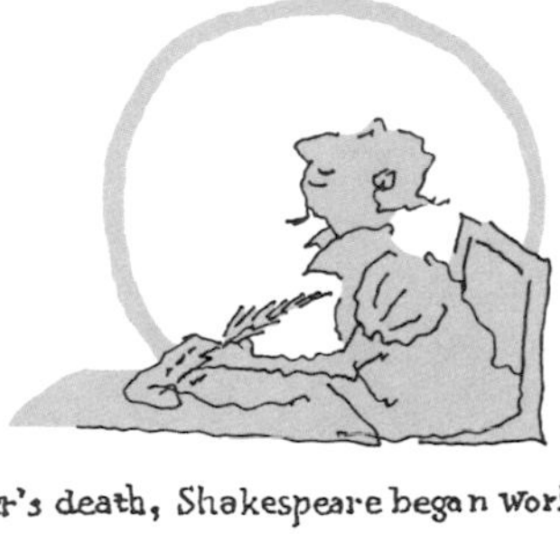

Inspired by his sister's death, Shakespeare began work on a new tragedy.

CHANGES

THE NEW YORK TIMES BOOK REVIEW, 2004

Goethe, as a 74 year old, proposed marriage to a 17 year old girl. Lust dies hard. I'm reminded of a quatrain written by William Butler Yeats in his later years:

> *You think it horrible that Lust and Rage*
> *Should dance attendant upon my old age;*
> *They were not such a plague when I was young.*
> *What else have I to spur me into song?*

CHANGES

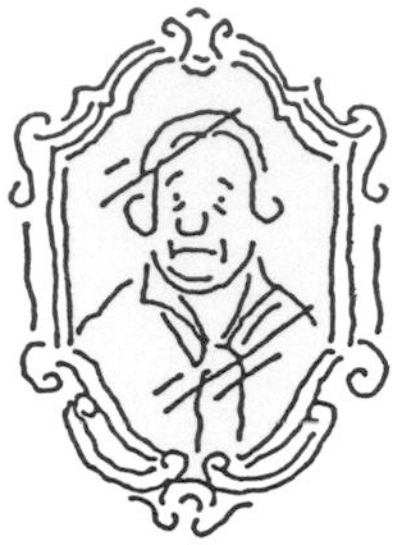

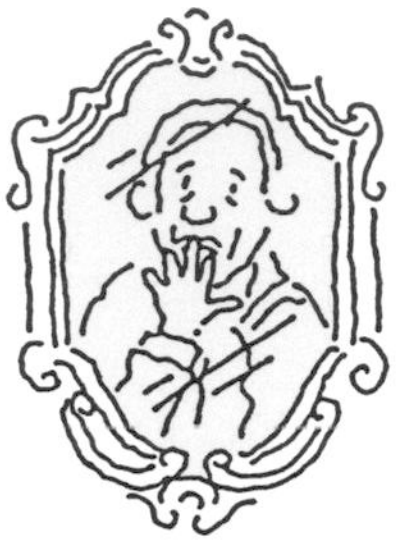

It was not possible--
no, it did not seem possible--
that this elderly gentleman
reflected in his mirror...

...was himself,
Johann Wolfgang Goethe.

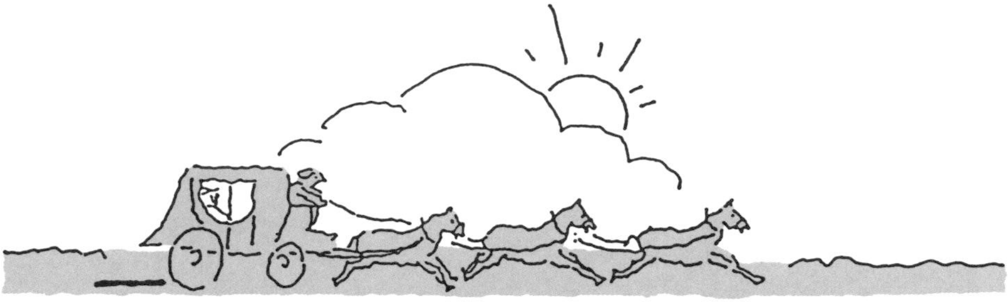

He must get away. A change. That was what was needed. Goethe left for the rejuvenating waters of Marienbad.

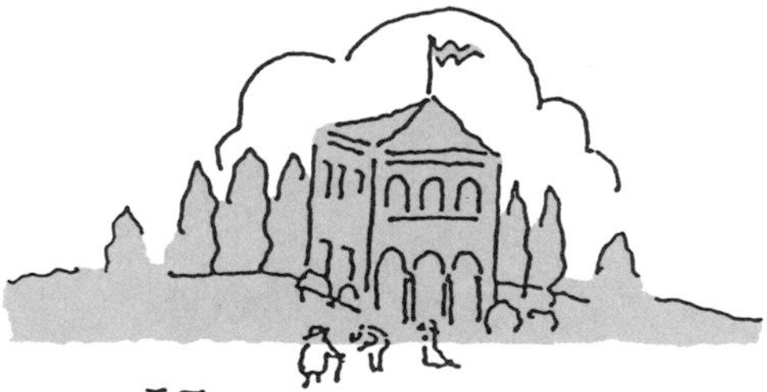

He was welcomed by
the proprietor of the
Pension Brösigke,
Herr von Levetzow...

A great honor.
Yes, surely.

... and his daughter, seventeen-year-old Ulrike. "Charming," Goethe thought. "She was charming."

My book, TRUTH & POETRY

But her chatter. Vacant. That must change.

"Sweets to the sweet." Shakespeare, Hamlet. 1601, dear child.

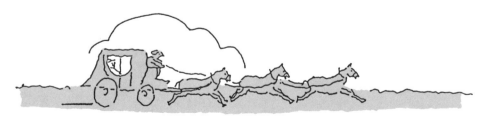

He felt young again.
Young. And so, when he returned the following year...

... he spoke to her mother,
asking for young Ulrike's hand
in marriage.

True, he had turned 74.
She was only 17.
But did it matter?

Age mattered to
Frau von Levetzow.

Goethe returned home.

He wrote a masterpiece,
the poem, *Elegy of Marienbad.*

"Yes," Johann Wolfgang Goethe
thought." The change. That was
what I needed."

Sacrifice

THE NEW YORK TIMES BOOK REVIEW, 2004

Virginia Woolf's husband, Leonard, was his wife's constant mentor, editor, and nurse. The price he paid to become her husband was to accept what the French call a "mariage blanc" (a sexless marriage). Could she have become-- or remained-- a writer without his constant ministrations? I doubt it.

Sacrifice

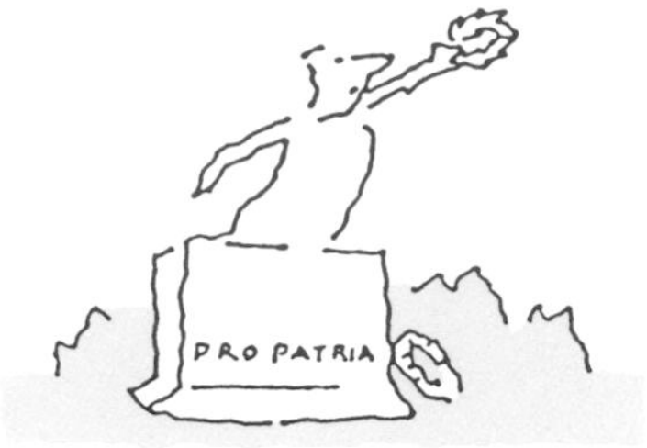
PRO PATRIA

"All life entails sacrifice."
That is what Leonard Woolf
believed.

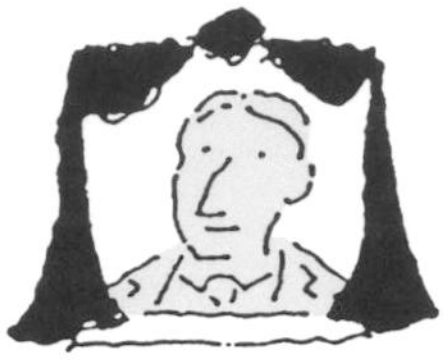

He learned that as
a child when his father,
a successful barrister,
suddenly died.

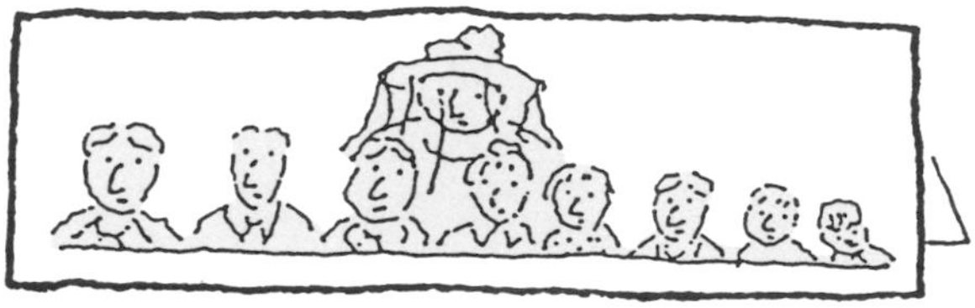

His death left the large family nearly destitute.

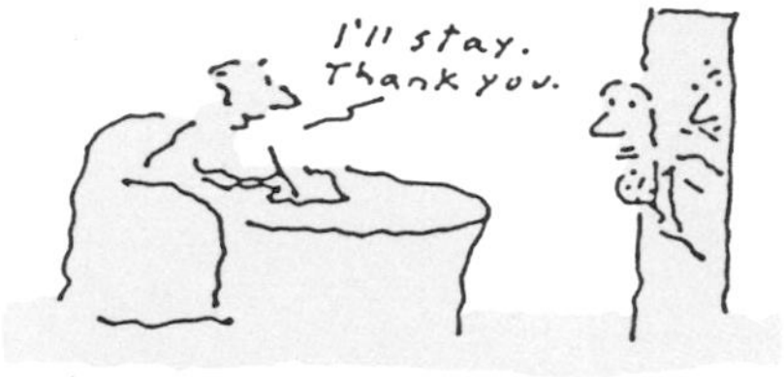
I'll stay.
Thank you.

He learned that as
a scholarship student
at Cambridge.

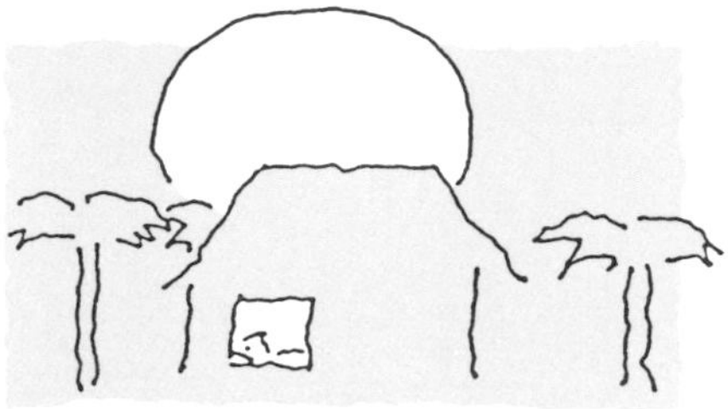

He learned that as a civil servant
spending seven years in Ceylon.

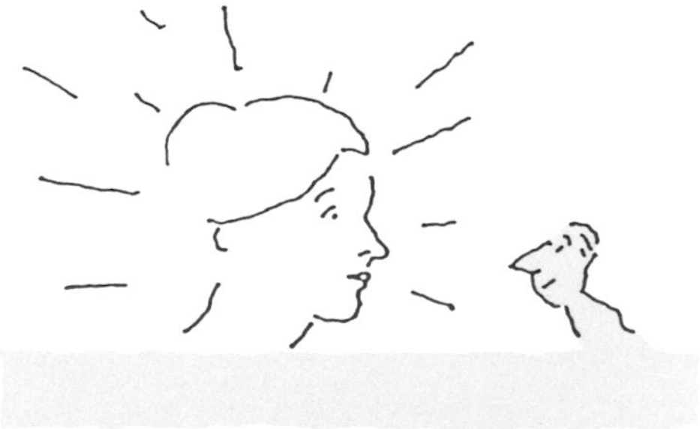

And then... he married Virginia!
A beauty! With the classic Stephens' look

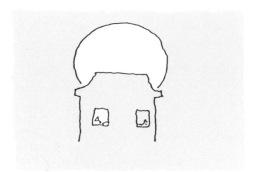

Cold, yes.
No doubt about it.
But brilliant. Brilliant.

A hobby — printing — will do you worlds of good.

And fragile.
He would be her nurse...
Her mentor...
Her Pygmalion.

Excellent, Excellent.
She is so fragile

Her genius must be encouraged.

Years later, he might have wondered.
Was it worth it? The long nights alone?
His Galatea would never turn to flesh.

"All life entails sacrifice."
That is what Leonard Woolf believed.

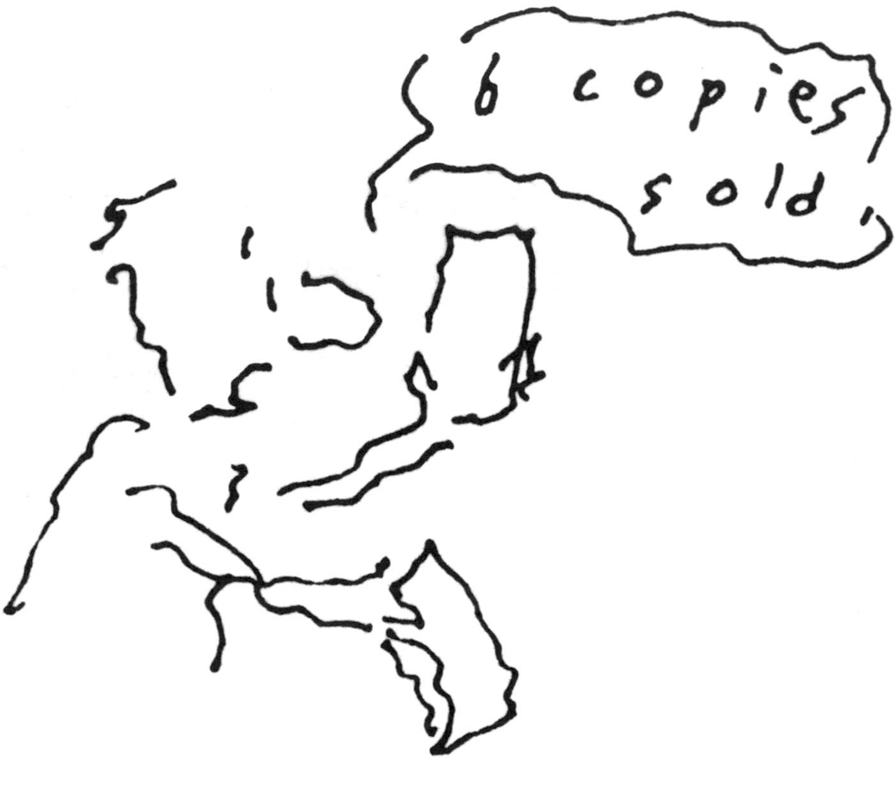
6 copies sold

SUCCESS

....

THE NEW YORK TIMES BOOK REVIEW, 2004

Success was based on my experience of having had three books pulped not too long after publication. I had to re-order them from Amazon— and when they came, a few bore the rubber stamp "Donated by Barnes and Noble."

SUCCESS

My royalty statement!
6 copies sold.

Success always eluded Milton Molar. His book (16 years in the writing), *The Life and Loves of Saint Ignatius*, was not selling well.

683 returns, Milton.
Give it time. The book's only been out two years.

There was a danger that the remaining copies might be pulped.

I have to do something.

Molar decided to visit several Barnes & Nobles . . .

I hope my books are still there.

. . . and move his books to the Recommended sections.

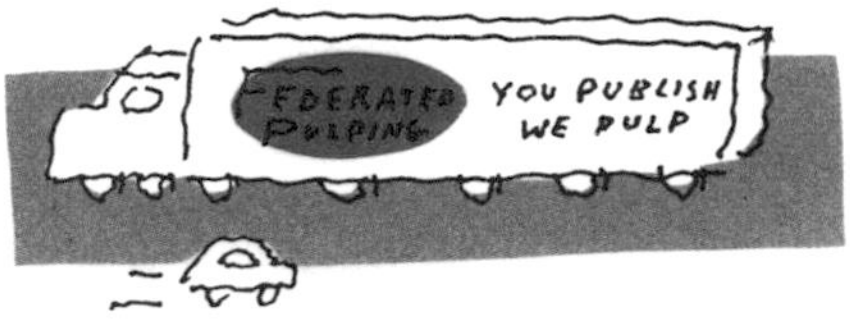
FEDERATED PULPING
YOU PUBLISH WE PULP

On the way he passed a huge tractor-trailer.

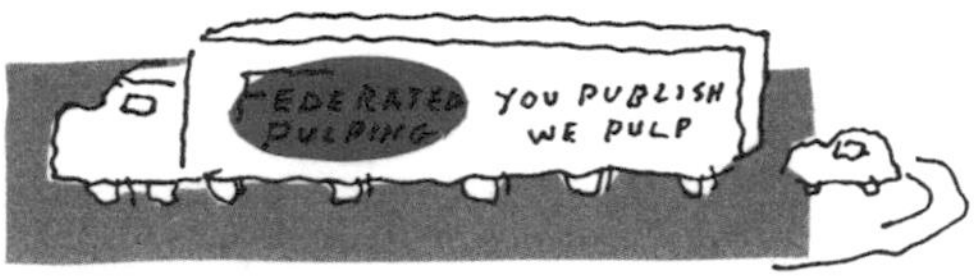
FEDERATED PULPING
YOU PUBLISH WE PULP

He followed it to the factory.

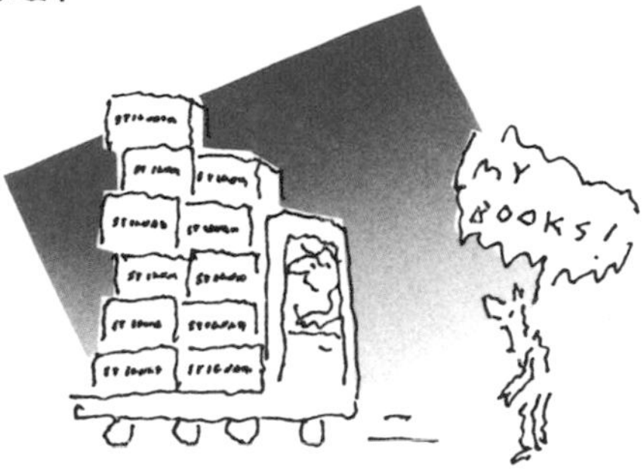
MY BOOKS!

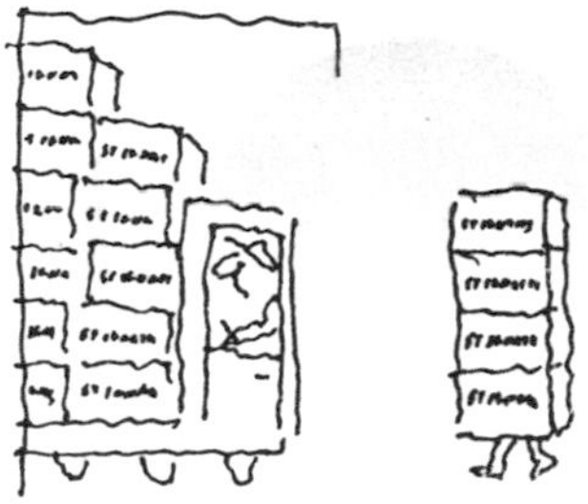

Disguised as his paperbacks, he entered the factory...

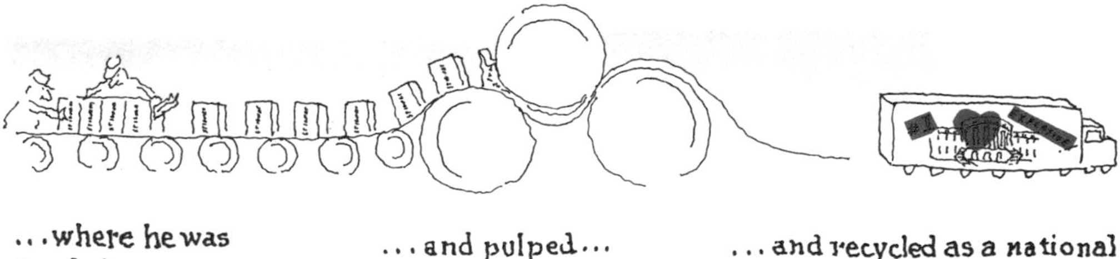

...where he was loaded onto a conveyor belt...

...and pulped...

...and recycled as a national best seller, *The Lives and Loves of Our Presidents.*

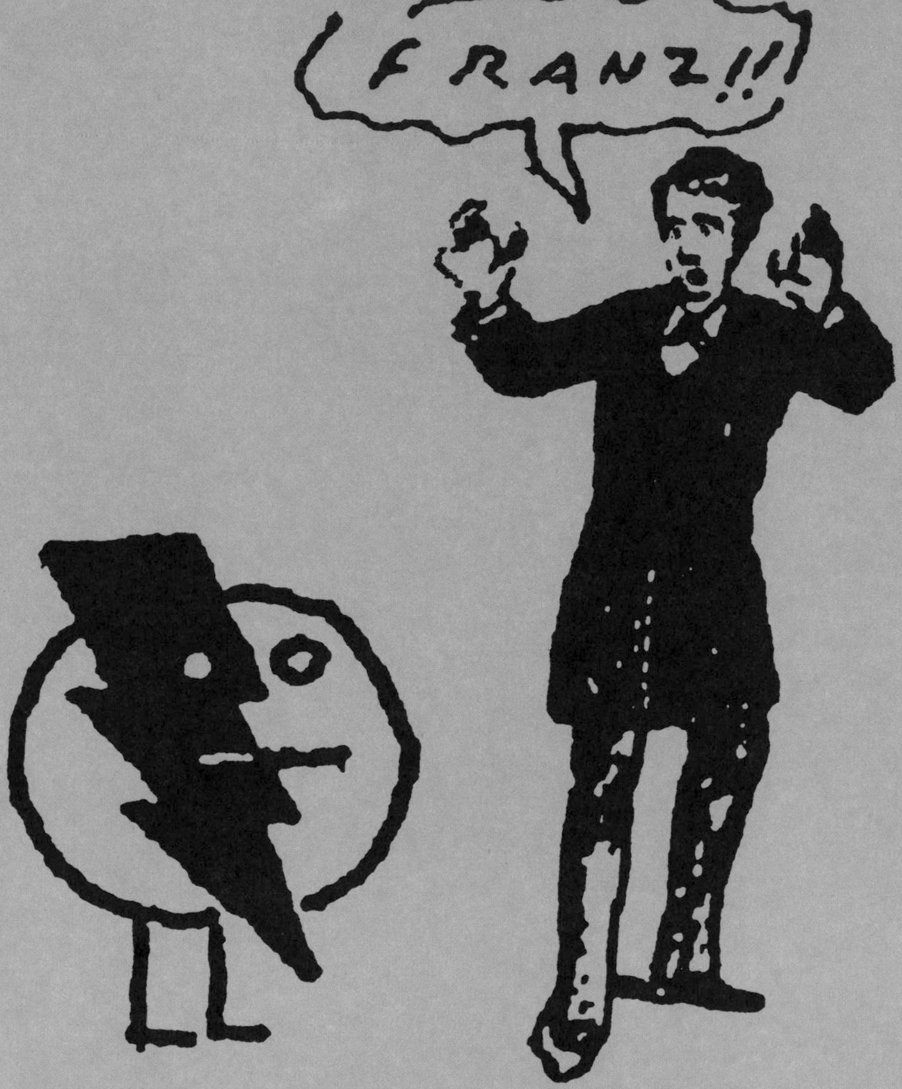
FRANZ!!

Metamorphosis

SKID, 1999

Metamorphosis appeared in *Skid*, a book "devoted to unpublished black and white work." In the introduction, Bruce McCall writes, "(Illustrators) are so conditioned to the idea... that what they create purely for their own personal pleasure or amusement or practice... is of no artistic value because it is of no commercial value."
This was done for my "personal pleasure"—as an experiment combining my drawings with collage elements.

Metamorphosis

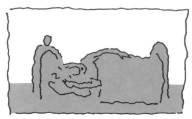

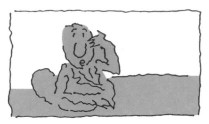

As Franz Kafka awoke one morning from an uneasy dream . . .

. . . he found that he had been transformed into a cartoon.

What has HAPPENED to me?

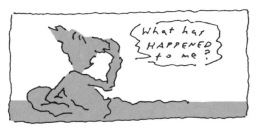

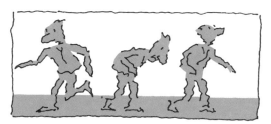

Kafka was disturbed.

Leaving his bed, he explored his surroundings. There were comic strip panels everywhere.

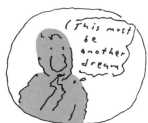

(This must be another dream

CLOCK
EASY CHAIR
LOOKING GLASS
TYPE-WRITER
UNPUBLISHED MANUSCRIPTS

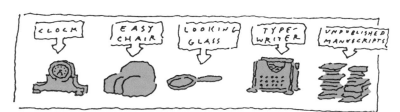

He looked about his room. Everything was there, all the familiar objects, all in their usual places, although transformed into drawings.

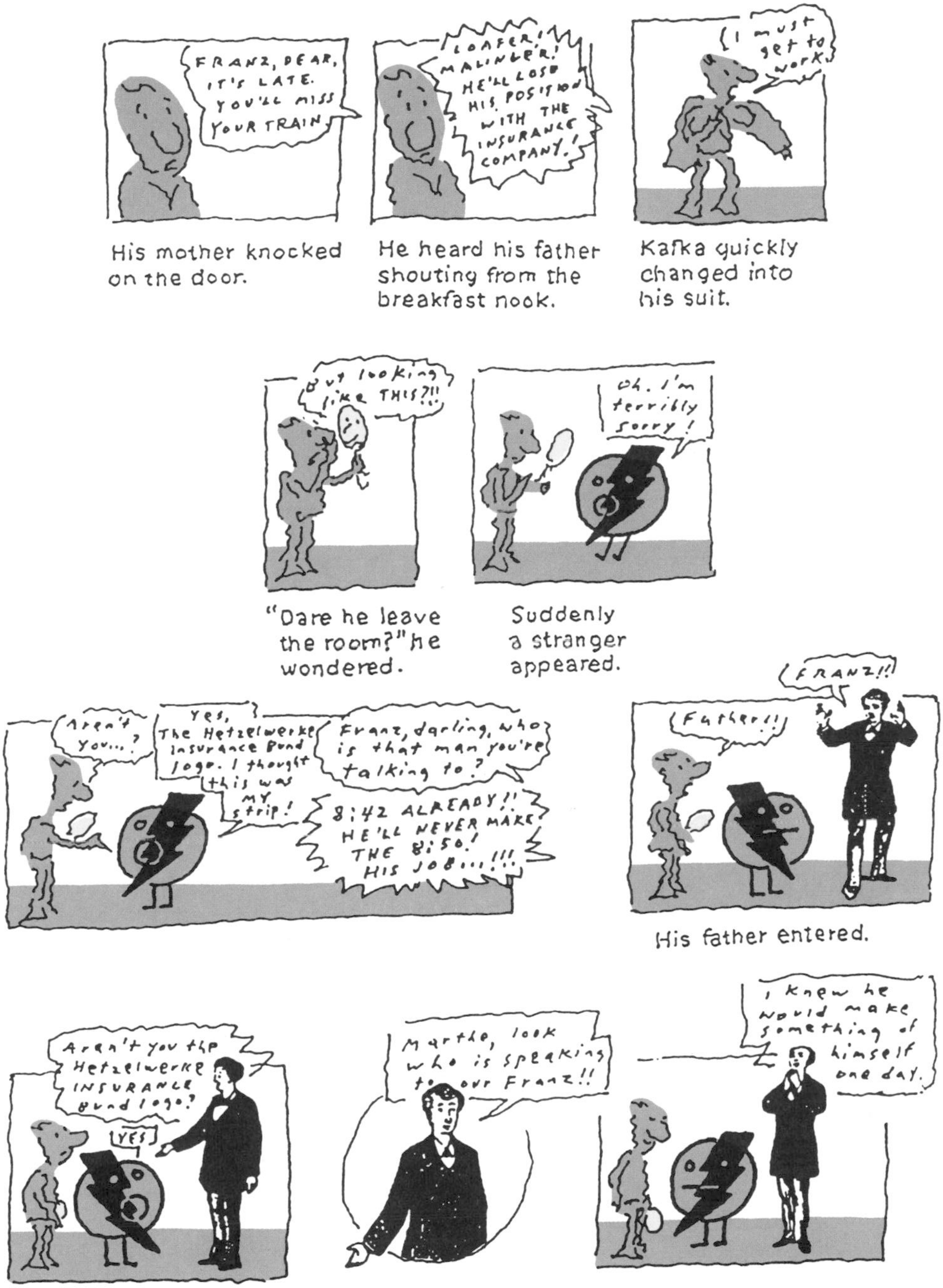
FRANZ, DEAR, IT'S LATE. YOU'LL MISS YOUR TRAIN.
His mother knocked on the door.
LOAFER! MALINGER! HE'LL LOSE HIS POSITION WITH THE INSURANCE COMPANY!
He heard his father shouting from the breakfast nook.
I must get to work.
Kafka quickly changed into his suit.
But looking like THIS?!!
"Dare he leave the room?" he wondered.
Oh. I'm terribly sorry!
Suddenly a stranger appeared.
Aren't you...?
Yes, The Hetzelwerke Insurance Bund logo. I thought this was my strip!
Franz, darling, who is that man you're talking to?
8:42 ALREADY!! HE'LL NEVER MAKE THE 8:50! HIS JOB...!!!
FRANZ!!!
Father!!
His father entered.
Aren't you the Hetzelwerke INSURANCE Bund logo?
YES
Marthe, look who is speaking to our Franz!!
I knew he would make something of himself one day.

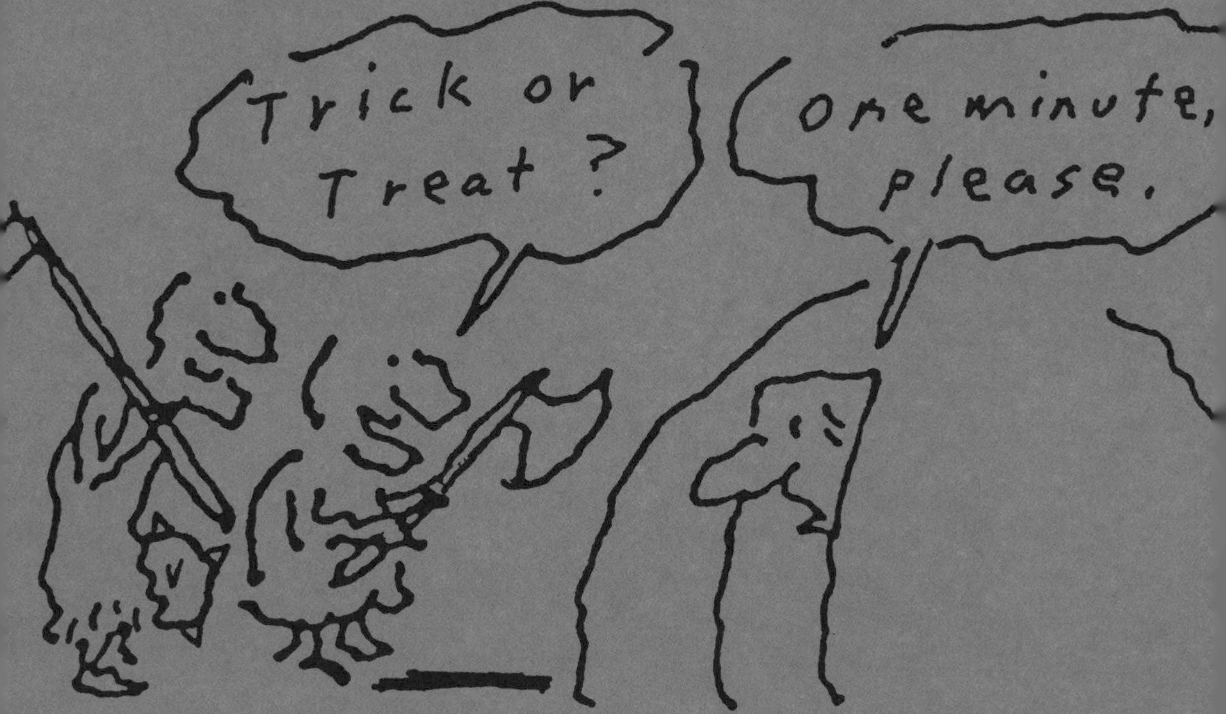
Trick or Treat?
One minute, please.

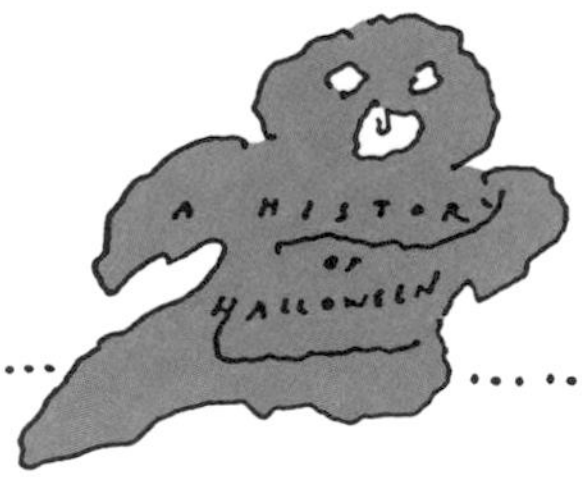
A HISTORY
OF
HALLOWEEN

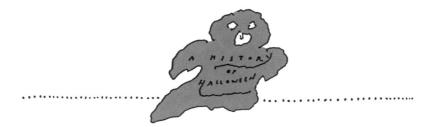

THE NEW YORK TIMES, 2003

Shortly after *The New York Times* published this, I received a letter from a reader accusing me of anti-Armenian prejudice. Can you even find a reference to Armenia? It's there... but still...?

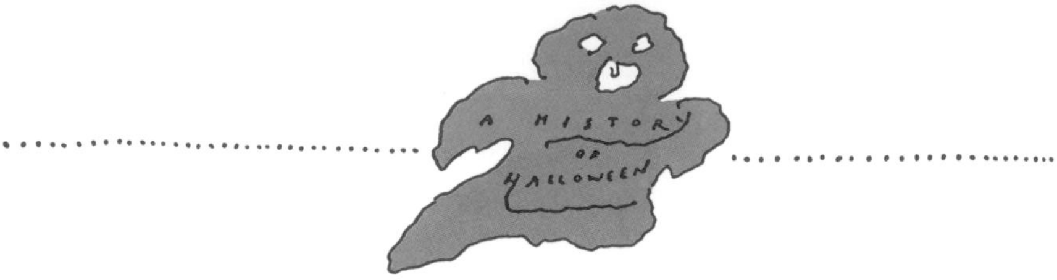
A HISTORY OF HALLOWEEN

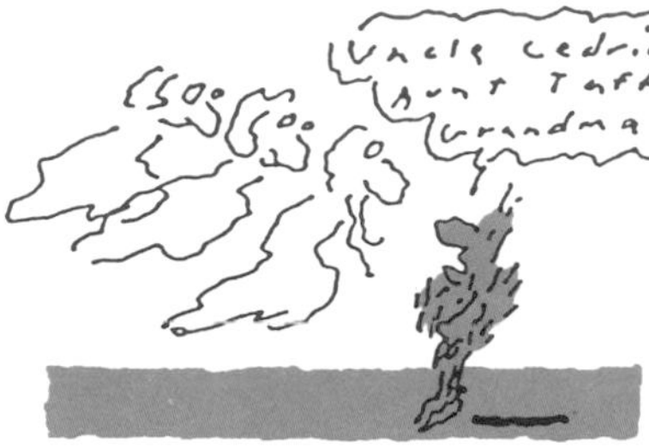
Uncle Cedric! Aunt Taffy! Grandma!!

Halloween began as a Celtic festival honoring the family dead.

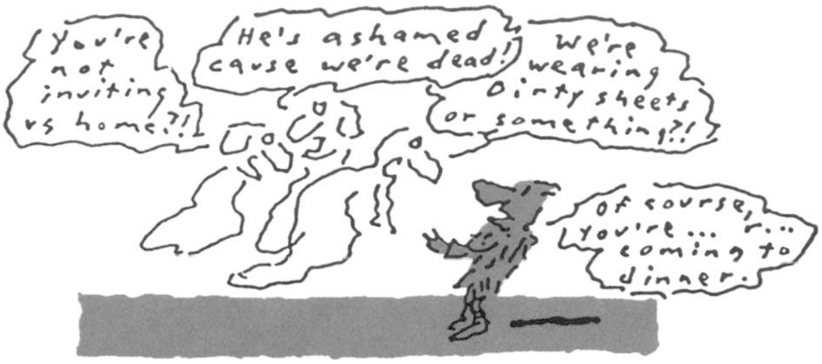
You're not inviting us home?!
He's ashamed 'cause we're dead!
We're wearing dirty sheets or something?!
Of course, you're... r... coming to dinner.

Their spirits were invited to visit the family hearth.

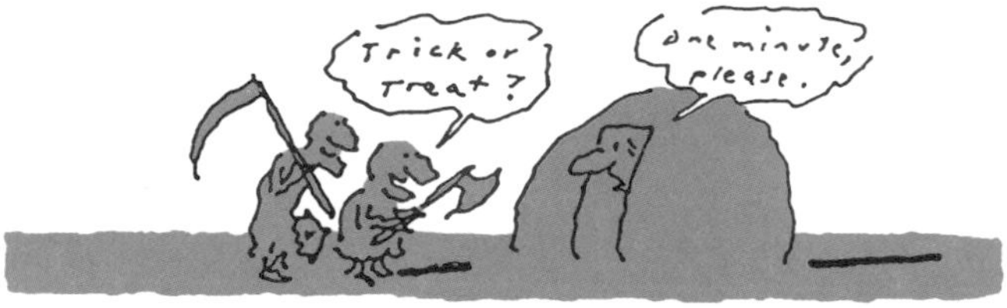
Trick or Treat?
One minute, please.

In the Middle Ages, bands of peasants roamed the countryside demanding food for the holiday festivities.

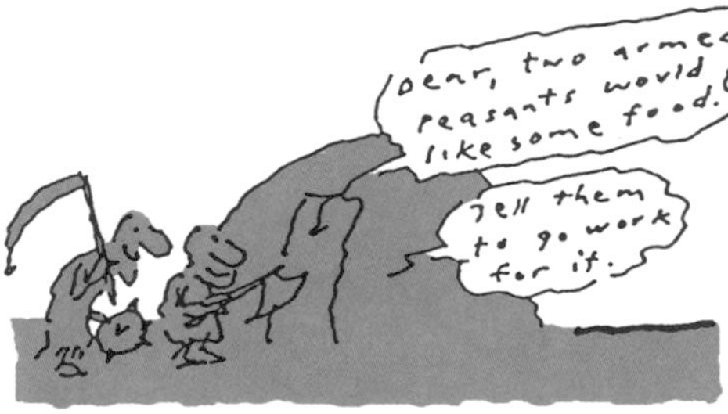
Dear, two armed peasants would like some food.
Tell them to go work for it.

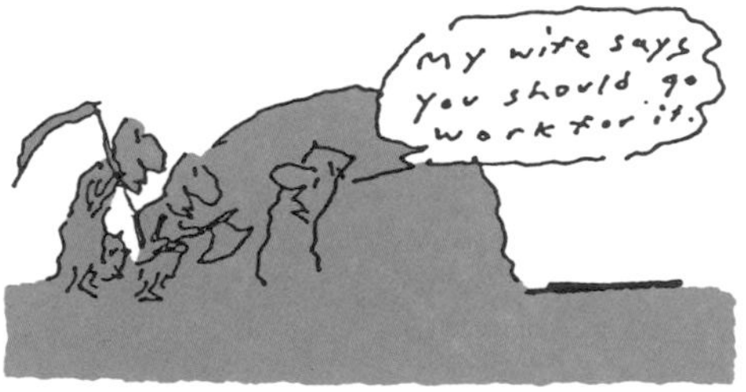
My wife says you should go work for it.

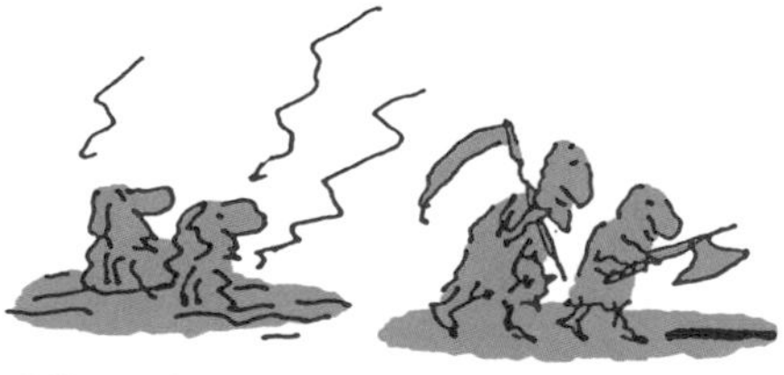

The observance of Halloween was often marked by mischief.

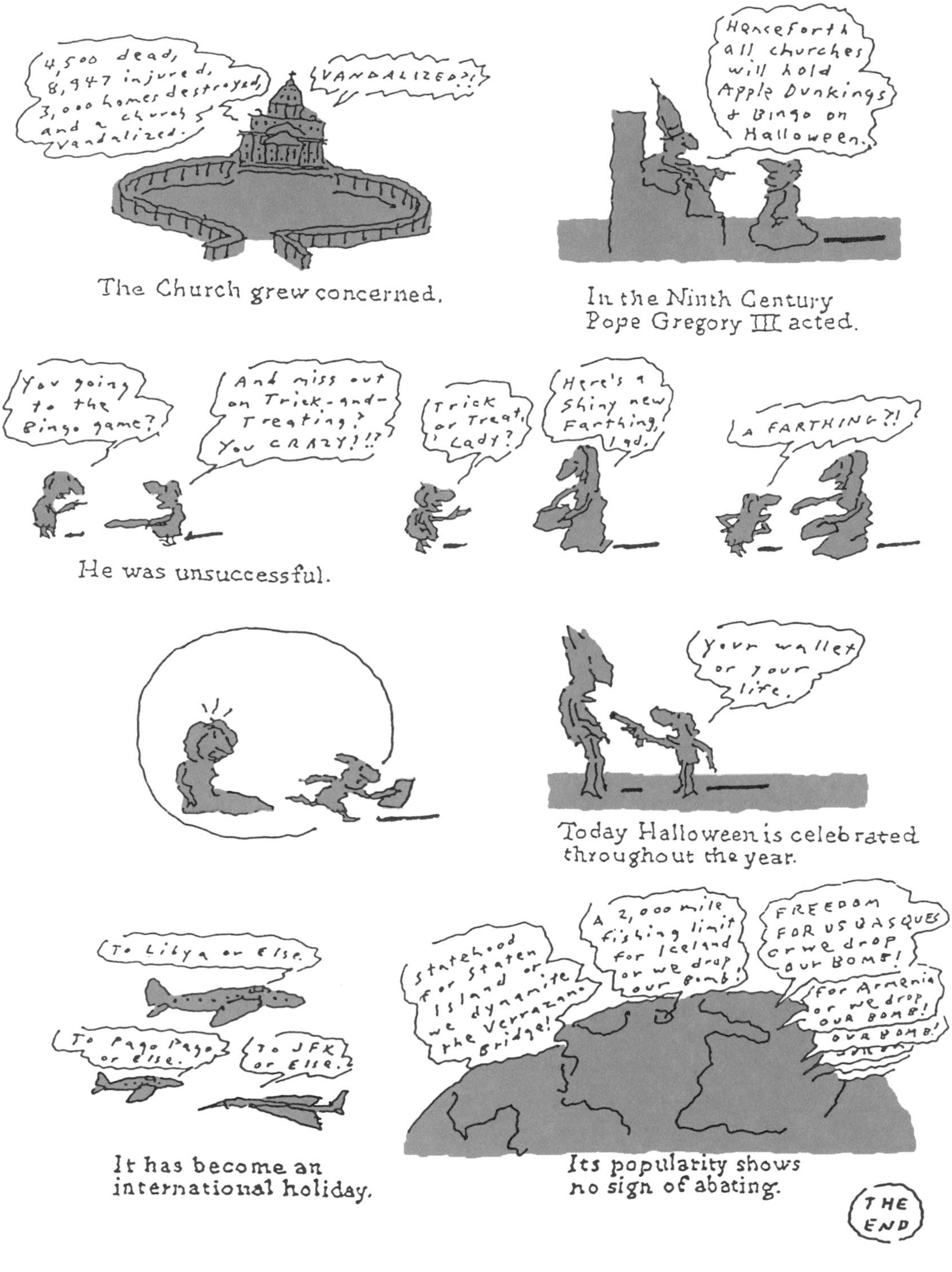
4,500 dead, 8,947 injured, 3,000 homes destroyed, and a church vandalized.
VANDALIZED?!
The Church grew concerned.
Henceforth all churches will hold Apple Dunkings & Bingo on Halloween.
In the Ninth Century Pope Gregory III acted.
You going to the Bingo game?
And miss out on Trick-and-Treating? You CRAZY!!?
Trick or Treat, Lady?
Here's a shiny new Farthing, 1 qd.
A FARTHING?!
He was unsuccessful.
Your wallet or your life.
Today Halloween is celebrated throughout the year.
To Libya or Else.
To Pago Pago or else.
To JFK or Else.
It has become an international holiday.
Statehood for Staten Island or we dynamite the Verrazano Bridge!
A 2,000 mile fishing limit for Iceland or we drop our Bomb!
FREEDOM FOR US BASQUES or we drop OUR BOMB!
For Armenia or we drop OUR BOMB!
OUR BOMB!
Its popularity shows no sign of abating.
THE END

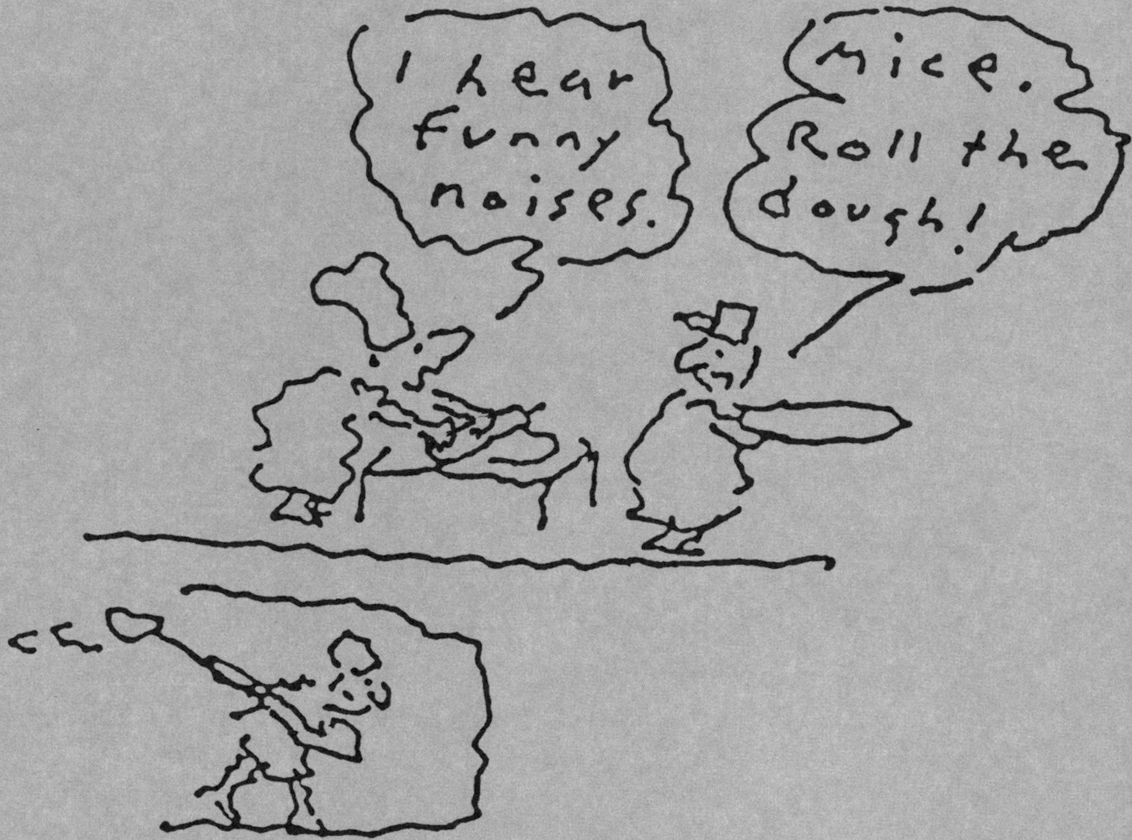
I hear funny noises.
Mice. Roll the dough!

THE BIRTH of THE CROISSANT & THE BAGEL

· ·

THE NEW YORK TIMES, 2009

About ten years ago, when Leanne Shapton was an art director at Toronto's *National Post*, I told her a curious story about the presumed birth of the bagel and croissant. She never forgot it. This year, as an art director at *The New York Times*, she asked me to draw it up. I did, somewhat reluctantly, because it's rather lightweight, and I prefer my art to make some kind of statement. But a job's a job — and maybe the world could use a little laugh.

THE BIRTH of THE CROISSANT & THE BAGEL

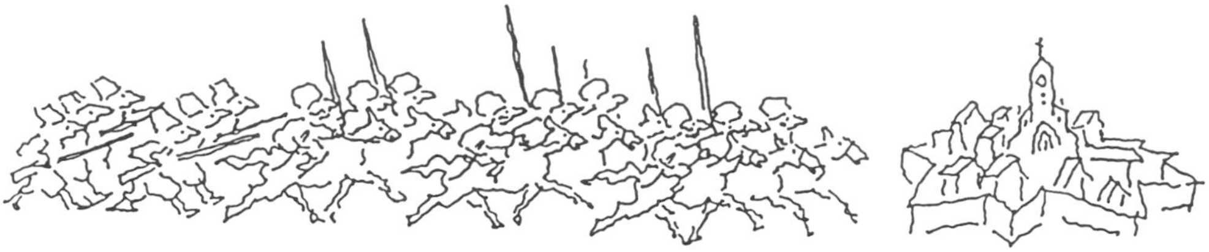

In 1683, 150,000 Ottoman soldiers attacked the imperial city of Vienna. This much we know is true. What follows is most likely true.

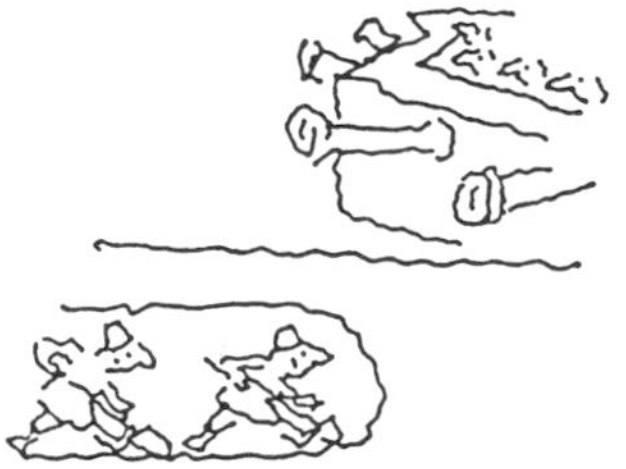

Traveling underground, the Ottomans hoped to evade the defenses.

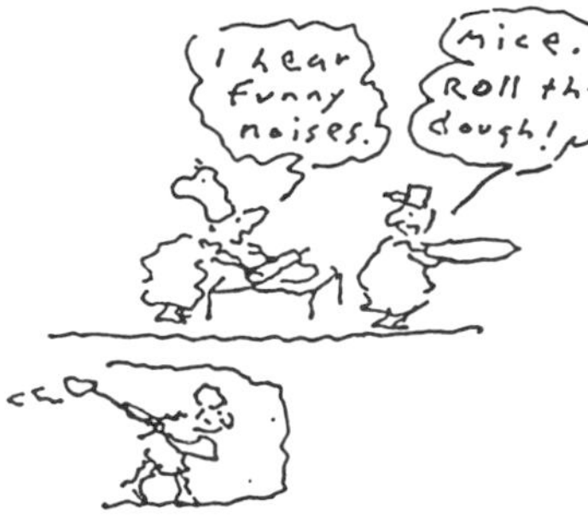

I hear funny noises.
Nice. Roll the dough!

A baker, working early in the morning, heard something suspicious.

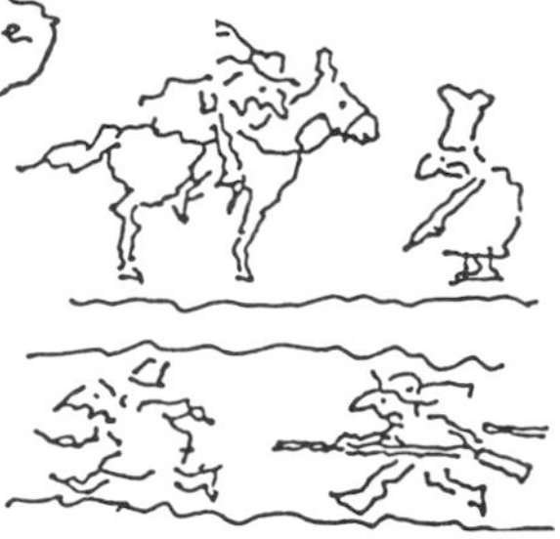

He alerted the imperial army, and the invaders were routed.

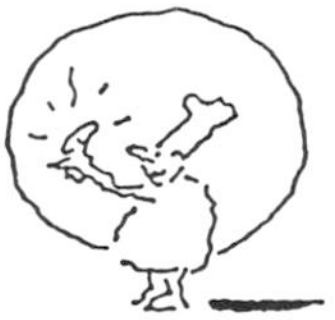

In celebration, a special pastry was baked in the shape of a crescent (a "croissant").

But the siege continued.

A relief force of Polish and German knights defeated the Ottoman Army. Vienna was saved.

a "bügel"

a Bagel

What a story behind this !

Pass the cream cheese.

The victory was commemorated with a pastry shaped like a German knight's stirrup (a "bügel").

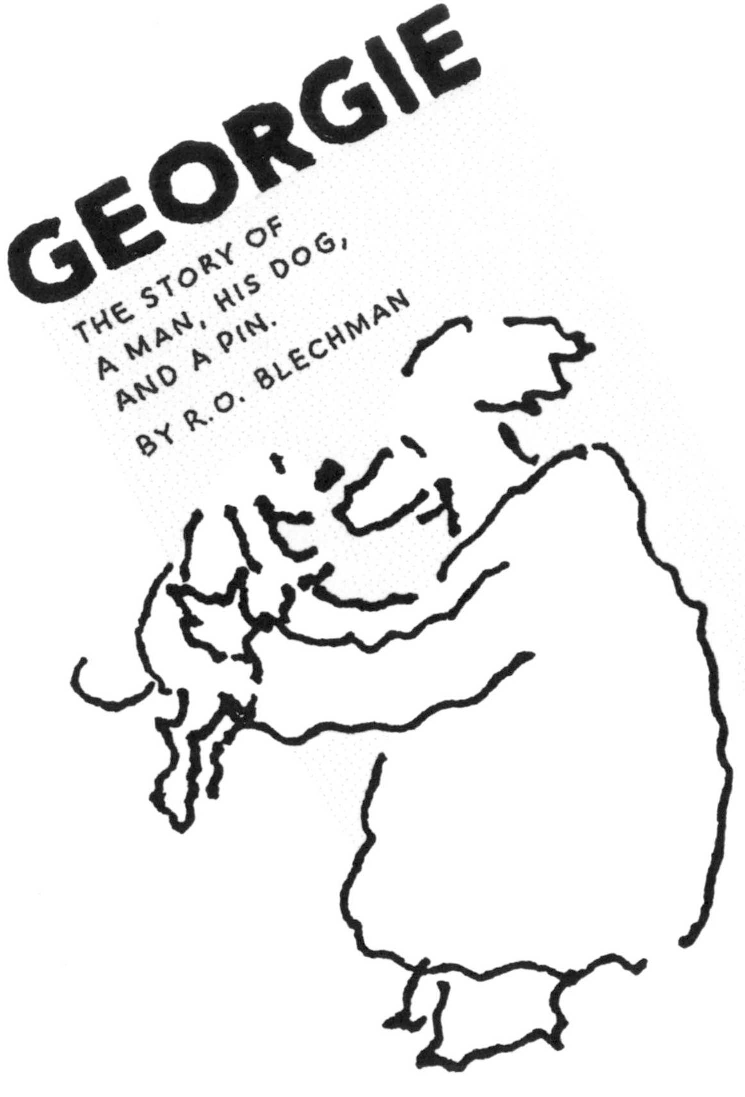
GEORGIE
THE STORY OF
A MAN, HIS DOG,
AND A PIN.
BY R.O. BLECHMAN

GEORGIE

UNPUBLISHED, 1992

I once read of a dog who was taught a few words (although maybe I dreamed this up). Anyway, it inspired me to write this piece. Its genesis, probably, also had something to do with the birth of my first son and all the anxieties that new fatherhood entailed.

It was like an appletree in winter...

...suddenly bearing fruit.

Minnie Goodwin had a baby.

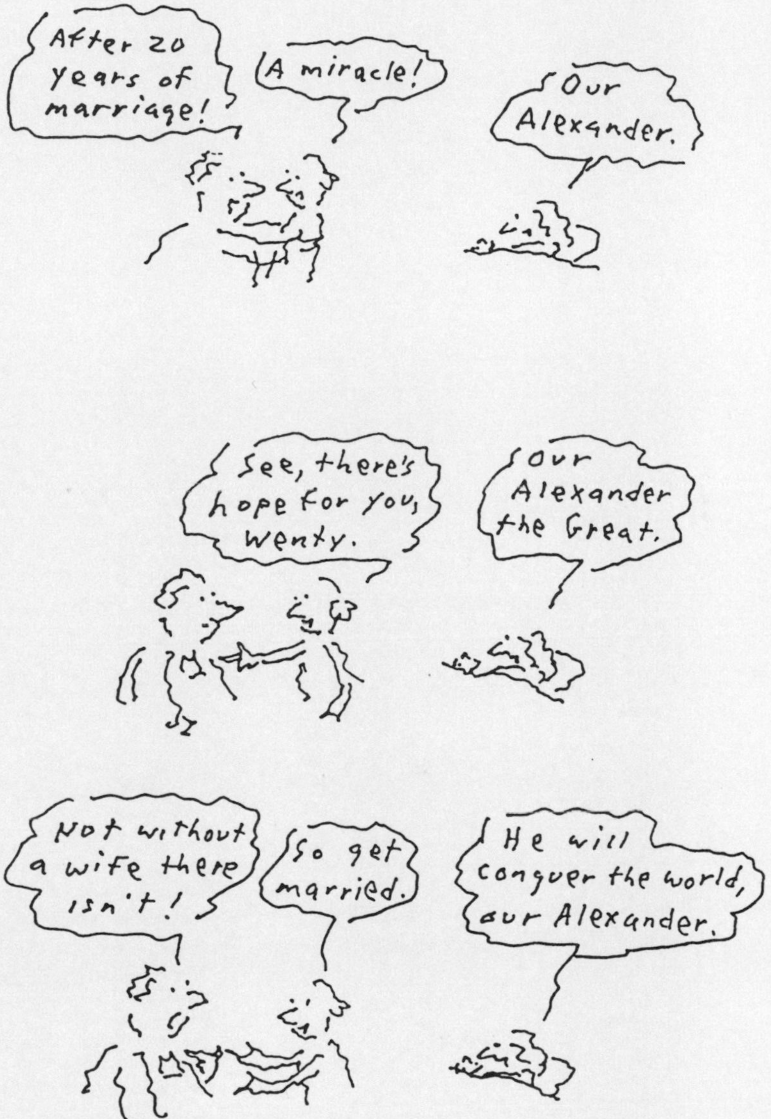
After 20 years of marriage!
A miracle!
Our Alexander.
See, there's hope for you, wenty.
Our Alexander the Great.
Not without a wife there isn't!
So get married.
He will conquer the world, our Alexander.

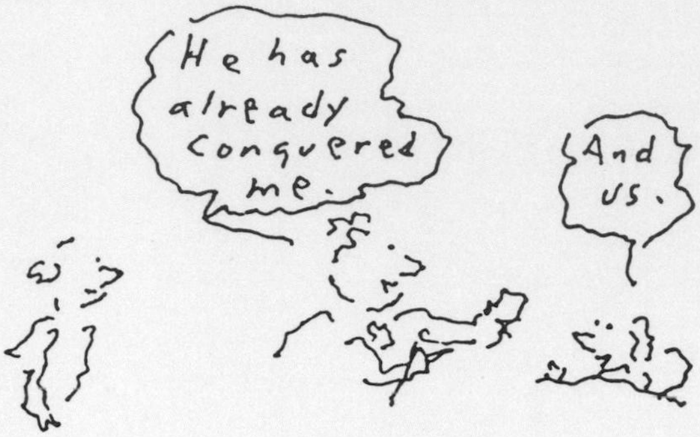
He has already conquered me.
And us.

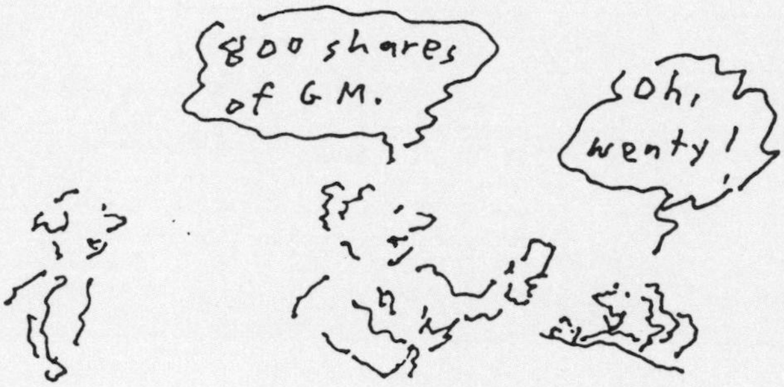
800 shares of GM.
Oh, wenty!

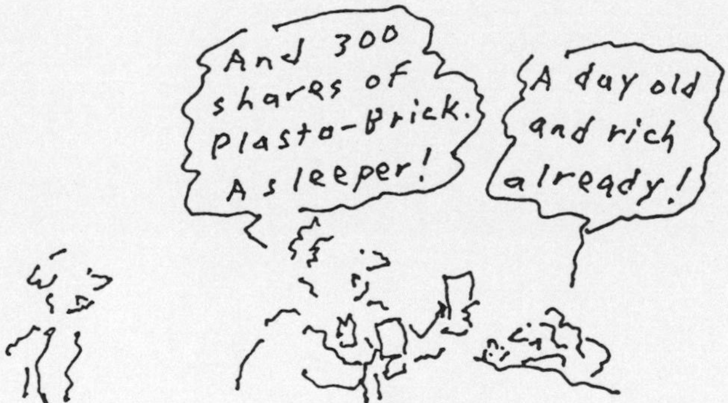
And 300 shares of plasto-brick. A sleeper!
A day old and rich already!

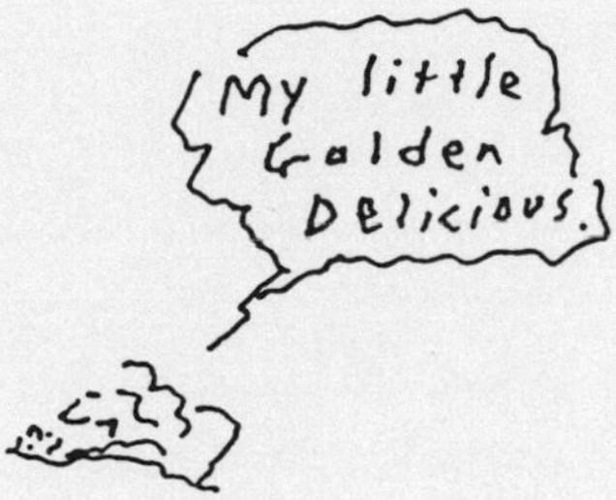
My little Golden Delicious.

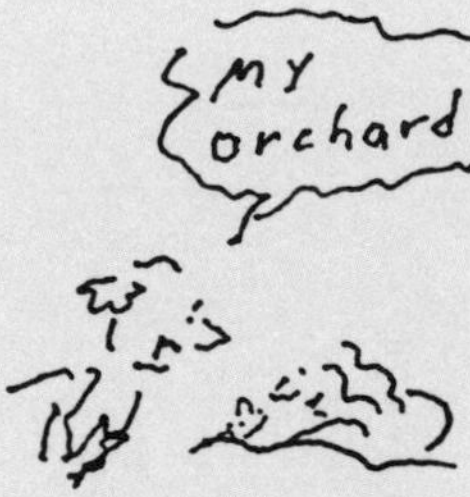
my orchard!

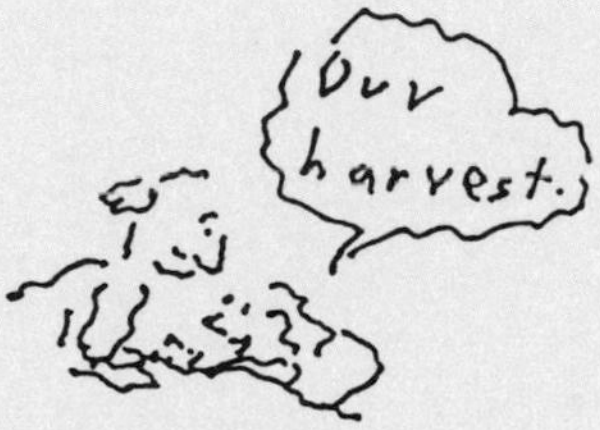
Our harvest.

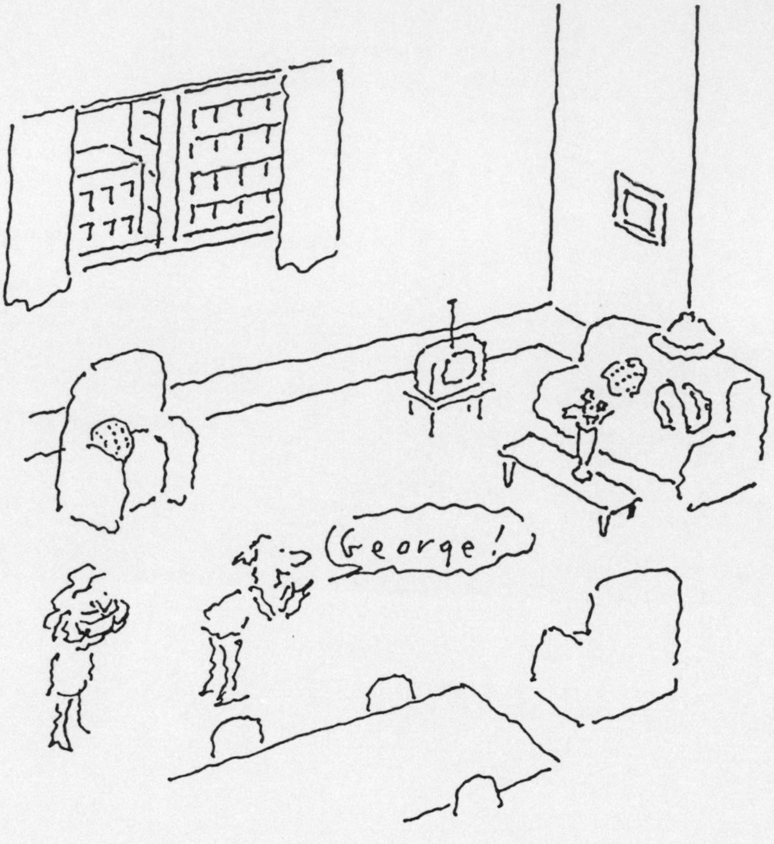
George!

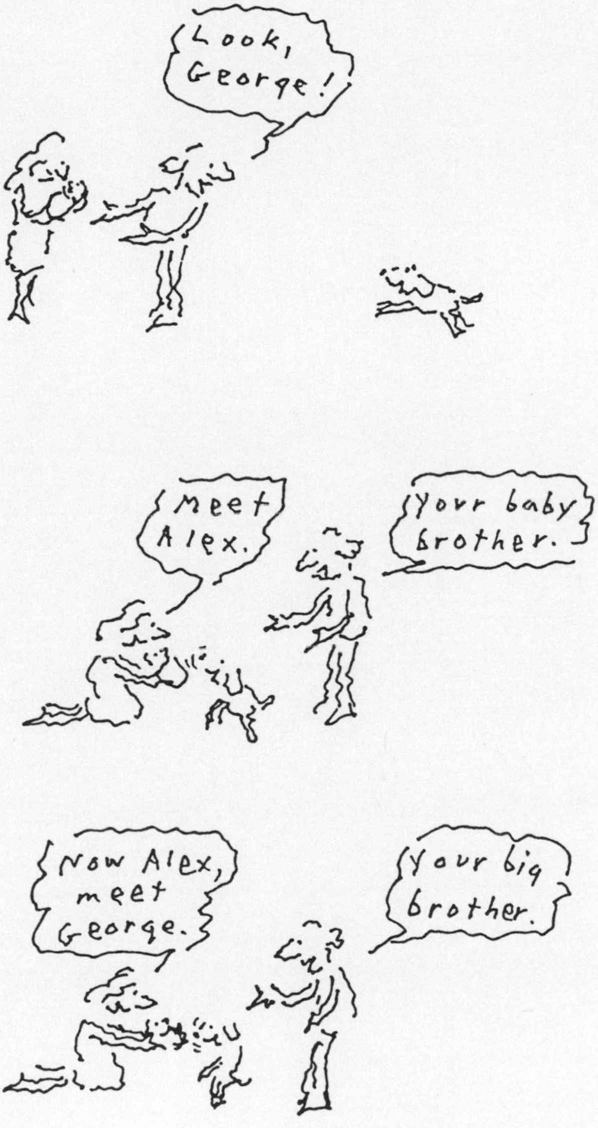
Look, George!
Meet Alex.
Your baby brother.
Now Alex, meet George.
Your big brother.

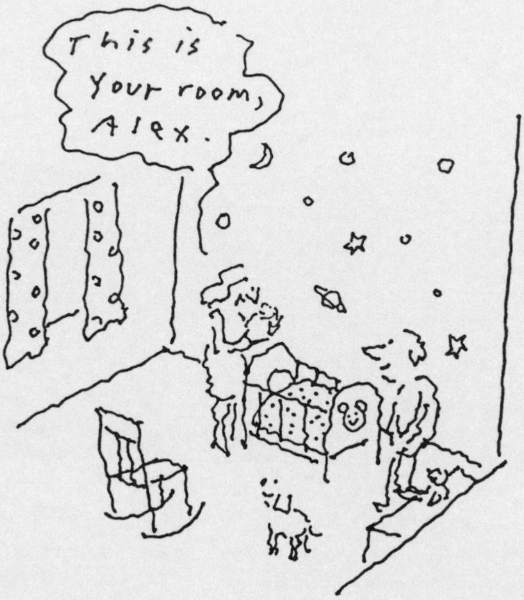
This is your room, Alex.

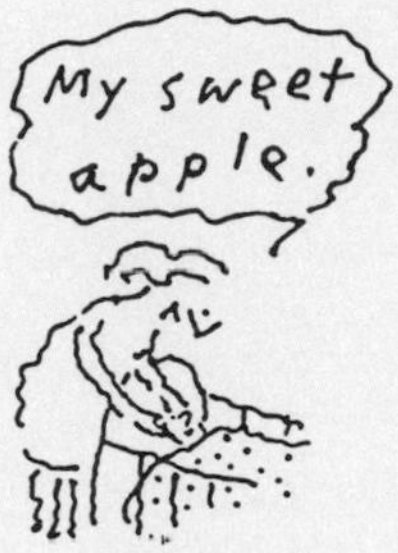
My sweet apple.

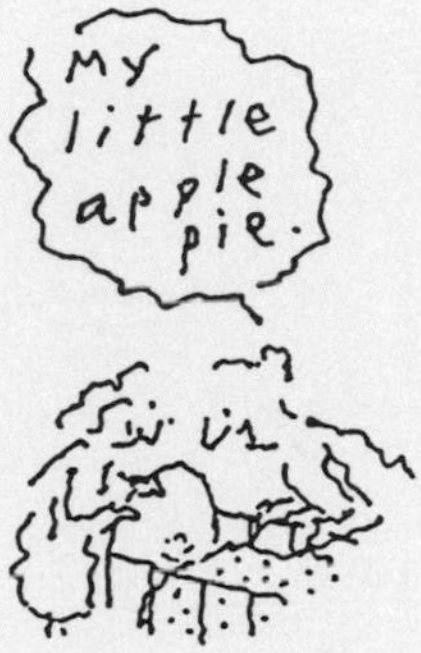
My little apple pie.

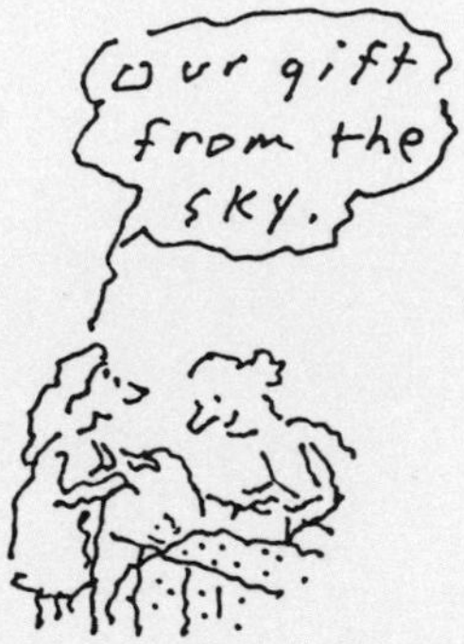
our gift from the sky.

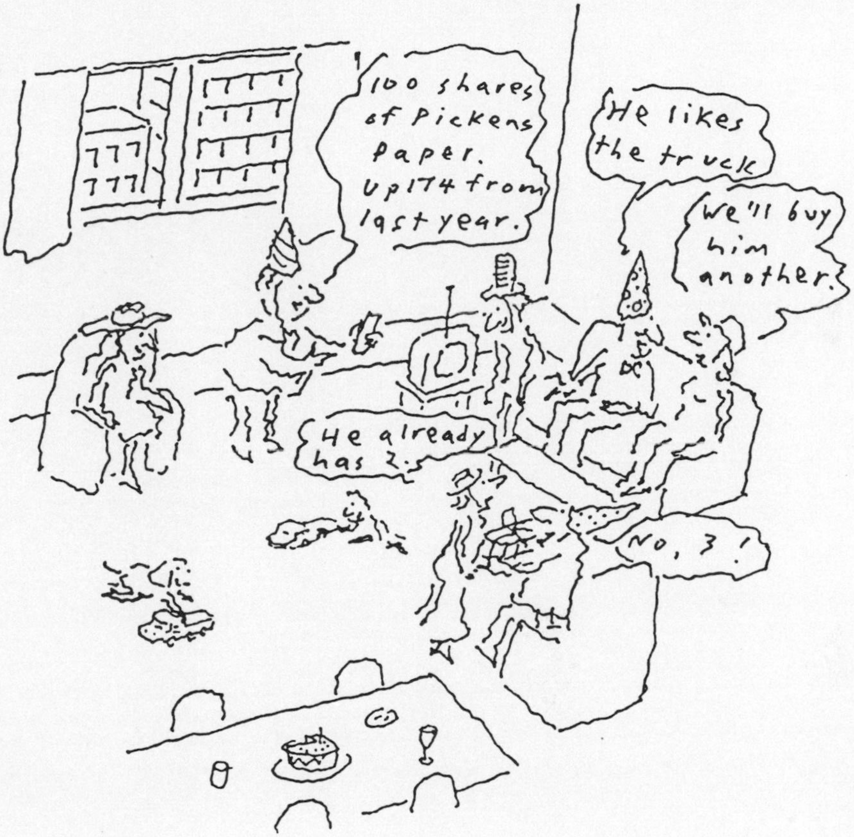
100 shares of Pickens paper. Up 17 4 from last year.
He likes the truck
We'll buy him another.
He already has 2.
No, 3!

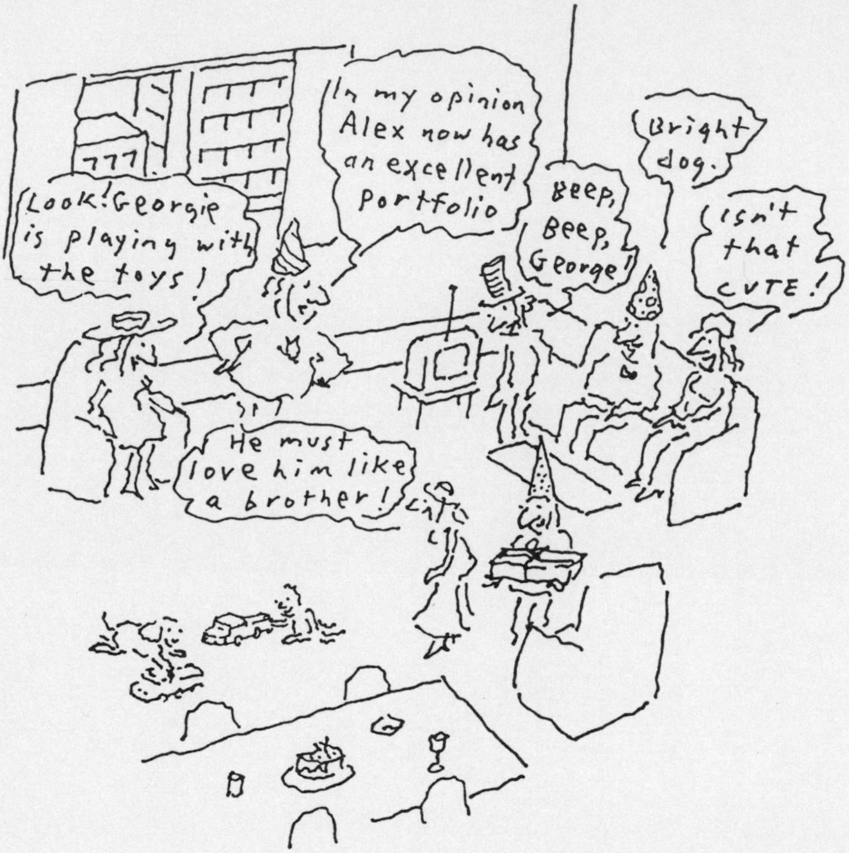
Look! Georgie is playing with the toys!
In my opinion Alex now has an excellent portfolio
Beep, Beep, George!
Bright dog.
Isn't that CUTE!
He must love him like a brother!

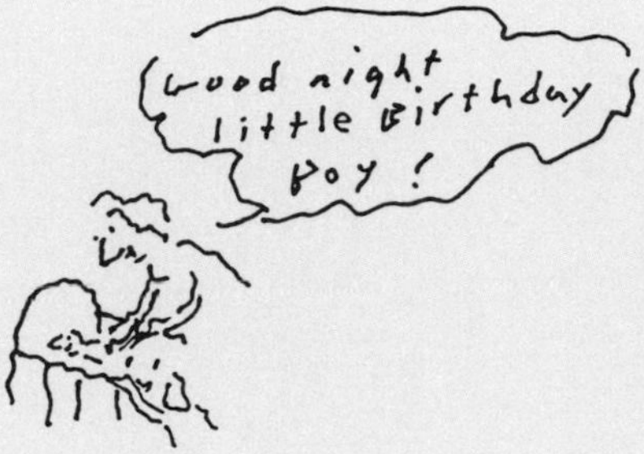
Good night little Birthday Boy!

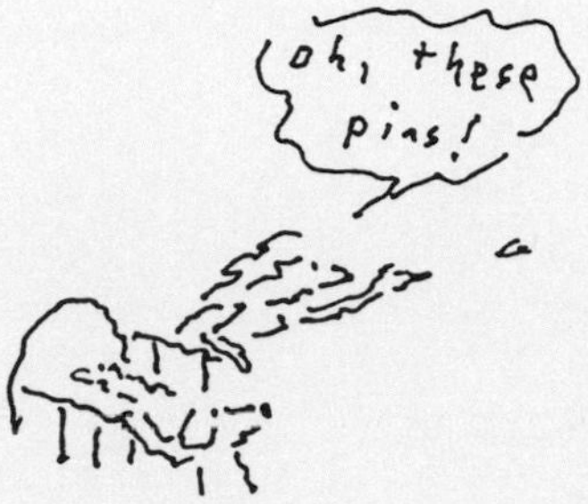
oh, these pins!

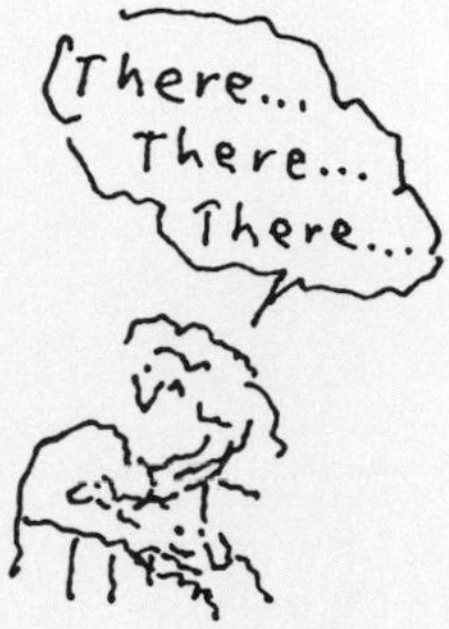
There... There... There...

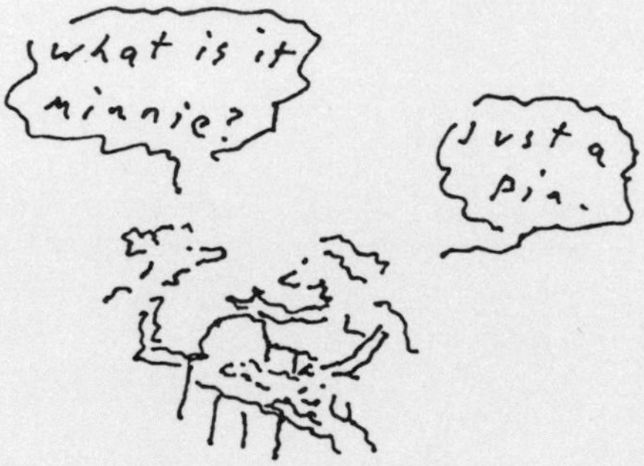
what is it minnie?
Just a pin.

I turned off the light, minnie.
There... there... there...

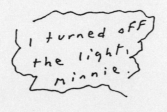

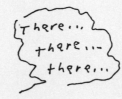

Now go to sleep.
Sleep, Alex, sleep.

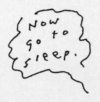

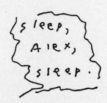

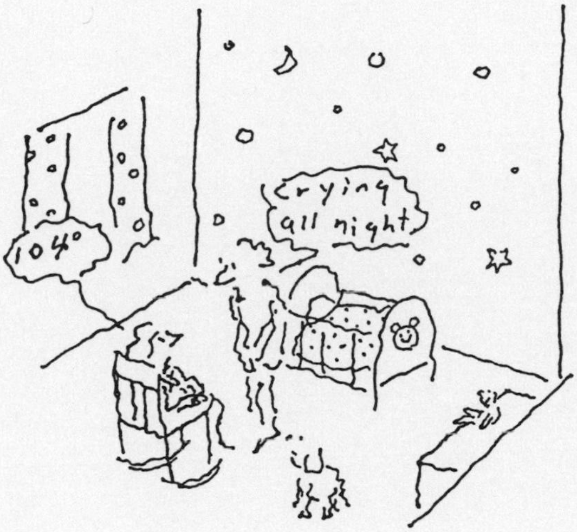
104°
crying
all night

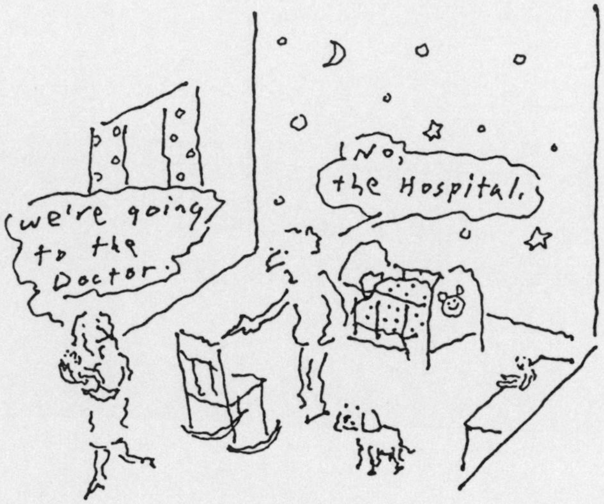
we're going to the Doctor.
No, the Hospital.

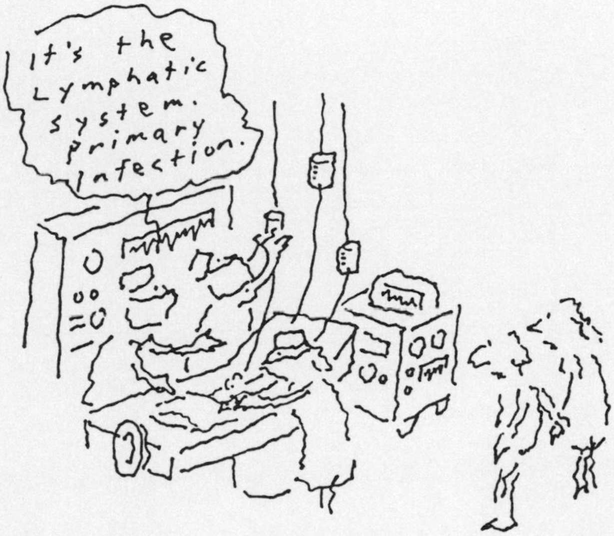
It's the Lymphatic system. primary infection.

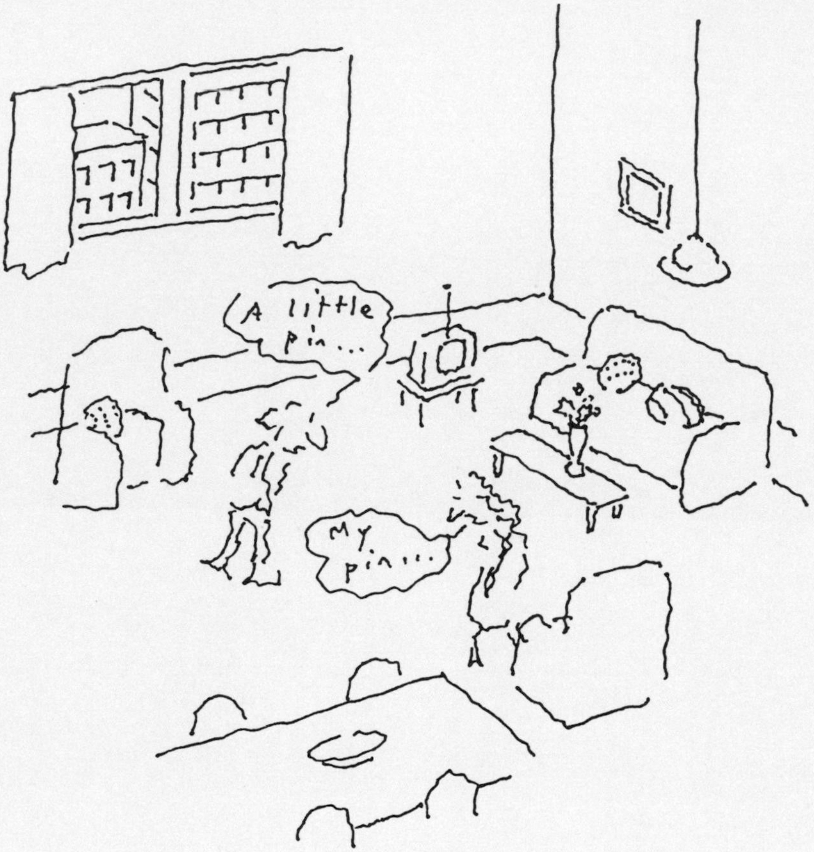
A little pin...
My pin...

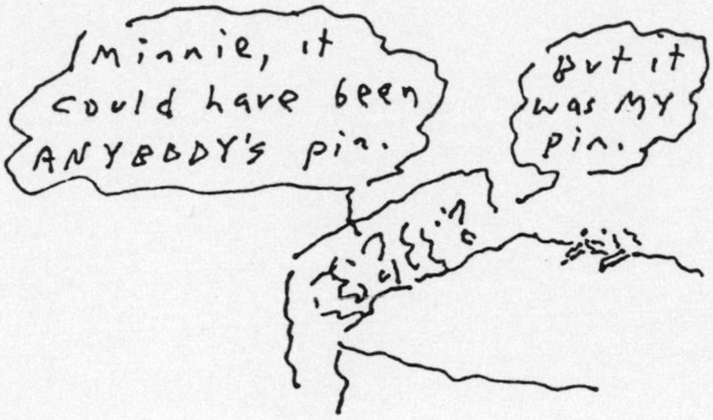
Minnie, it could have been ANYBODY's pin.
But it was MY pin.

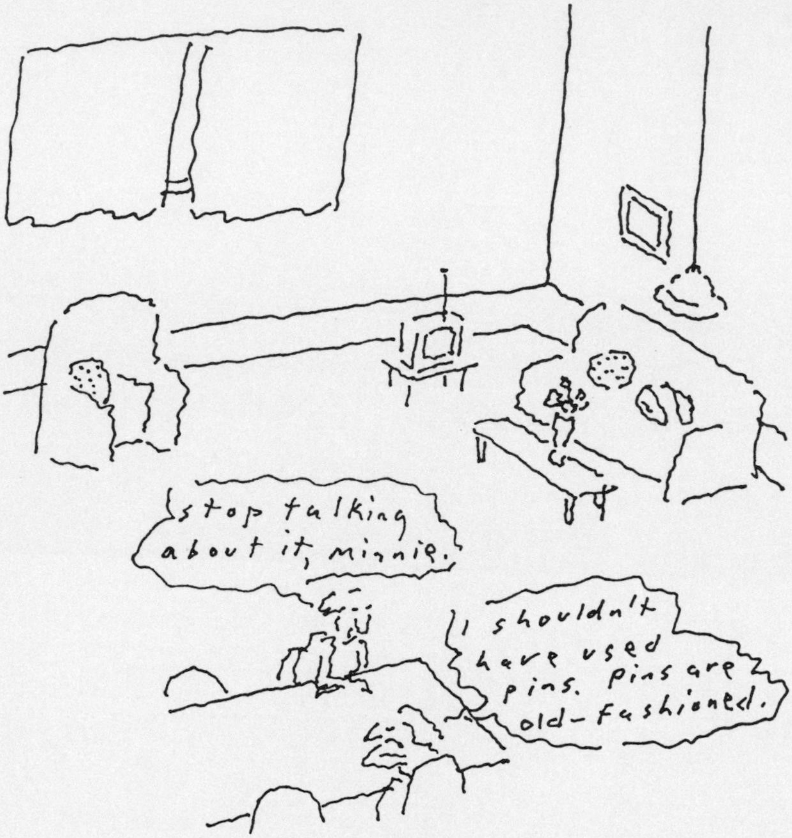
stop talking about it, minnie.
I shouldn't have used pins. pins are old-fashioned.

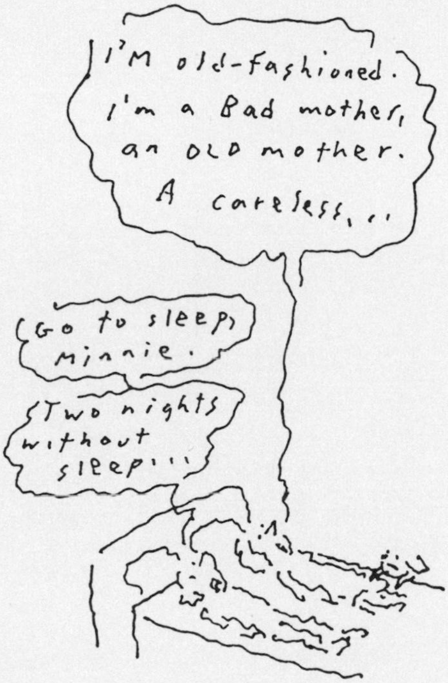
I'M old-fashioned. I'm a Bad mother, an OLD mother. A careless...
Go to sleep, Minnie.
Two nights without sleep...

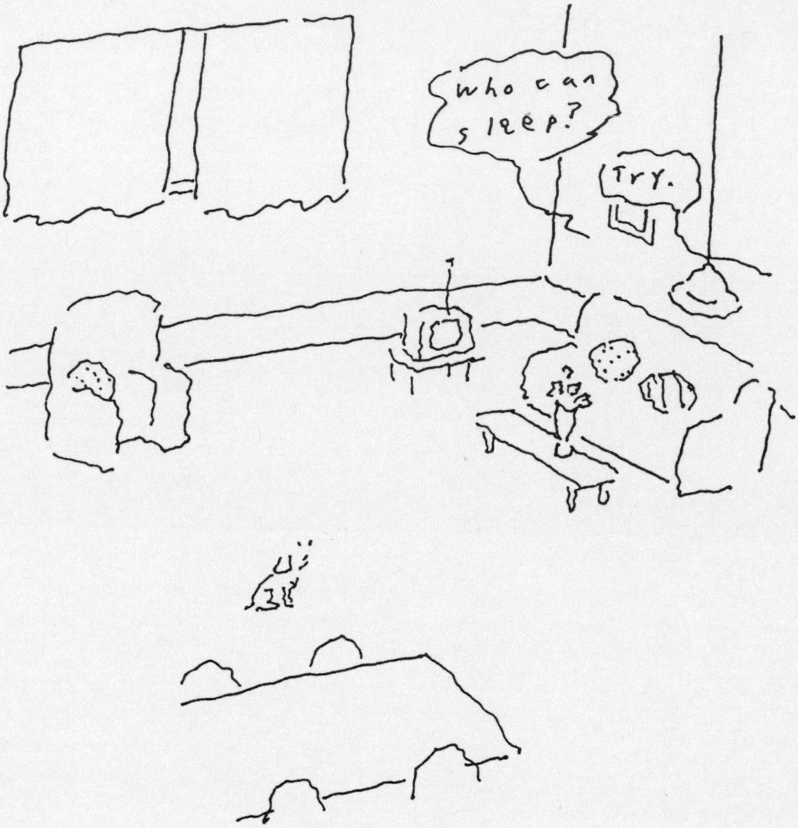
who can sleep?
Try.

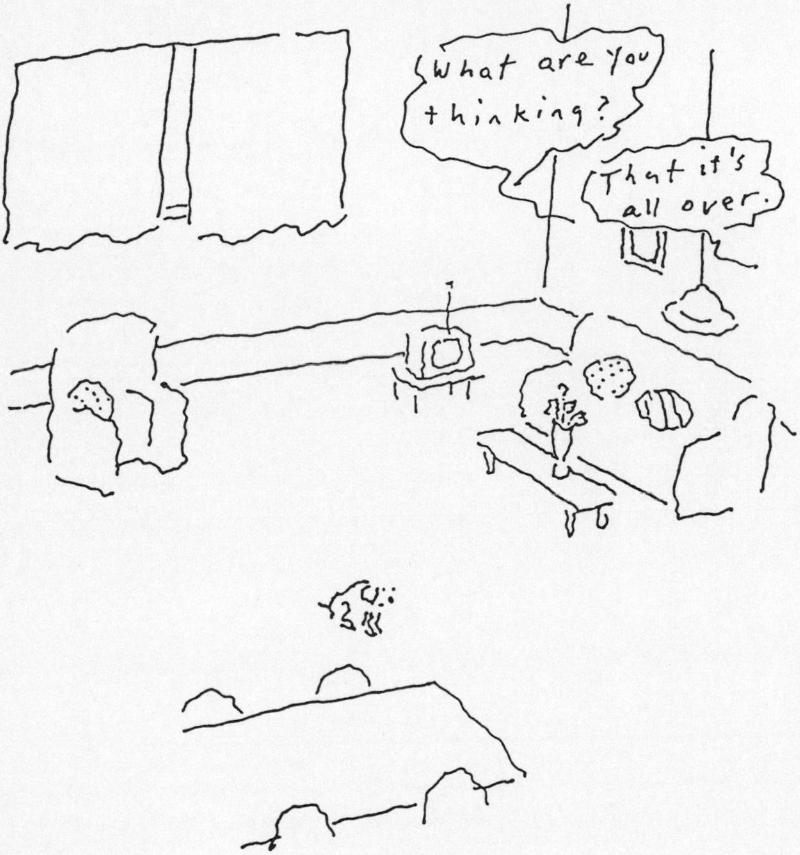
What are you thinking?
That it's all over.

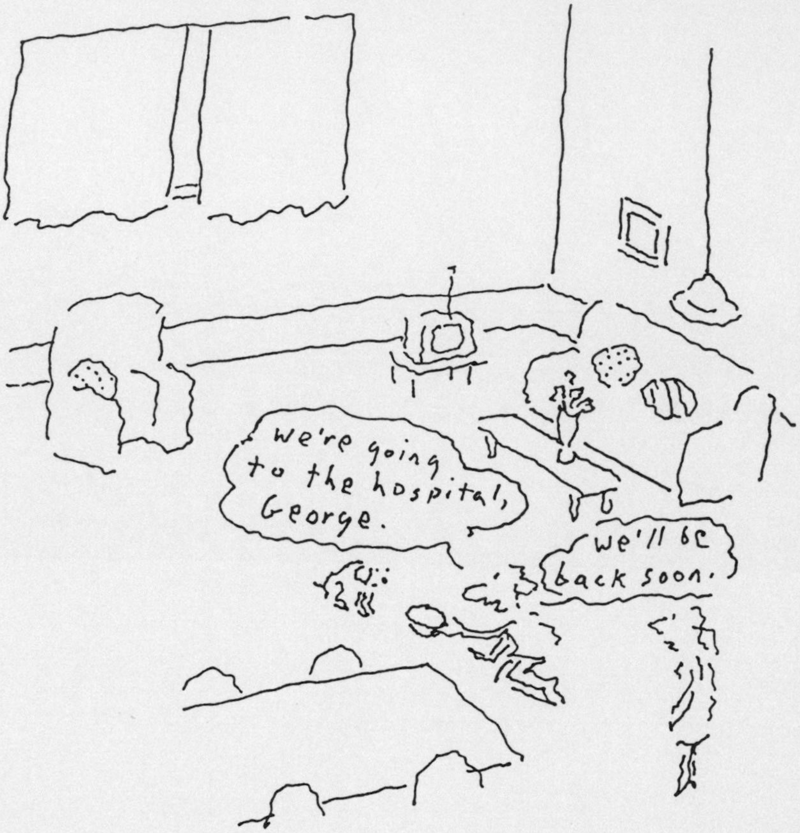
we're going to the hospital, George.
we'll be back soon.

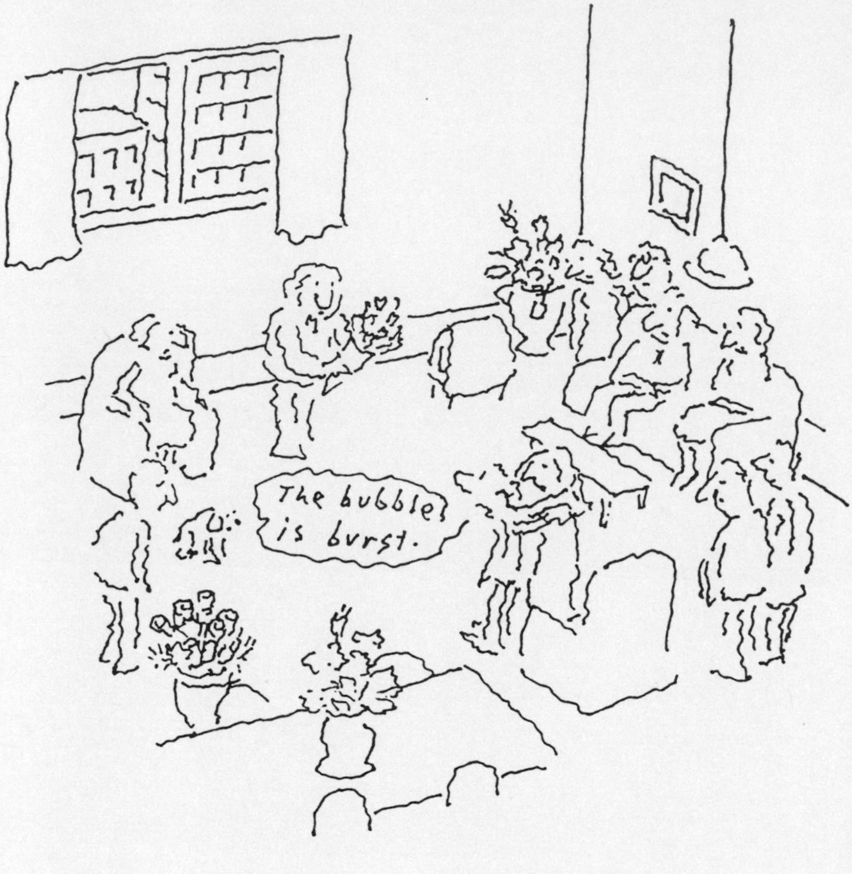
The bubble is burst.

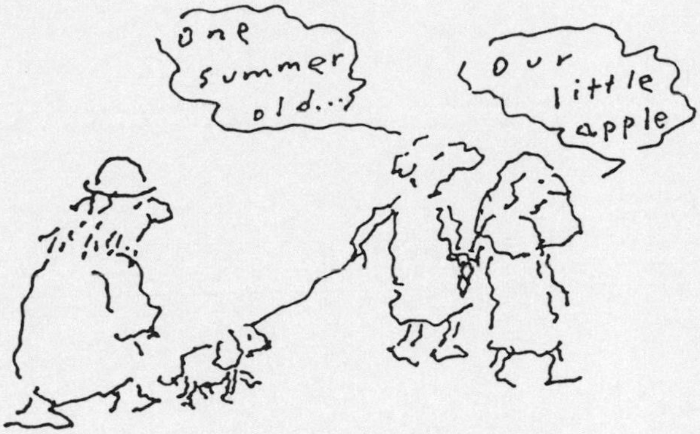
one summer old...
our little apple

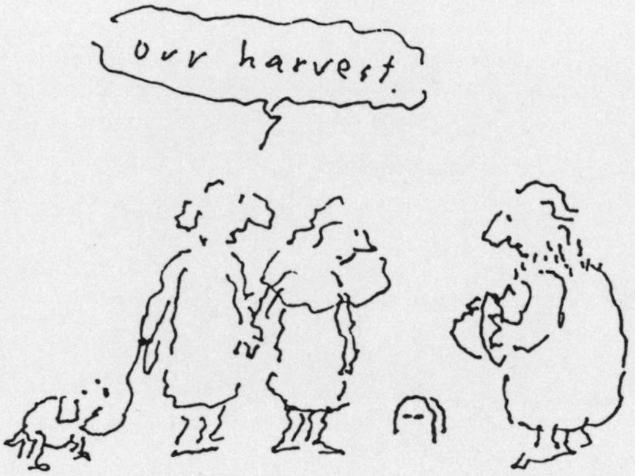
our harvest.

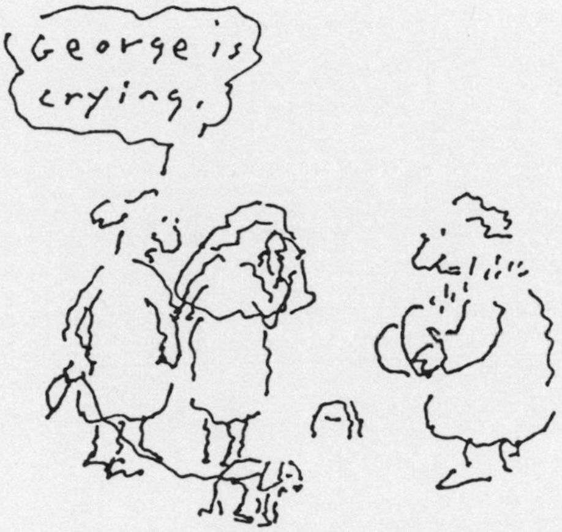
George is crying.

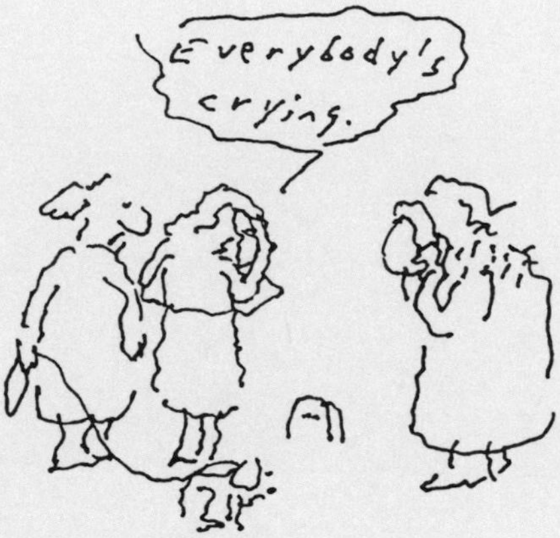
Everybody's crying.

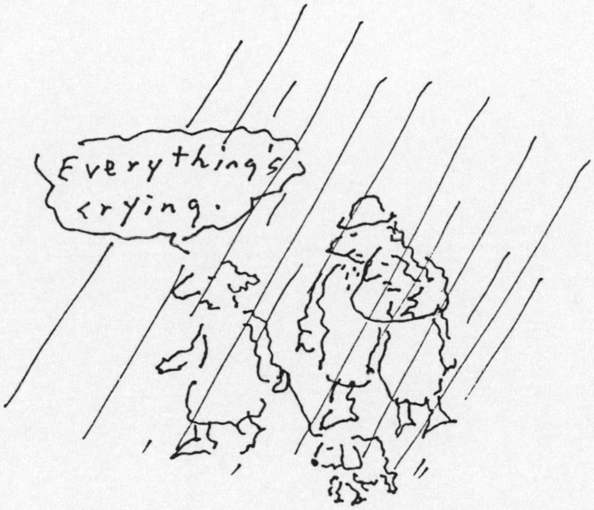
Everything's crying.

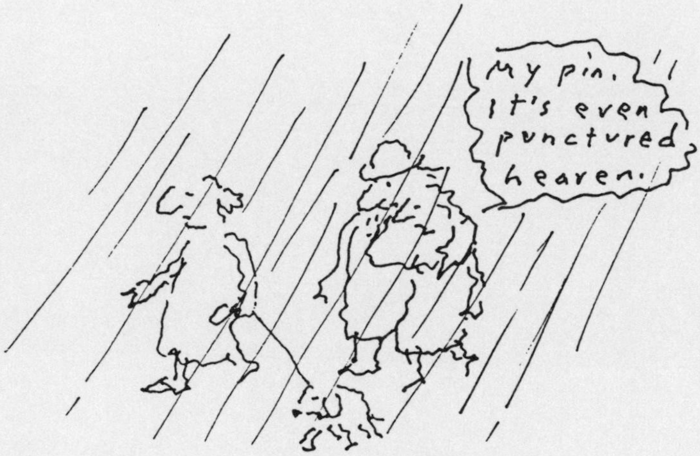
My pin. It's even punctured heaven.

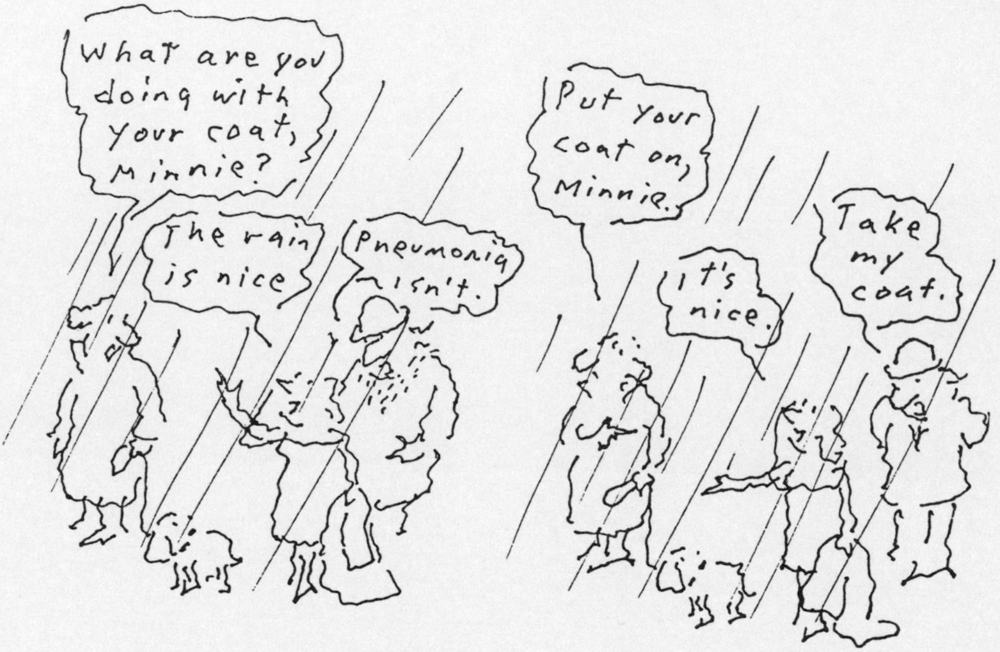
What are you doing with your coat, Minnie?
The rain is nice
Pneumonia isn't.
Put your coat on, Minnie.
It's nice.
Take my coat.

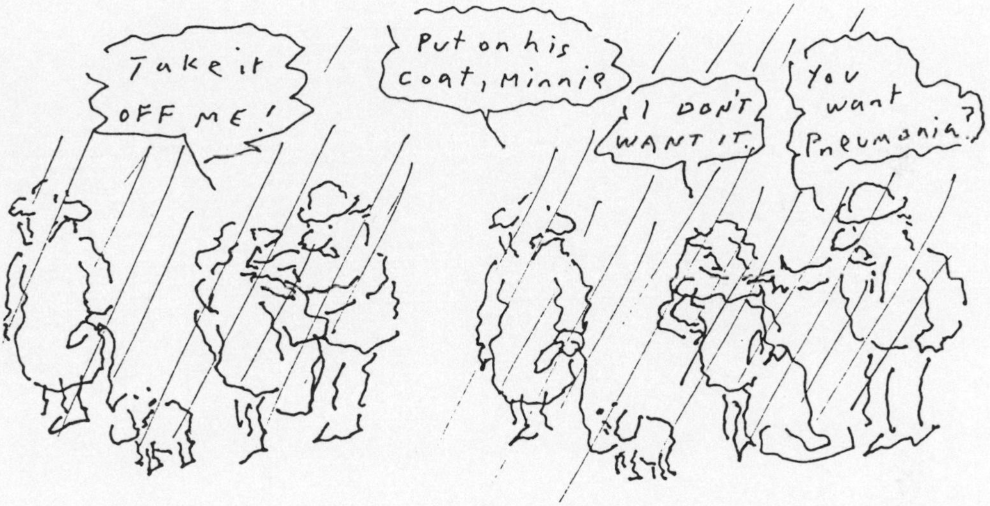
Take it OFF ME!
Put on his coat, Minnie
I DON'T WANT IT.
You want Pneumonia?

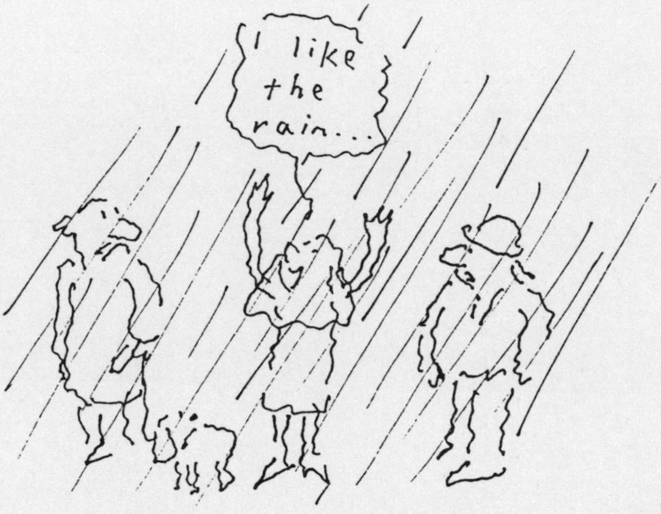
I like the rain...

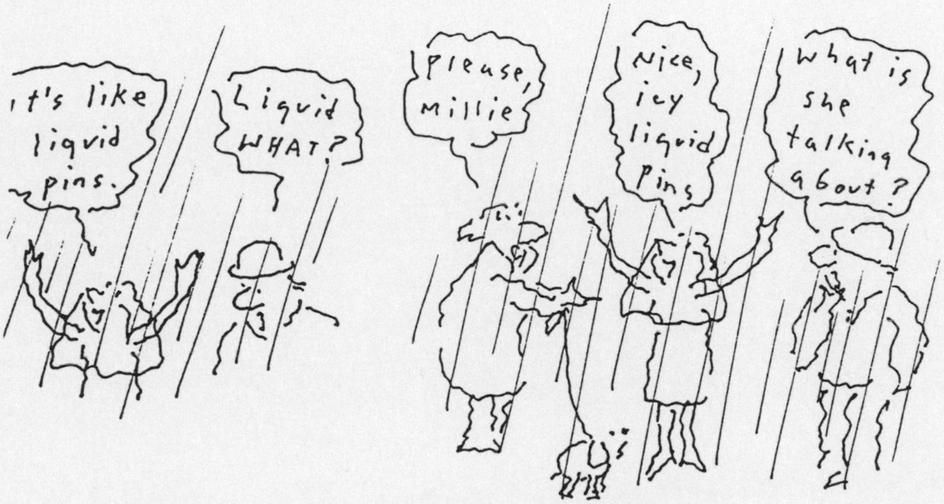
it's like
liquid
pins.
Liquid
WHAT?
please,
millie
Nice,
icy
liquid
pins
what is
she
talking
about?

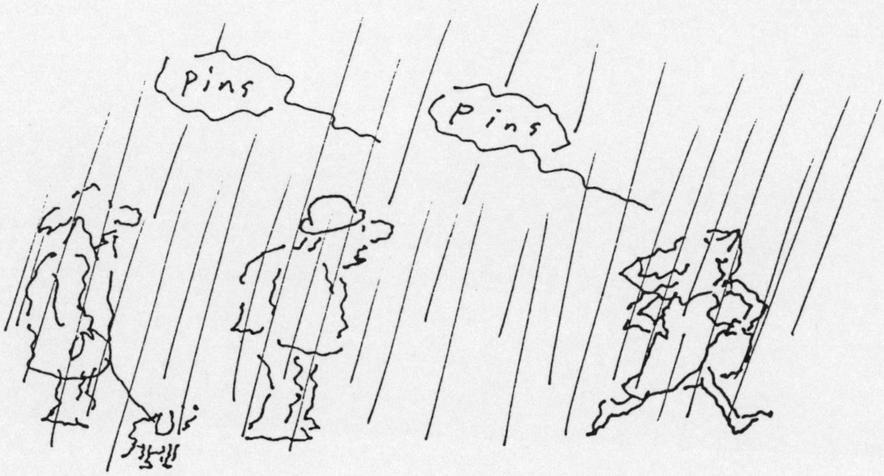
pins
pins

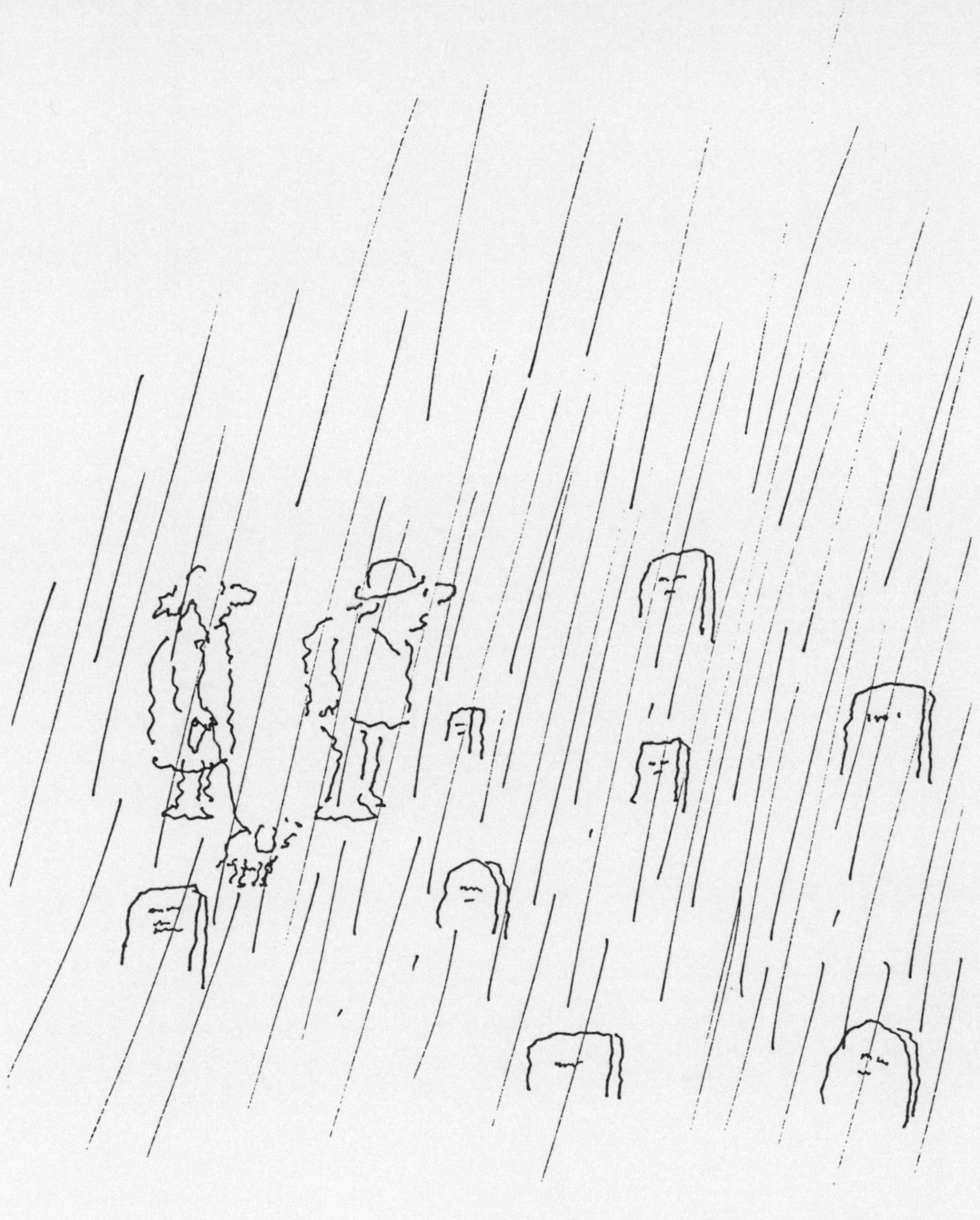

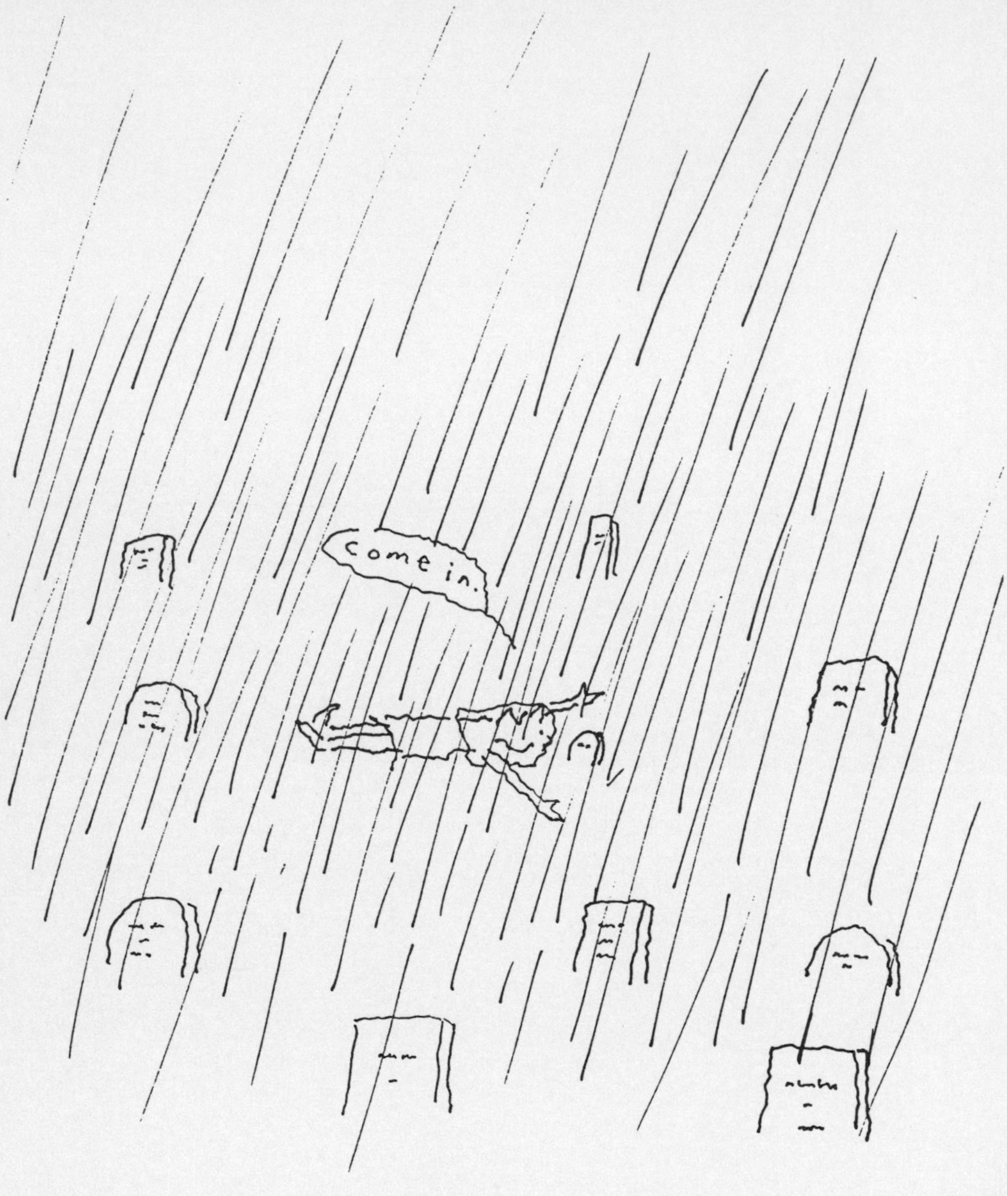
come in.

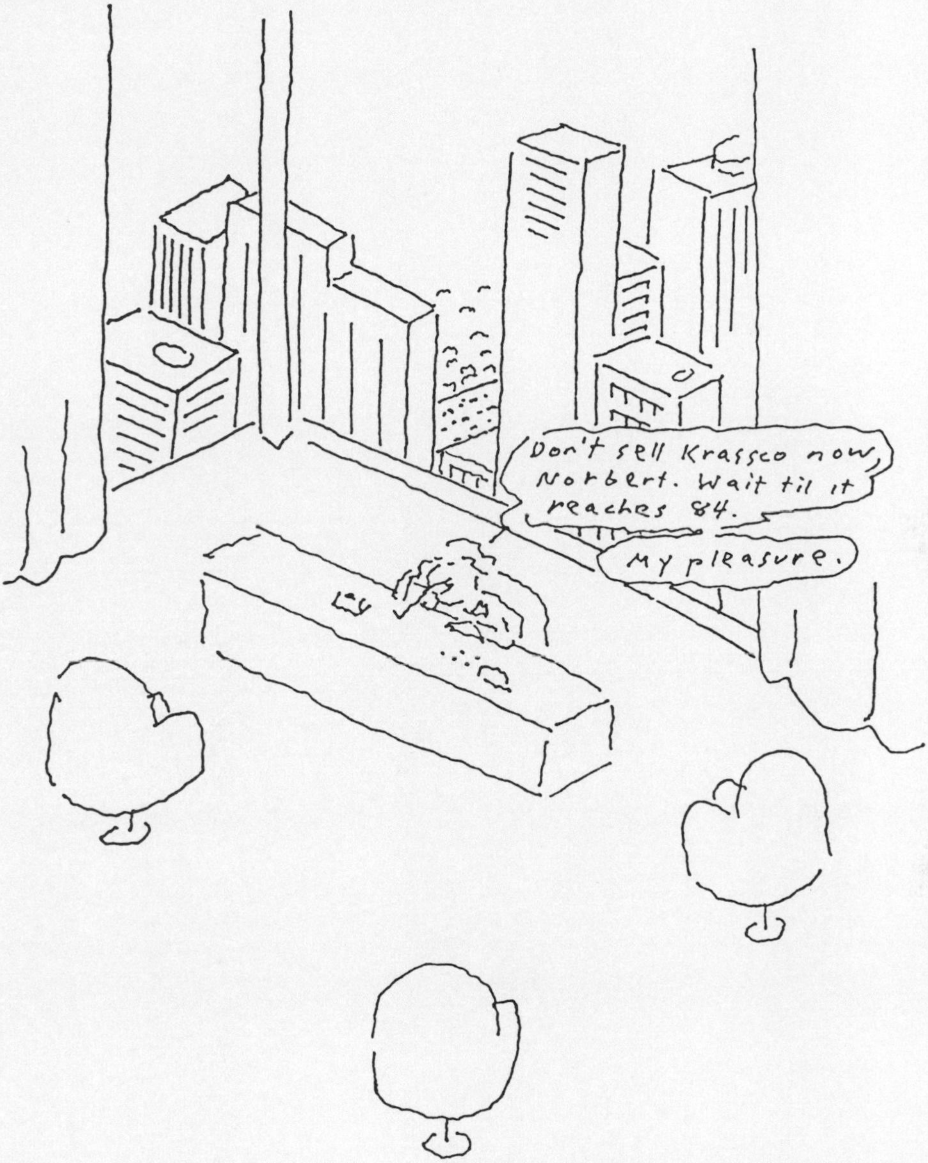
Don't sell Krassco now, Norbert. Wait til it reaches 84.
My pleasure.

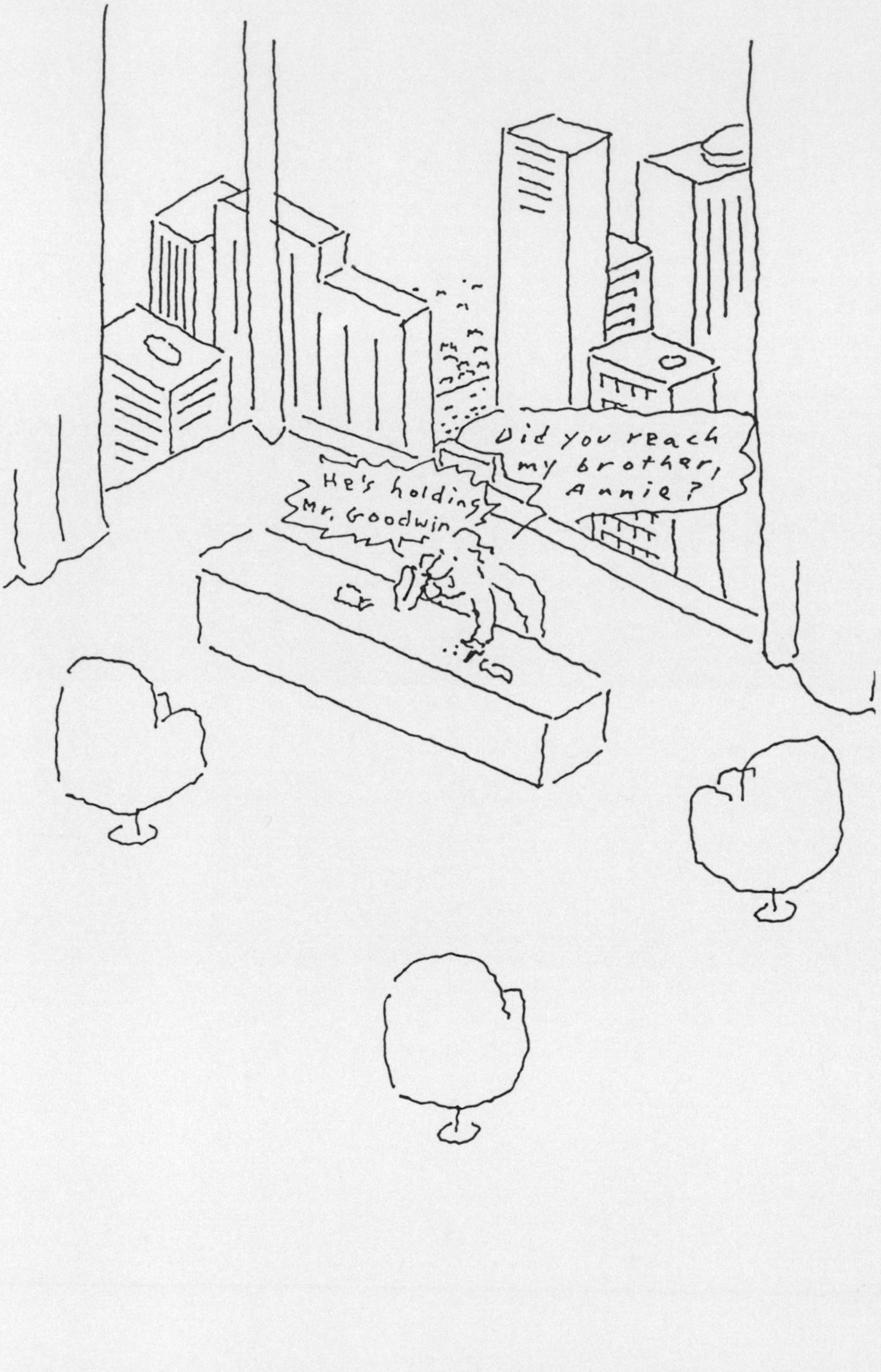
Did you reach my brother, Annie?
He's holding Mr. Goodwin.

Hello, Arnold, it's Wenty.
I transferred Alex's stocks to your account. And Minnie's too, of course.

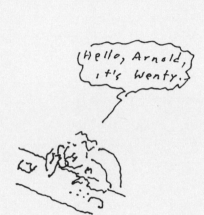

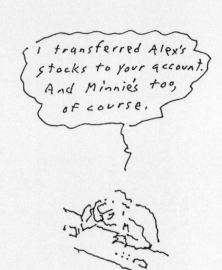

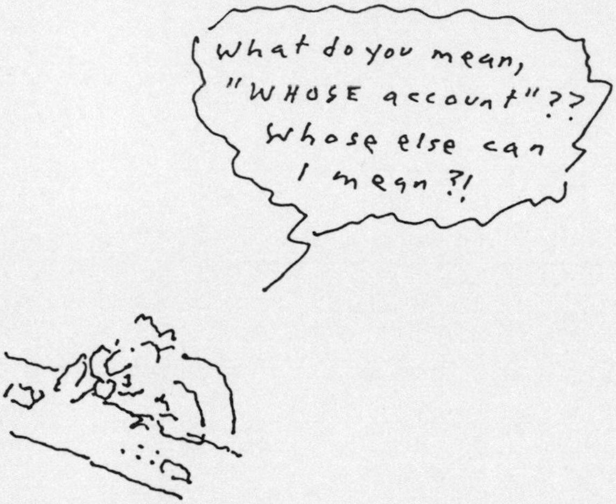
What do you mean, "WHOSE account"?? Whose else can I mean?!

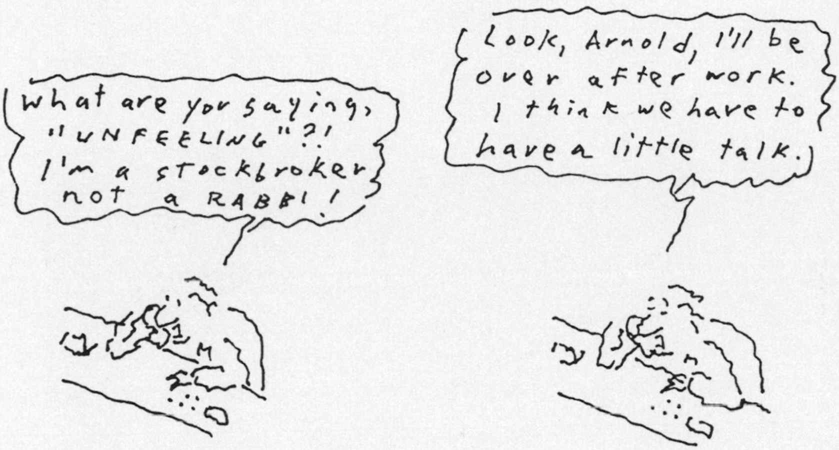
What are you saying, "UNFEELING"?! I'm a stockbroker not a RABBI!
Look, Arnold, I'll be over after work. I think we have to have a little talk.

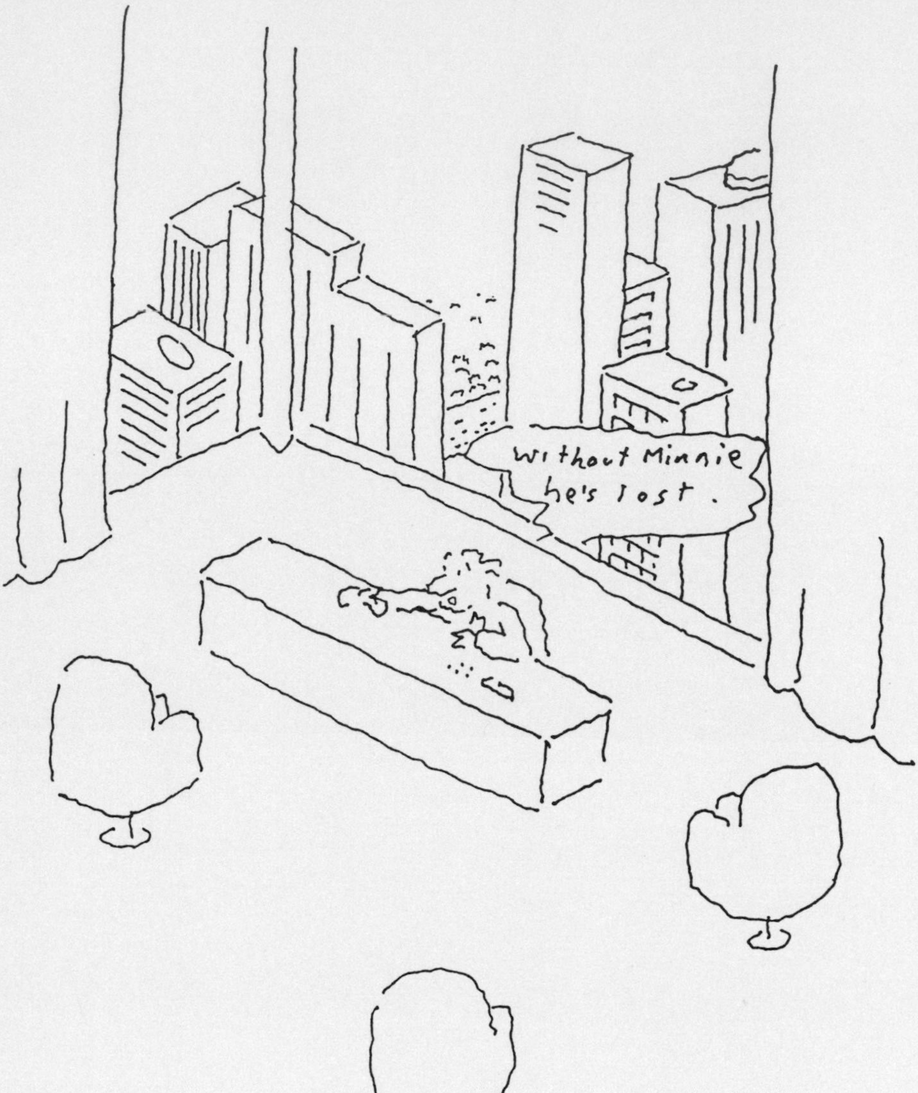
without Minnie he's lost.

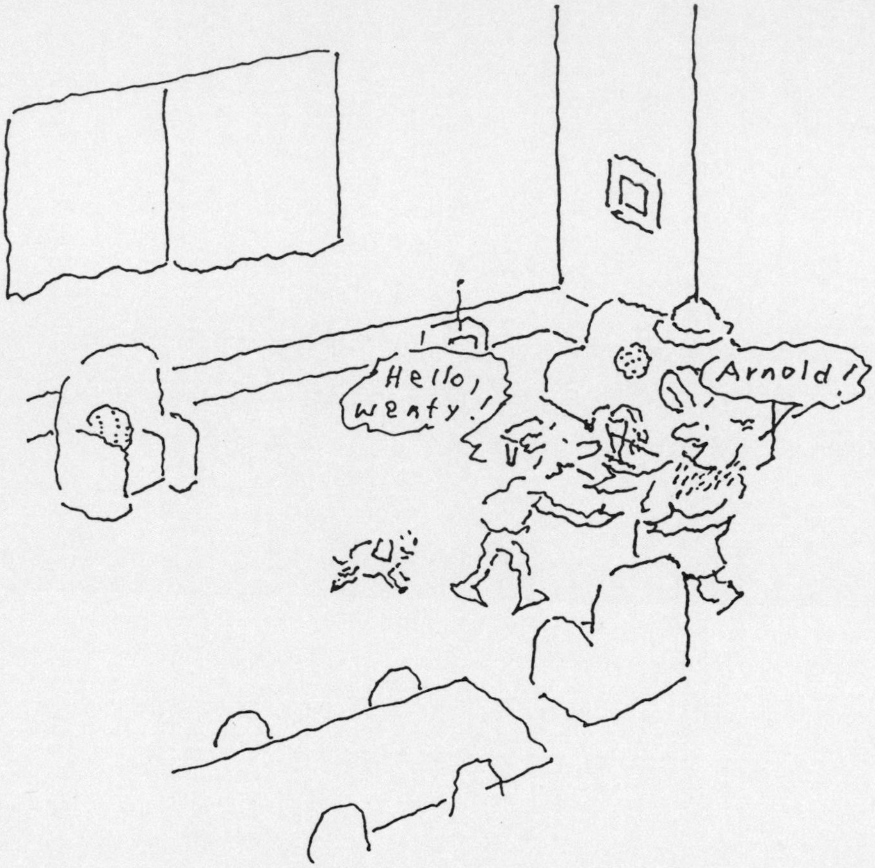
Hello, wenty!
Arnold!

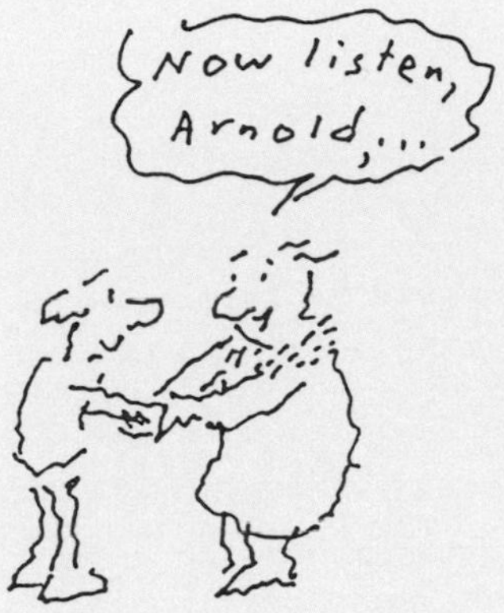
Now listen, Arnold,...

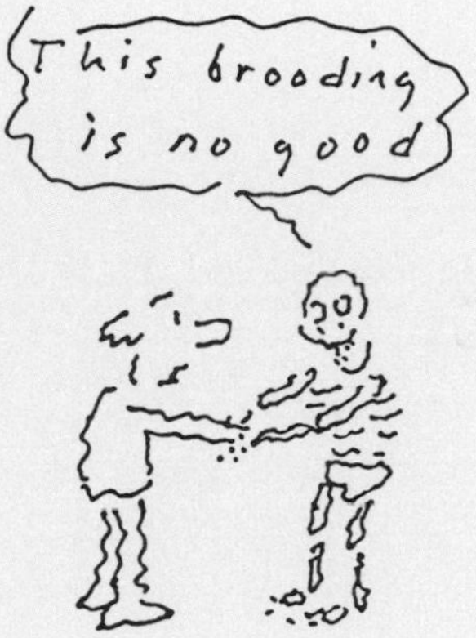
This brooding is no good

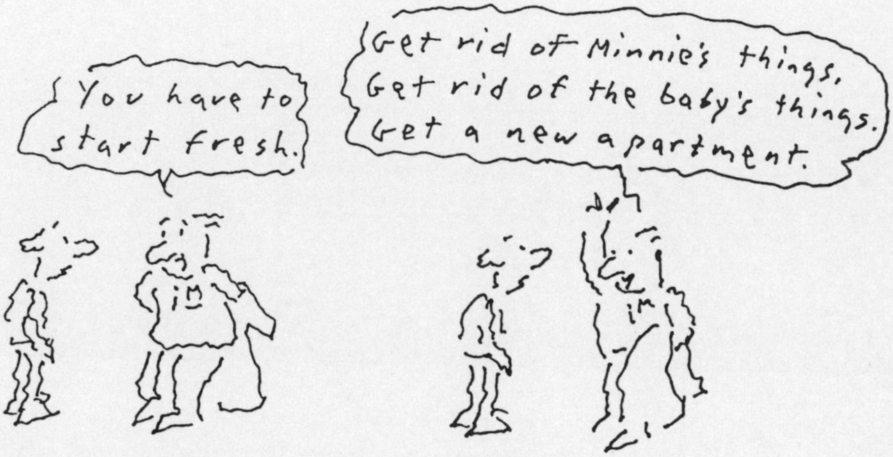
You have to start fresh.
Get rid of Minnie's things, Get rid of the baby's things. Get a new apartment.

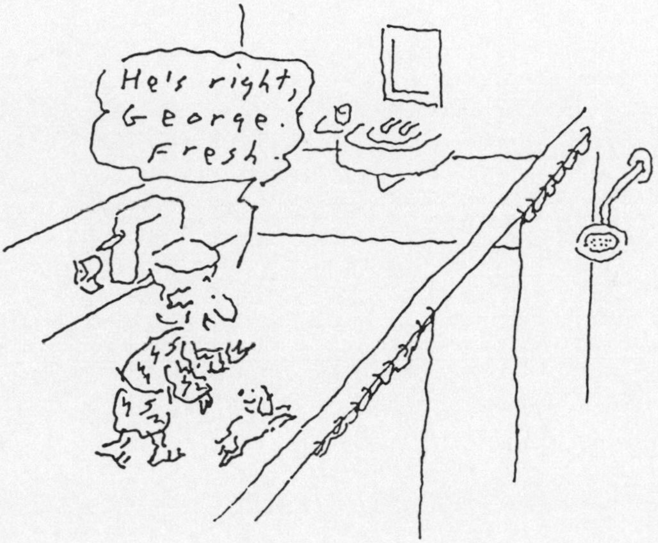
He's right, George. Fresh.

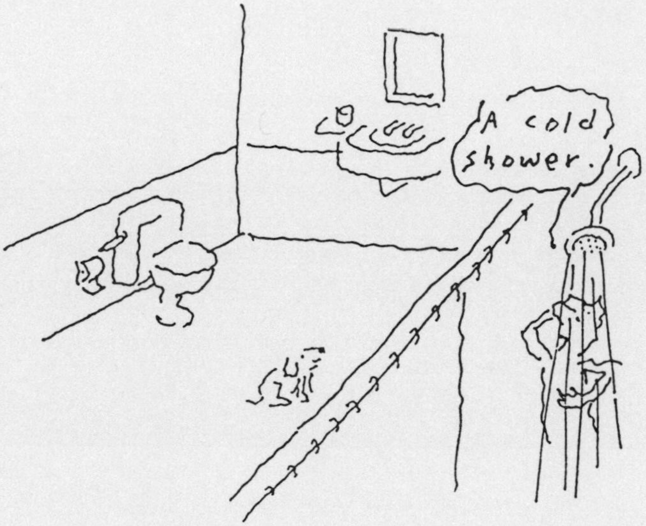
A cold shower.

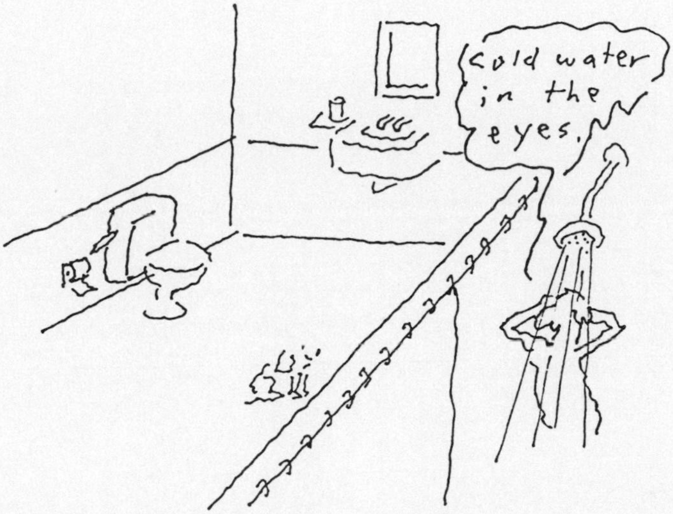
cold water
in the
eyes.

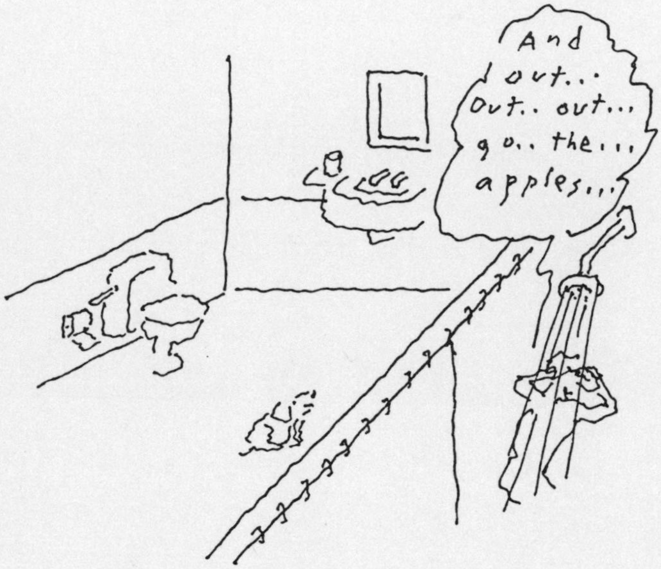
And out.. Out.. out... go.. the... apples...

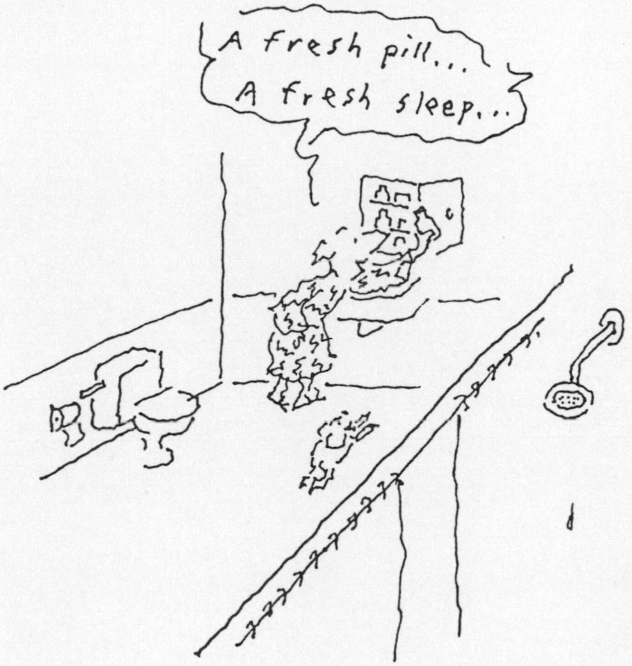
A fresh pill...
A fresh sleep...

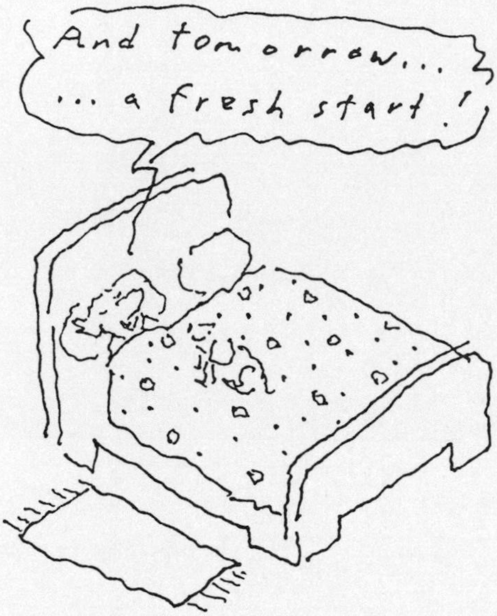
And tomorrow...
... a fresh start!

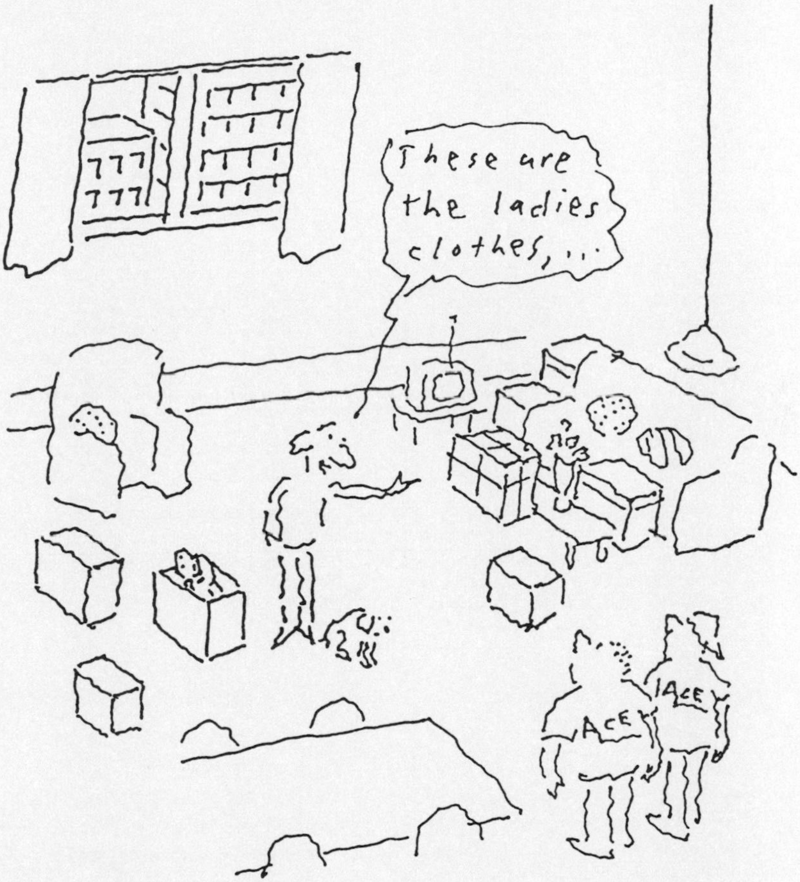
These are the ladies clothes, ...
ACE
ACE

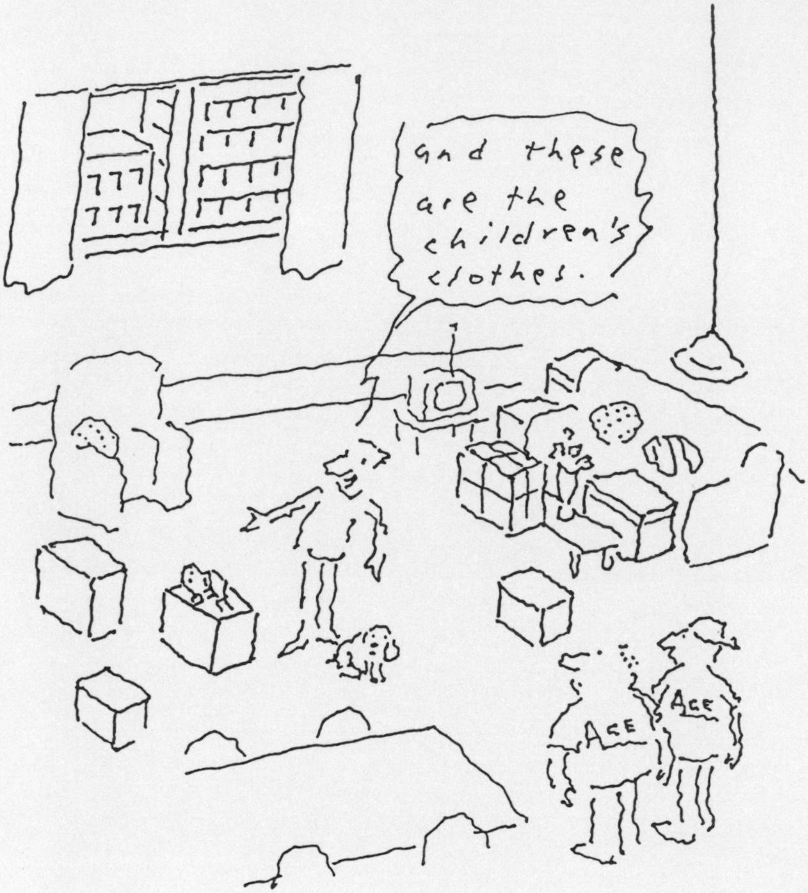
and these are the children's clothes.
ACE
ACE

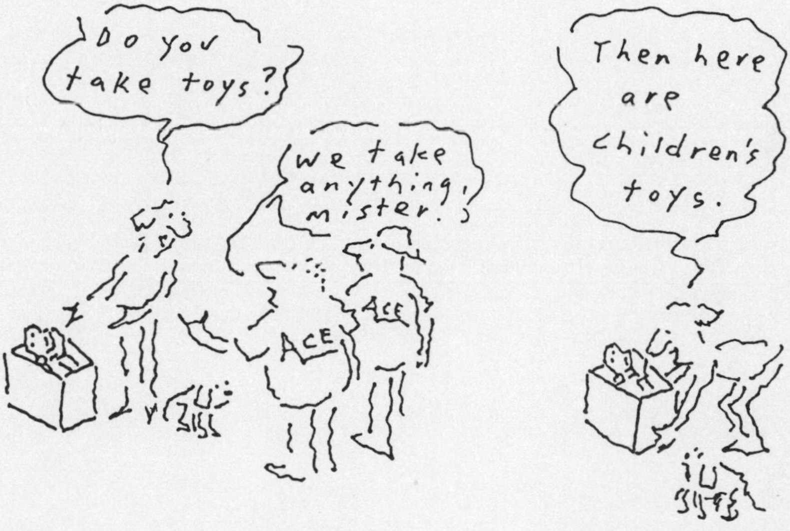
Do you take toys?
We take anything, mister.
ACE
ACE
Then here are children's toys.

ACE
ACE
ACE
ACE

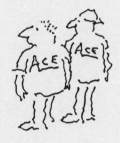

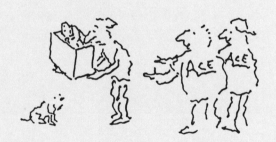

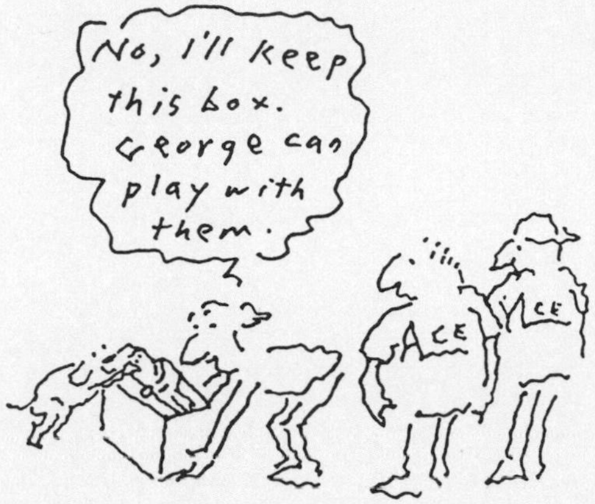
No, I'll keep this box. George can play with them.

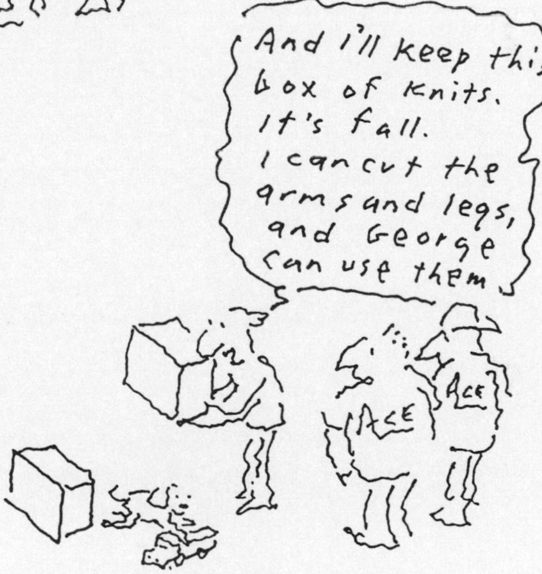
And I'll keep this box of knits. It's fall. I can cut the arms and legs, and George can use them.

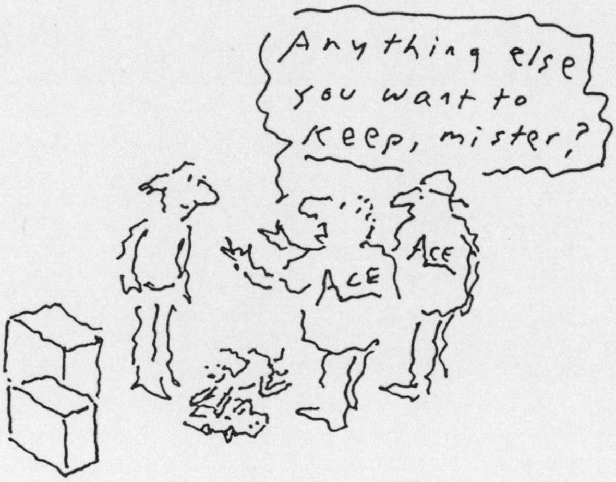
Anything else you want to keep, mister?
ACE
ACE

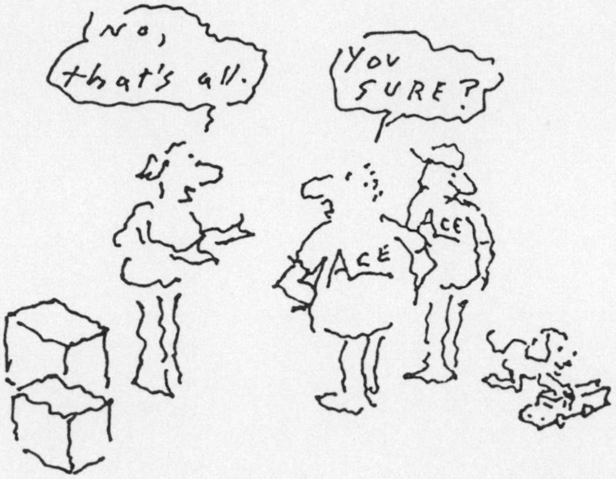
No, that's all.
You SURE?
ACE
ACE

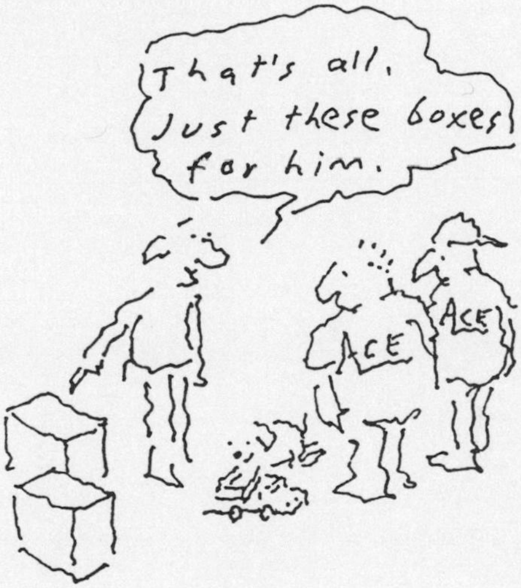
That's all. Just these boxes for him.
ACE
ACE

ACE
ACE

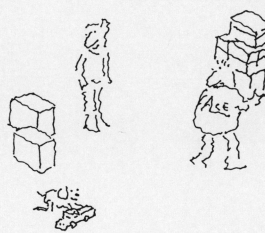

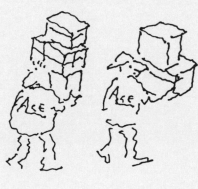

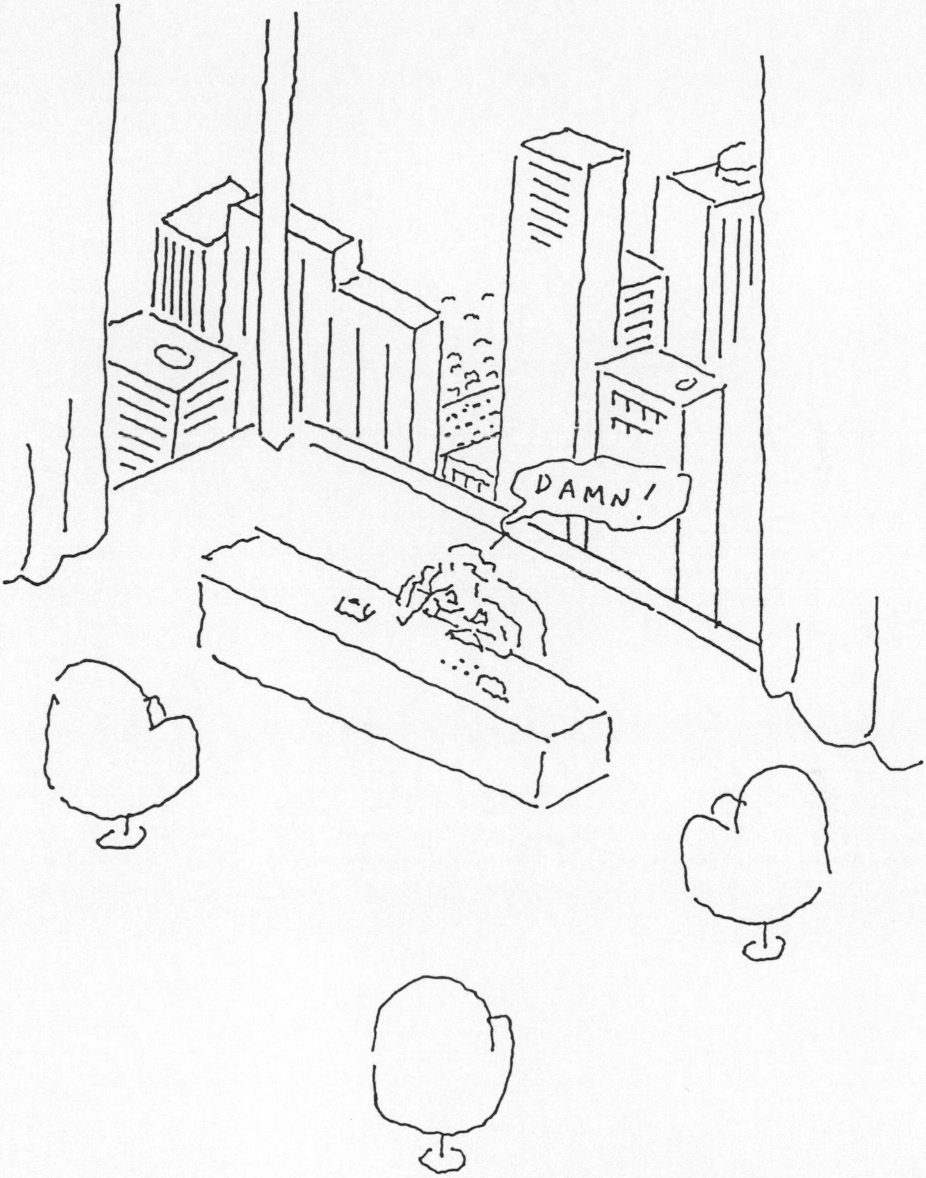
DAMN!

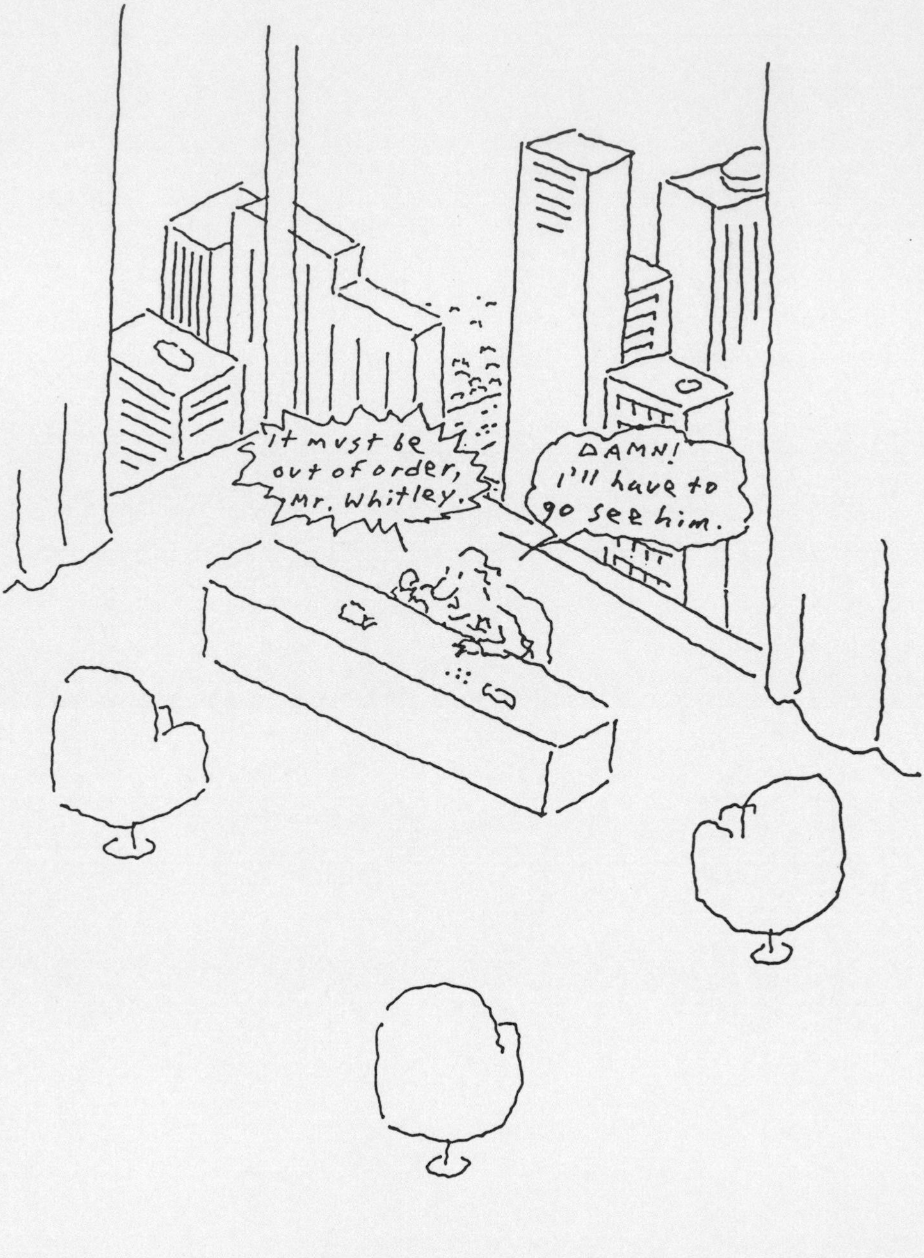
It must be out of order, Mr. Whitley.
DAMN! I'll have to go see him.

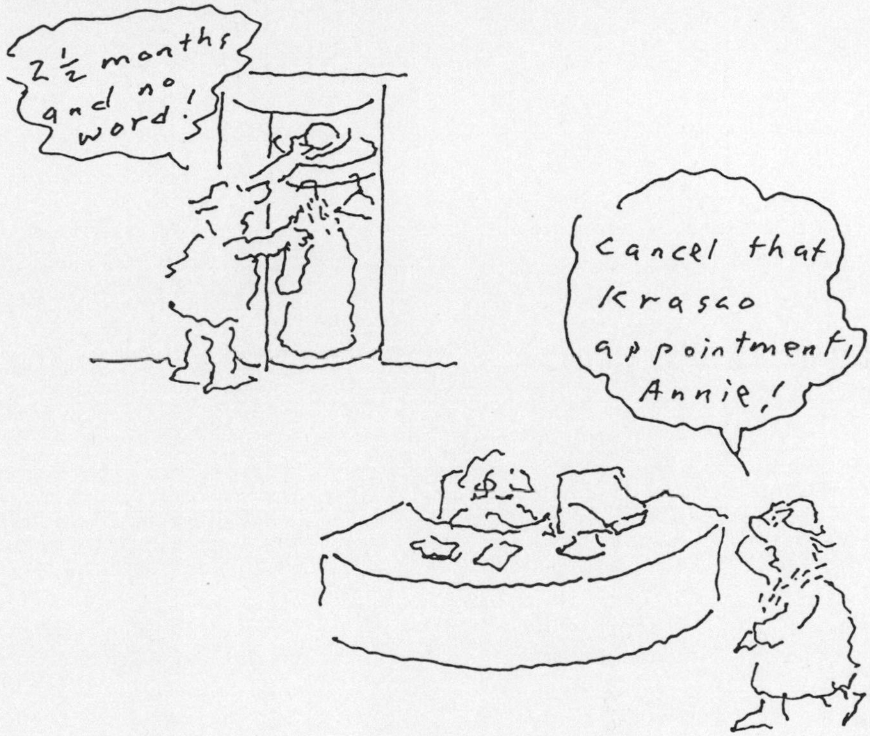
2½ months and no word!
Cancel that Krasco appointment, Annie!

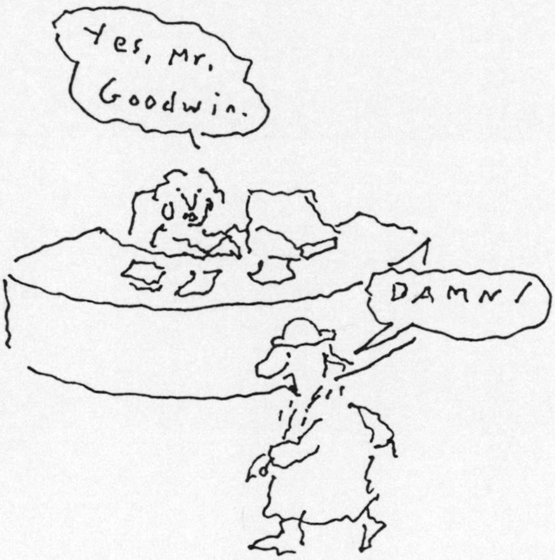
Yes, Mr. Goodwin.
DAMN!

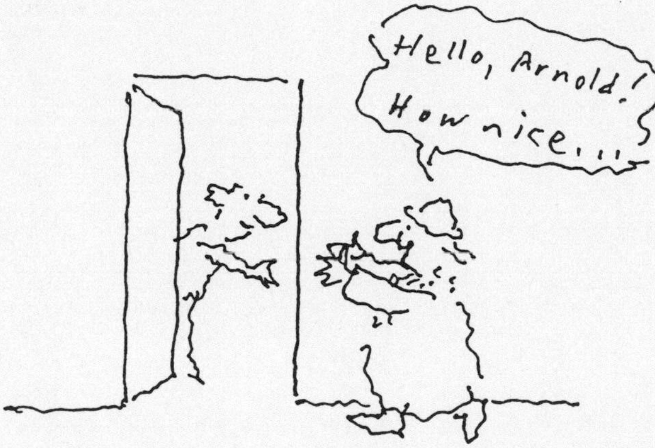
Hello, Arnold! How nice...

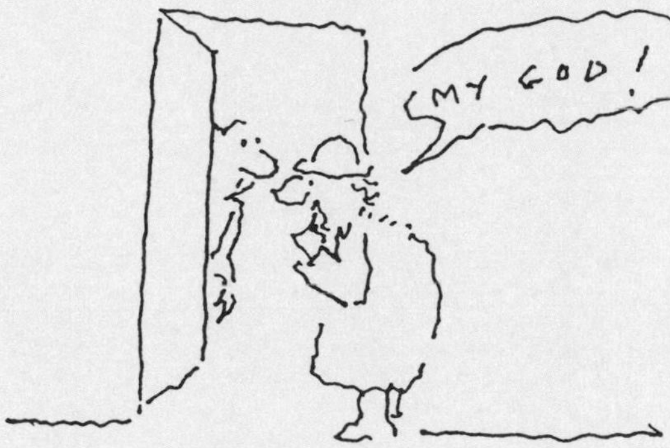
MY GOD!

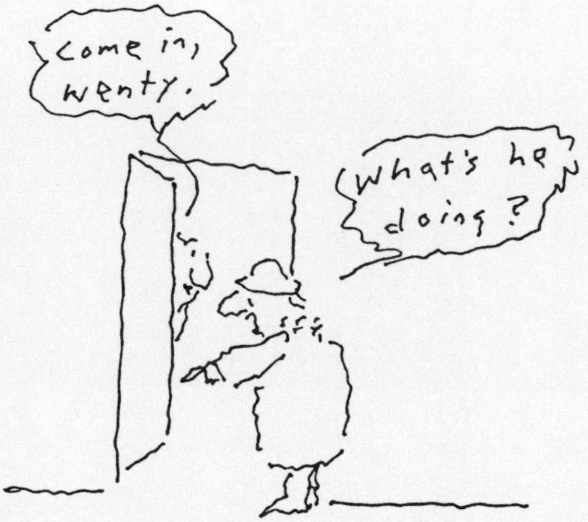
come in, wenty.
what's he doing?

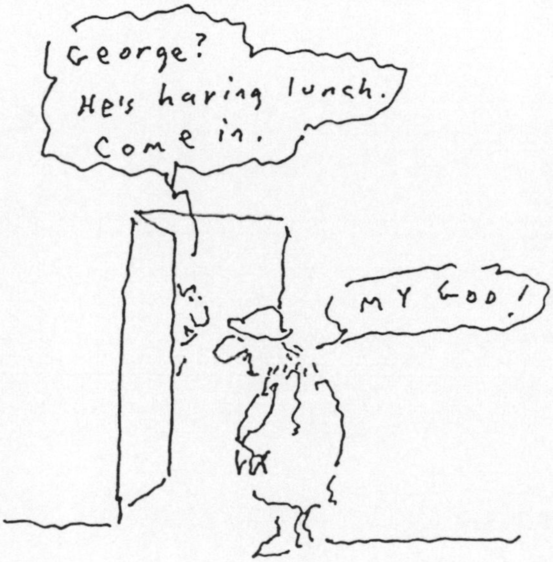
George? He's having lunch. Come in.
MY GOD!

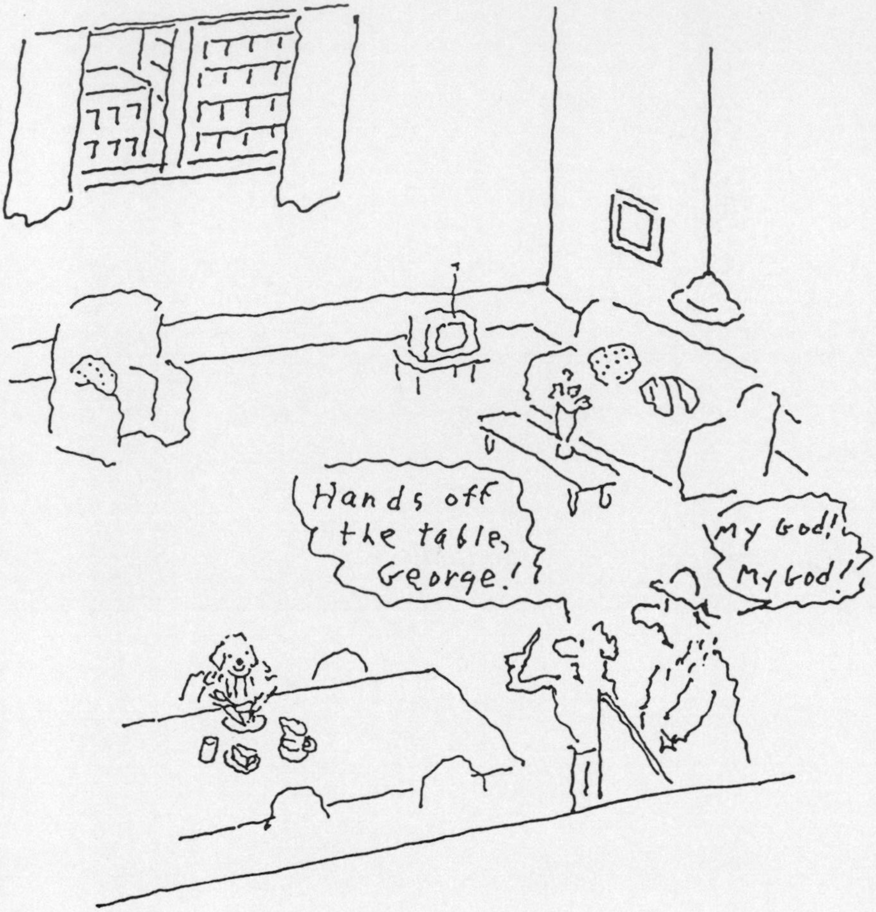
Hands off the table, George!
My God! My God!

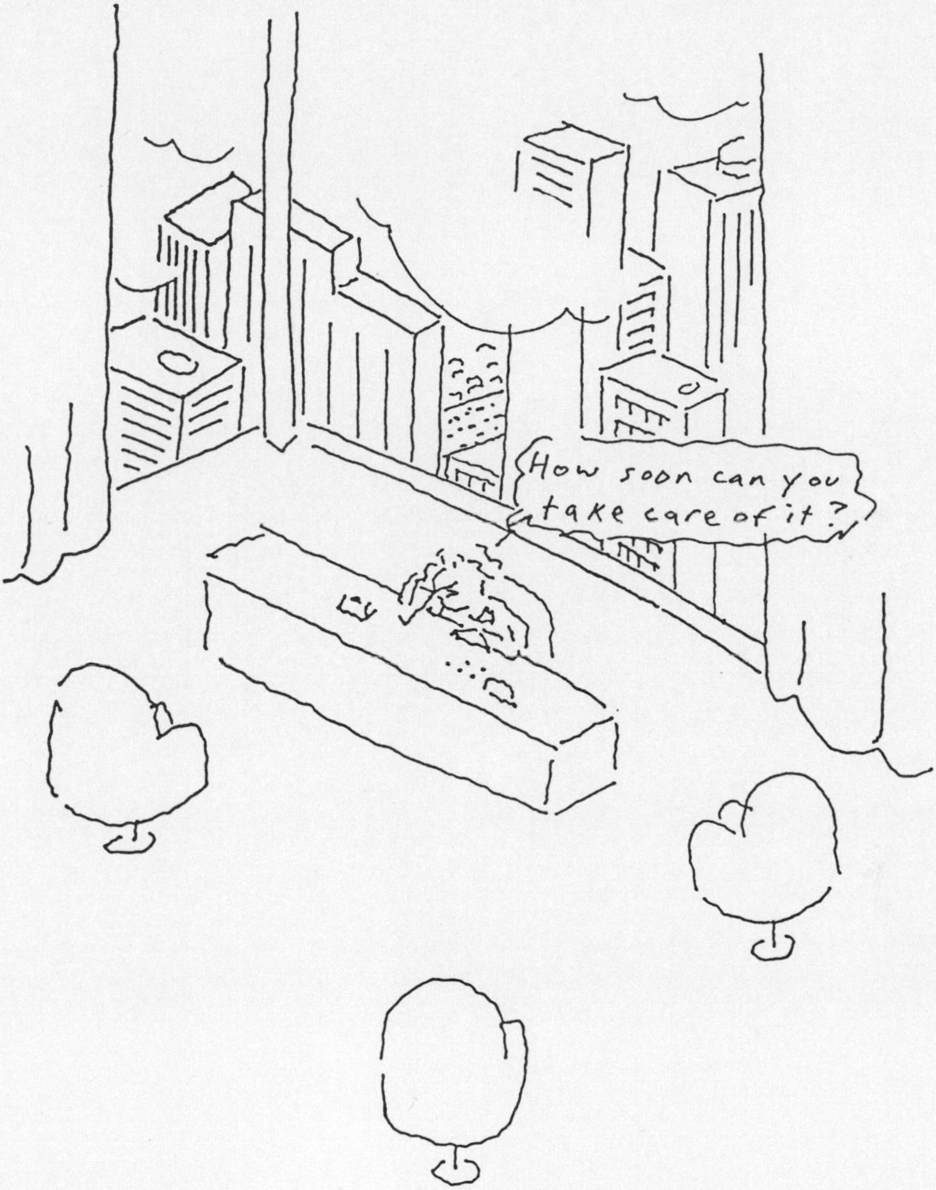
How soon can you take care of it?

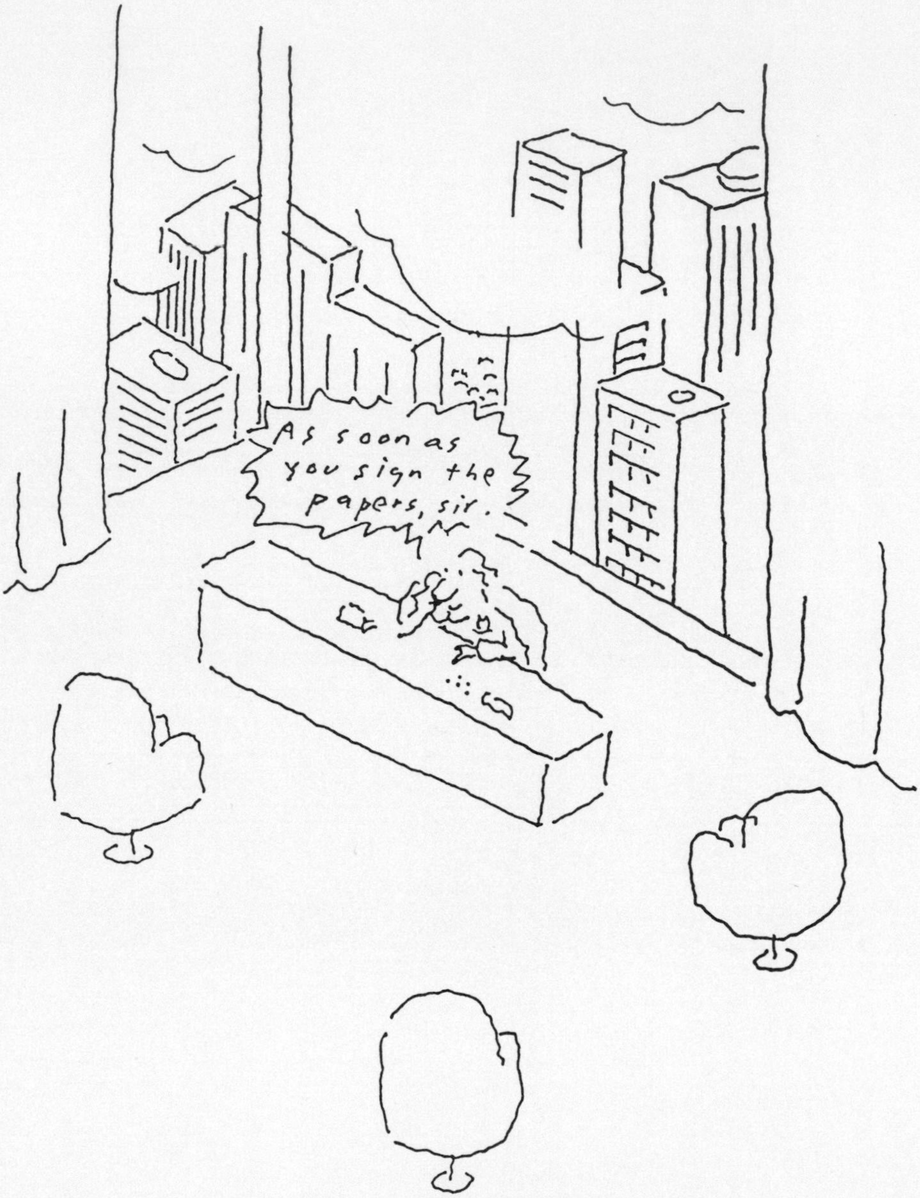
As soon as you sign the papers, sir.

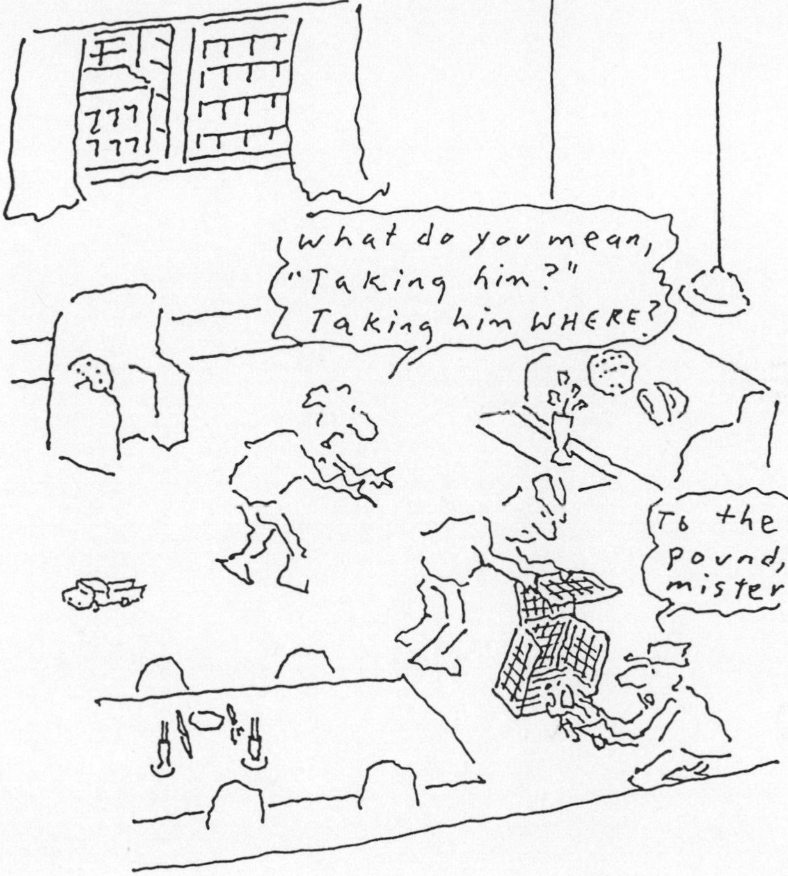
What do you mean, "Taking him?" Taking him WHERE?
To the pound, mister.

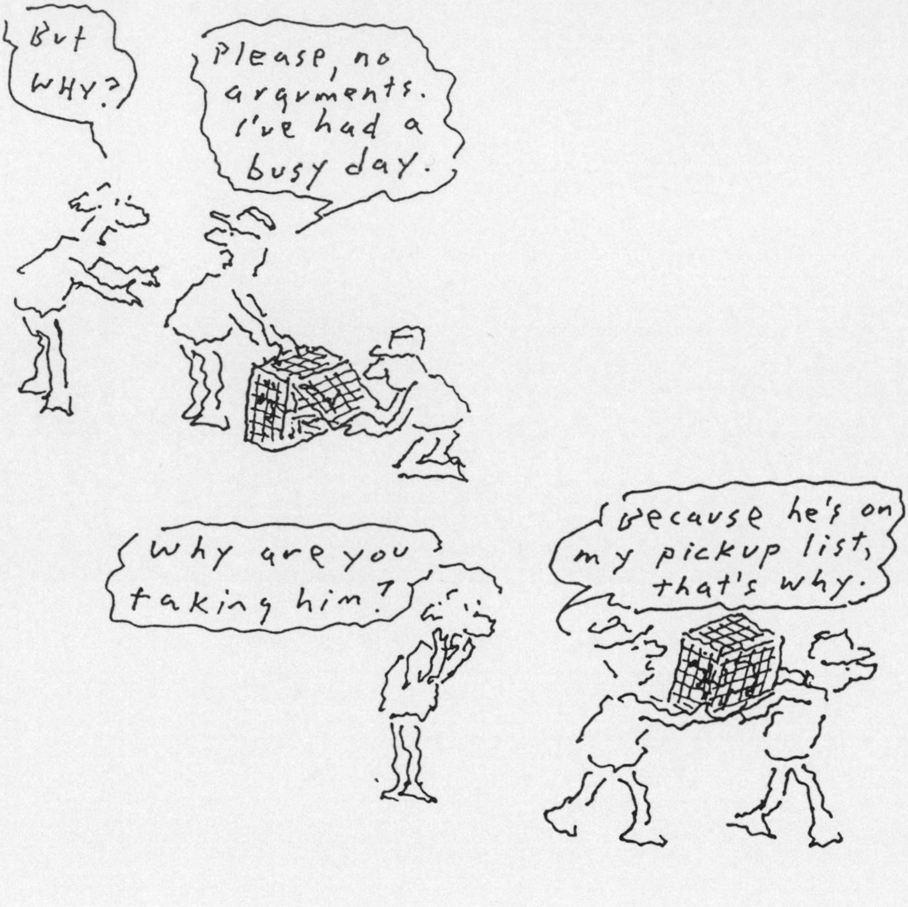
But WHY?
Please, no arguments. I've had a busy day.
Why are you taking him?
Because he's on my pickup list, that's why.

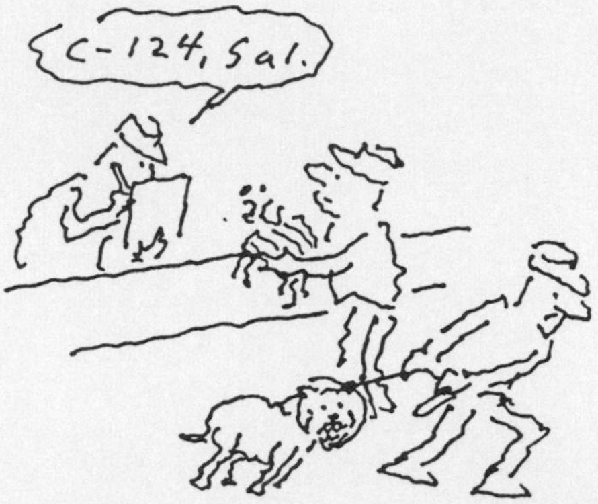
C-124, Sal.

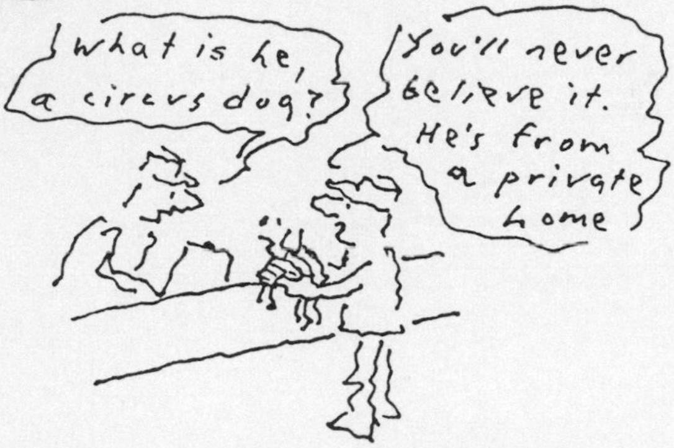
What is he, a circus dog?
You'll never believe it. He's from a private home

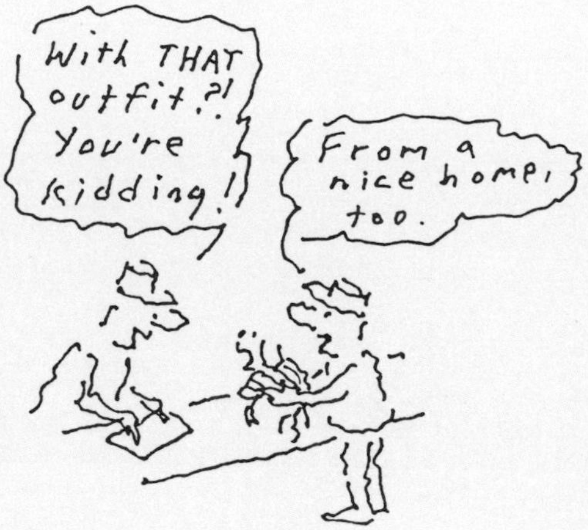
With THAT outfit?! You're kidding!
From a nice home, too.

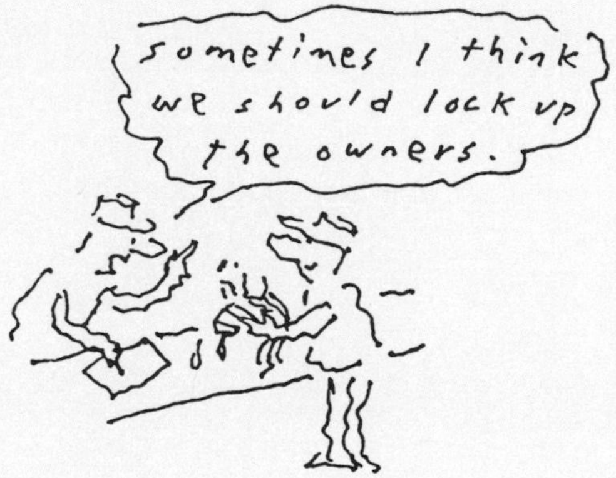
sometimes I think we should lock up the owners.

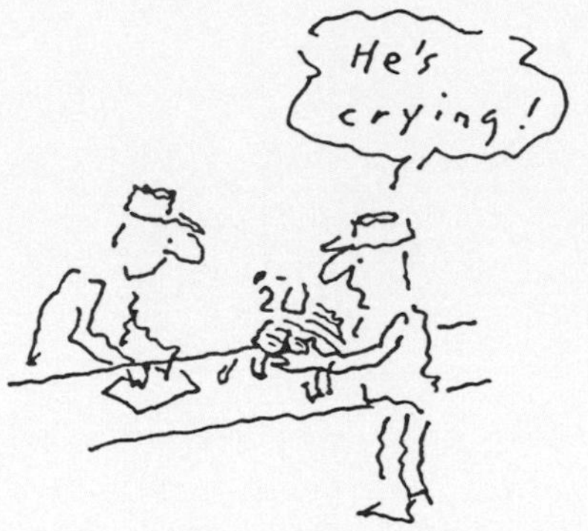
He's crying!

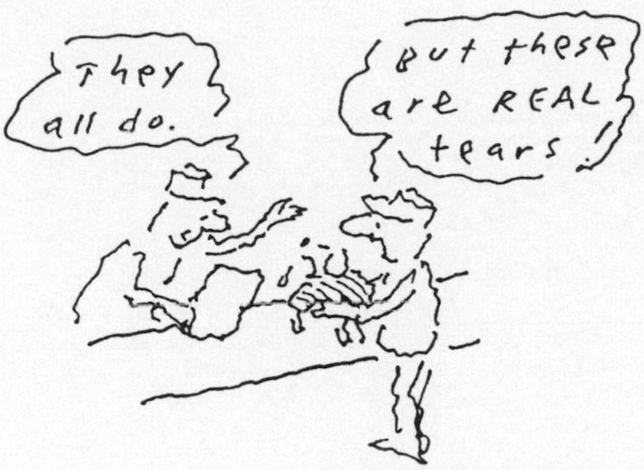
They all do.
But these are REAL tears!

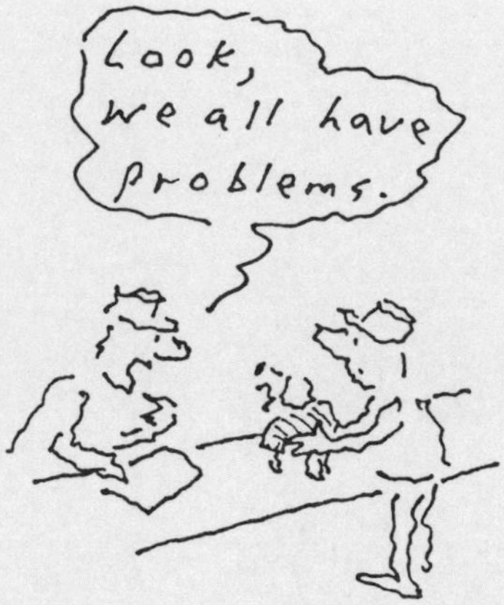
Look, we all have problems.

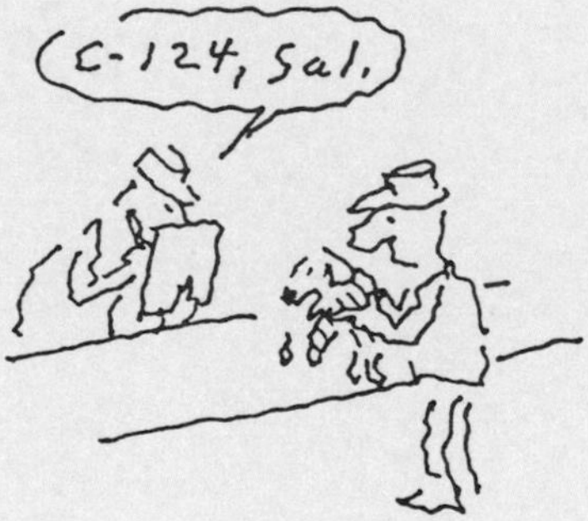
C-124, Sal.

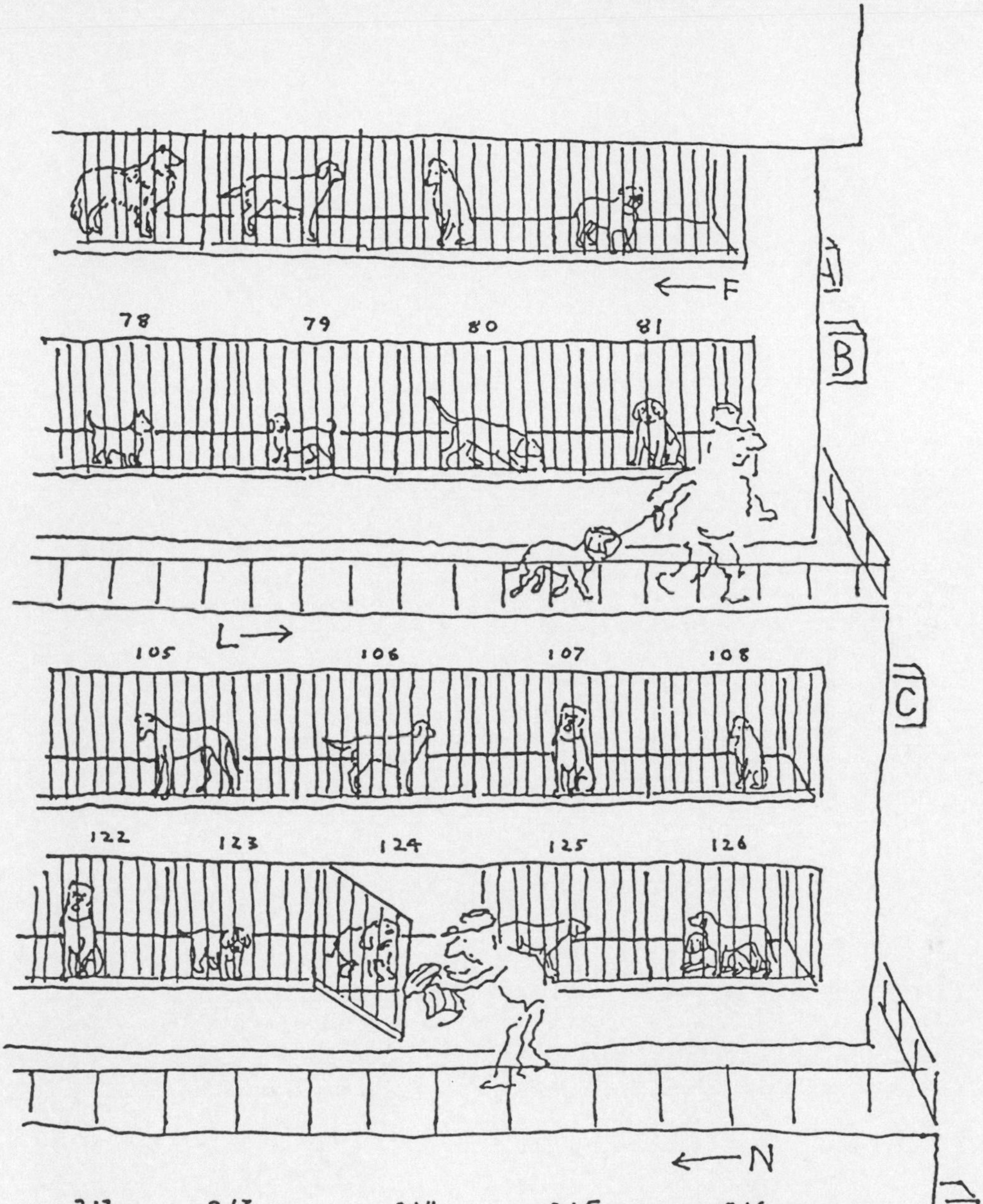
A
←F
78
79
80
81
B
L→
105
106
107
108
C
122
123
124
125
126
←N
212
213
214
215
216
D

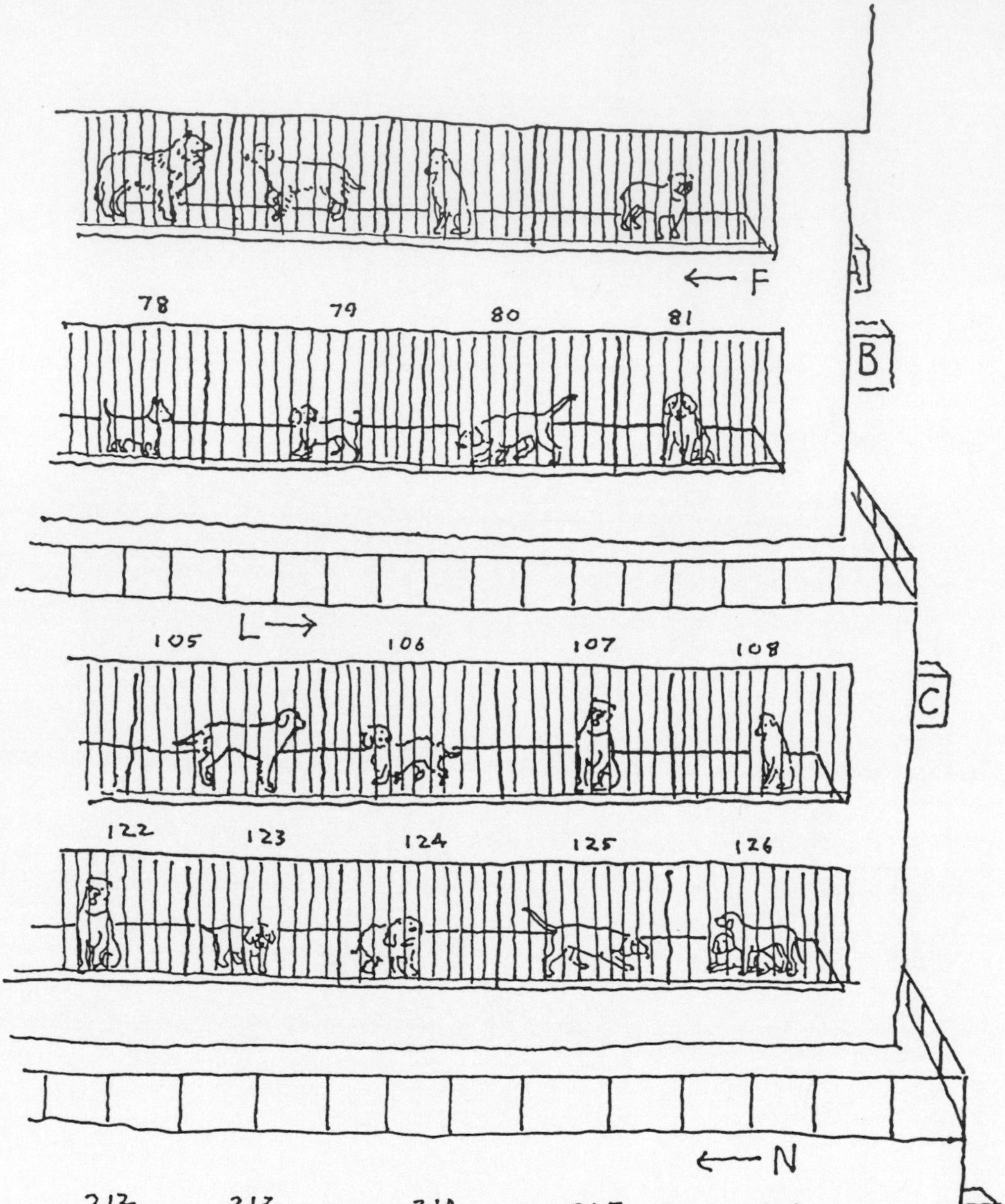
F
78
79
80
81
A
B
L
105
106
107
108
C
122
123
124
125
126
N
212
213
214
215
216
D

124

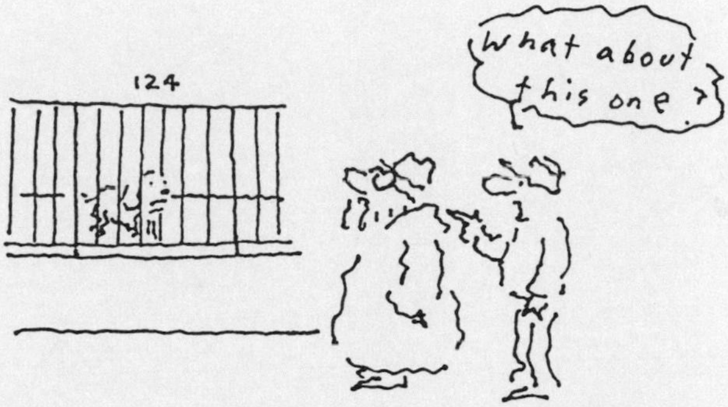
124
What about this one?

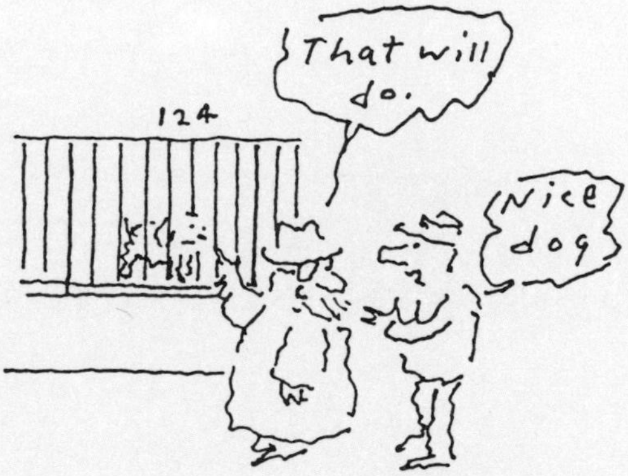
That will do.
124
Nice dog

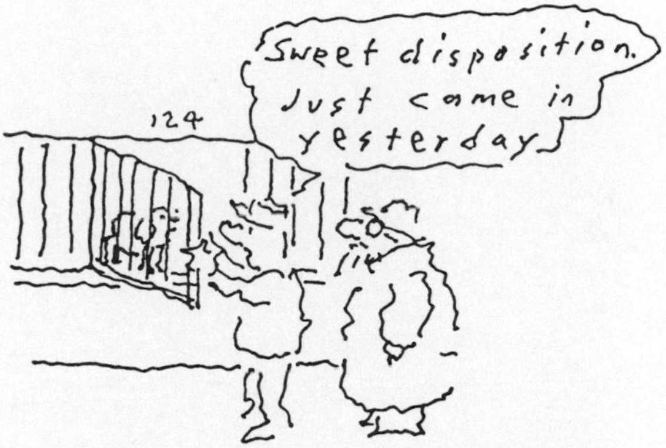
124
Sweet disposition. Just came in yesterday.

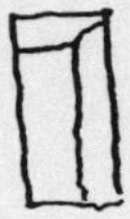

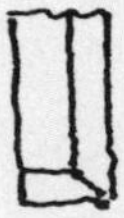

Hello, Georgie.

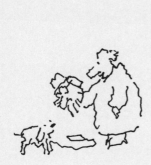

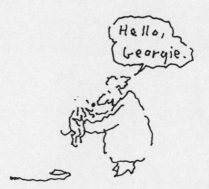

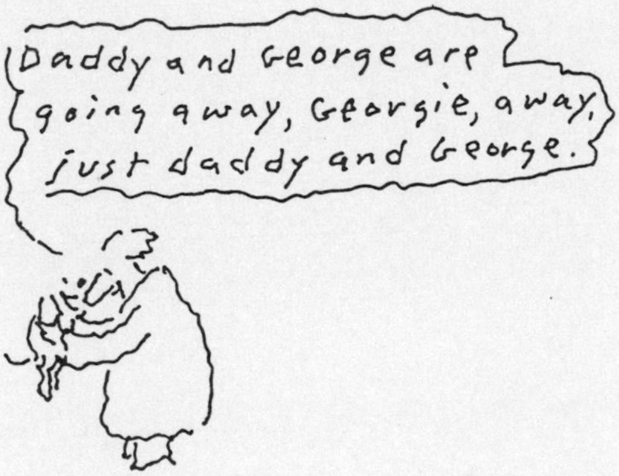
Daddy and George are going away, Georgie, away, just daddy and George.

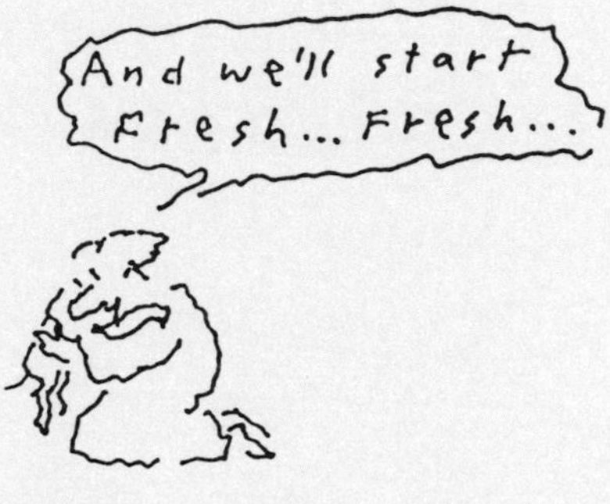
And we'll start fresh... fresh...

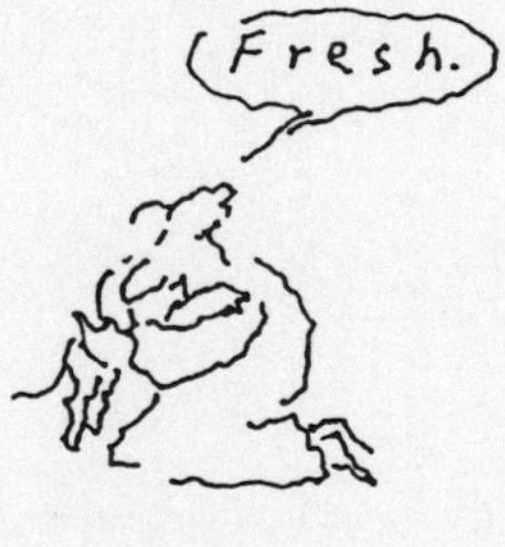
Fresh.

REFLECTIONS

UNPUBLISHED, 2006

This really happened. A few years ago I looked in my mirror
and my grandfather appeared. In my mirror!

In 1948, I
entered college...

... graduating
in 1952, not much
changed.

Over the decades,
I married (once), and
had children (two).

But I remained
basically the
same person.

Then in the
1970s something
changed.

My father
replaced me.

I wanted him
to leave -- after all,
it was my mirror! --
but he wouldn't.

He finally left
in the 1990s.

My grandfather
replaced him.

I was puzzled.

Here I was,
still the person
I had always been --

... so what was
my grandfather
doing in MY
mirror?